Human Laterality

This is a volume in

PERSPECTIVES IN
NEUROLINGUISTICS, NEUROPSYCHOLOGY,
AND PSYCHOLINGUISTICS

A Series of Monographs and Treatises

A complete list of titles in this series appears at the end of this volume.

Human Laterality

MICHAEL C. CORBALLIS

Department of Psychology
The University of Auckland
Auckland, New Zealand

 1983

ACADEMIC PRESS

A Subsidiary of Harcourt Brace Jovanovich, Publishers
New York   London
Paris   San Diego   San Francisco   São Paulo   Sydney   Tokyo   Toronto

ACADEMIC PRESS, INC.
111 Fifth Avenue, New York, New York 10003

United Kingdom Edition published by
ACADEMIC PRESS, INC. (LONDON) LTD.
24/28 Oval Road, London NW1 7DX

Library of Congress Cataloging in Publication Data

Corballis, Michael C.
 Human laterality.

 (Perspectives in neurolinguistics, neuropsychology,
and psycholinguistics)
 Bibliography: p.
 Includes index.
 1. Cerebral dominance--Addresses, essays, lectures.
2. Laterality--Addresses, essays, lectures. I. Title.
II. Series. [DNLM: 1. Laterality. WL 335 C789h]
QP385.5.C66 1983 612'.825   83-10019
ISBN 0-12-188180-6

PRINTED IN THE UNITED STATES OF AMERICA

83 84 85 86   9 8 7 6 5 4 3 2 1

This book is dedicated to the memory of Dalbir Bindra

Contents

Preface

Human right-handedness has been a source of curiosity throughout the ages. It is fascinating in part because it seems to be purely functional, contradicting the structural symmetry of the hands. Moreover it seems to be unique to human beings, at least among the mammals—we are truly the lopsided apes. Given these properties, it is even more curious that some individuals should apparently be born left-handed. Small wonder, then, that the phenomenon of handedness should have attracted such a storehouse of myth, superstition, prejudice, and religious symbolism.

Although human handedness has been apparent since the dawn of recorded history, the functional asymmetry of the human brain is a relatively recent discovery. In degree and scope, it too seems to belie the structural symmetry of the brain, and it too seems uniquely human. And it has also attracted its share of myth and superstition, especially in some of the more fanciful of contemporary ideas on so-called ''left-hemispheric'' and ''right-hemispheric'' modes of consciousness.

Part of my objective in this book is to set the record straight and to establish the main facts of human laterality as they are currently known. Given the explosion of research, especially over the past decade, I have not attempted an exhaustive coverage; indeed, this is the place to apologize to those whose work is not mentioned, and to assure them that no malice is intended. While not claiming exhaustiveness, I have nevertheless tried to examine laterality from as many perspectives as possible. I have therefore drawn on evidence from normal, intact human beings as well as from neurological patients, and where it has seemed appropriate I have also covered material on asymmetries in other species. I have devoted separate chapters to the development of laterality (Chapter 5), the evolution of laterality (Chapter 6), and the inheritance of laterality (Chapter 7). In Chapter 8 I have tried to sort out the voluminous literature on the relation between laterality and developmental disorders of speech and language, including dyslexia and stuttering. In the final chapter, Chapter 9, I speculate about the possible origins of laterality in the fundamental asymmetries of living molecules and of particle physics.

In a topic so myth-laden as laterality, there is a natural temptation to graft the left–right dimension onto the cultural and philosophical fads of the moment; there can be few dichotomies in contemporary culture, for instance, that have escaped association with one or the other cerebral hemisphere of the human brain. One antidote to this is to examine the development of knowledge and ideas about laterality over the course of history, if only because it helps convey a sense of the evanescence of some of the more extravagant theories. I have therefore tried throughout to maintain a historical perspective.

Although I have tried to document the facts, I make no claim to total objectivity—as if that were ever possible! On the contrary, I have tried to interpret the evidence in as comprehensive and coherent a fashion as possible. In so doing I have no doubt contributed my own share of myth-making. Myths have a positive as well as a negative function; without some degree of interpretation beyond the evidence, all would be chaos.

This book has therefore been guided by a number of broad themes. I have written in the conviction that there is a common basis to both handedness and cerebral lateralization, and indeed to other manifestations of human laterality such as eyedness and footedness. I have maintained that lateralization is fundamentally biological rather than sociocultural, that it is an innate disposition rather than a matter of learning or imitation—although experience may well be a prerequisite to its expression. Although the particular pattern of human laterality may be unique, I have assumed that it shares principles in common with other asymmetries, including those in other species. Although I believe that such generalizations make best sense of the evidence, they are by no means overwhelmingly supported, and I hope my conclusions will not deter the reader who chooses to disagree.

ACKNOWLEDGMENTS

This book would have been impossible without the help of colleagues and friends. Michael J. Morgan did most to set the stamp on my thinking about laterality, but is of course not responsible for my heresies. Lauren J. Harris, both in his writing and in informal discussion, has done most to provide information and sources of reference, especially about historical matters. I also thank Ivan L. Beale, Brenda Milner, and Karl Stead. Barbara, my wife, and Paul and Timothy, my sons, were extraordinarily patient while I struggled in the weekends and evenings to tame the manuscript; my grateful thanks to them all. Finally, I thank Mary-Ellen and her dog, who between them managed to type the manuscript.

1 Laterality and Myth

The Maoris of New Zealand are said to have believed that if a person experienced a tremor during sleep the body had been seized by a spirit. It was critically important to observe which side of the body was afflicted, for a tremor on the right side foretold good fortune and life, whereas a tremor on the left meant ill fortune and even death (Hertz, 1909). In remarkably similar fashion, the native people of Morocco attach great importance to the twitching of an eyelid. Twitching of the right eyelid signifies return of a member of the family or some other good news, whereas twitching of the left eyelid is a warning of impending death in the family (Wieschhoff, 1938). These examples from unrelated cultures illustrate the universality of left–right symbolism.

According to Hertz (1909), the dominant polarity associated with right and left was that between the sacred and the profane. To the Maoris, the right was the side of the gods, as well as the side of strength and life, whereas the left was associated with profanity, demons, weakness, and death. We need look no further than the Bible to discover the same theme, as in Matthew 5:25:

> And He will set the sheep upon His right hand and the goats upon His left. Then shall the King say to those upon His right, ''Come ye blessed of my Father, and inherit the kindgom prepared for you from the beginning of the world.'' . . . Then shall He also say to those on the left, ''Depart from me, ye accursed, into everlasting fire prepared for the Devil and His angels.''

In the Pythagorean Table of Opposites, recorded by Aristotle, the right was associated with the limited, the odd, the one, the male, the state of rest, the straight, the light, the good, and the square, whereas the left signified the unlimited, the even, the many, the female, the moving, the curved, the dark, the evil, and the oblong (Lloyd, 1962). Remarkably similar tables can be constructed from the symbols of other, quite unrelated cultures. Among the Nyoro of East Africa, for instance, properties associated with the right include man, brewing, health, wealth, fertility, life, the even, the hard, the moon, fidelity, and cattle, whereas the opposing properties associated with the left are woman, cooking, sickness, poverty, barrenness, death, the odd, the soft, the sun, and chickens or sheep (R. Needham, 1967). Essentially the same associations are found among the Gogo of Tanzania (Rigby, 1966).

HANDEDNESS AND MYTH

There can be little doubt that the different values attached to left and right have their origins in handedness itself. There is occasional homage to the left—for instance, the Chinese are said to be rare among human societies in that they bestow special honor to the left hand (Granet, 1953)—but in the vast majority of cases, the right is granted the superior status or assigned the more positive pole of a dichotomy. Sometimes the reference to the hands themselves is explicit: The right hand is used for shaking hands, saluting, making the sign of the cross, laying on of hands, and swearing on the Bible, whereas the left hand is the "hand of the privy" and the hand that delivers the *coup de grâce* to a dying adversary. A "right-hand man" is a trusted ally, but a "left-handed compliment" is an insult. It is better to be termed "adroit" or "dexterous" than "gauche" or "sinister." But even in cases where reference to the hands is not explicit, the right clearly enjoys the superior status—the good, the clean, the true, the strong, and (regrettably) the male. The nearly universal symbolic superiority of the right is therefore testimony to the universality of right-handedness itself.

The association of right with male and left with female also appears to be universal, even though there is no basis for this in handedness; if anything, left-handedness appears to be more prevalent among men than women (Oldfield, 1971). Yet in Maori, for example, the expression *tama tane,* meaning "male side," referred to the right, whereas *tama wahine,* "female side," referred to the left (Hertz, 1909). *Tama tane* also connoted strength, virility, paternal descent, creative force, and offensive magic, whereas *tama wahine* stood for the antitheses of these. Hertz quoted a Maori proverb: "All evils, misery and death come from the female element [p. 559]." According to J. J. Bachofen, a nineteenth-century Swiss historian, we may find a reversal of traditional values in matriarchal societies and a corresponding emphasis on the left. In the Isis cult of ancient Egypt, for instance, honor was given to Isis, the wife, over

Osiris, the husband, as well as to mother over son and to night over day, and the Isis procession was headed by a priest carrying an image of the left hand (Bachofen, 1861/1967).

Empedocles, the Sicilian philosopher of the fifth century B.C., thought that males were hotter than females and the right hotter than the left, so that the sex of a child was determined by rightward or leftward location in the womb (Russell, 1946). He is also said to have thrown himself into the crater of Mt. Etna in a vain attempt to prove that he was a god. There is of course no basis for the idea that sex is determined by location in the womb, yet something of the flavor of Empedocles' theory does survive in modern biology. Ursula Mittwoch (1977), in an article called "To Be Born Right Is to Be Born Male," notes that in hermaphrodites with mixed sex organs testes are more often found on the right and ovaries on the left. She suggests that the same opposing tendencies are present in normal males and females, though overridden by the influence of the sex chromosome.

We might perhaps see a further manifestation of the Empedoclean principle in the report by Levy and Levy (1978), daughter and father, that in most human males the right foot is larger than the left, whereas in females the left is larger than the right. The Levys also reported that these tendencies are reversed among left-handers. Yet the Levys may have been influenced as much by the myth as by the evidence. In unpublished research at the University of Auckland, Sharon Cullen and Barbara Burkitt failed to observe any systematic differences in foot size associated with sex or handedness, and similar negative results have been obtained by several others (Mascie-Taylor, MacLarnon, Lanigan, & McManus, 1981; Peters, Petrie, & Oddie, 1981; Yanowitz, Satz, & Heilman, 1981).

The possibility that there might be a link between handedness and sex did not escape the notice of the psychoanalytic school, which added a subtle twist of its own. Wilhelm Fliess, a friend and colleague of Sigmund Freud, wrote as follows:

> Where left handedness is present, the character pertaining to the opposite sex seems more pronounced. This sentence is not only invariably correct, but its converse is also true: Where a woman resembles a man, or a man resembles a woman, we find the emphasis on the left side of the body. Once we know this we have the diviner's rod for the discovery of left handedness. This diagnosis is always correct [Fliess, 1923, quoted in translation in Fritsch, 1968, p. 133].

Freud himself did not accept this absurd and dogmatic theory. Indeed, he wrote a psychoanalytic study of Leonardo da Vinci without ever suggesting that there might be a relation between Leonardo's left-handedness and his homosexuality (Freud, 1948), although in a letter to Fliess he did suggest Leonardo as a possible example (Freud, 1954).

Why, then, should handedness have exerted so powerful an influence on human mythology, folklore, and value systems—an influence that goes well beyond, and indeed often against, the facts? There are perhaps two general reasons. One is that the phenomenon of handedness is itself poorly understood, despite centuries of observation and speculation. It is rendered all the more baffling because the hands appear to form a structurally symmetrical pair. Handedness is apparent in function rather than in structure; one cannot easily tell a person's handedness by inspecting the hands, but it is immediately clear which is the preferred hand if the person is asked to write or to throw a ball with each hand in turn. As Hertz (1960, p. 92) exclaimed: "What resemblance more perfect than that between the two hands! And yet what a striking difference there is!" No wonder handedness has invited the intervention of gods and demons, for how else might one explain the remarkable difference between members that *look* so much alike!

The second reason is that handedness appears to be uniquely human, at least in the sense that the majority of our species are right-handed. Other animals do not seem to show this consistent bias; if preferences do exist, they appear to be distributed equally between left and right limbs. Our right-handedness, therefore, serves to reassure us that we are different from other animals, and it may in fact help to preserve the myth that we are superior to them. Indeed, the transcendental quality of handedness, in which functional right-handedness transcends the apparent structural symmetry of the hands, may have reinforced this argument. There is a philosophical view, going back at least to Descartes's (1644/1905) *Principia Philosophiae,* that animals act merely as automatons, governed by the laws of physics, whereas human beings possess a soul that transcends physical laws. It is this soul that bestows on human beings, but not on animals, the privilege of consciousness and free will. The phenomenon of human handedness may have lent support to this view. Although this connection has never to my knowledge been made explicit, it may help explain the powerful symbolism associated with handedness and the often extreme vilification of those who are left-handed.

CEREBRAL ASYMMETRY AND MYTH

If the argument of the previous paragraph seems far-fetched, it may gain in plausibility if cerebral lateralization is substituted for handedness, for in this context the link with consciousness and human uniqueness *has* been made explicit. Eccles (1965; Popper & Eccles, 1977) has proposed that, at least in the majority of people, only the left cerebral hemisphere is conscious, whereas the right hemisphere is a mere "computer," comparable to the brains of lower species. The nature of hemispheric specialization is discussed in detail in later chapters of this book, but suffice it to say for the moment that I think Eccles's view belongs more in the realm of myth than of science. Zangwill (1976), for instance, describes it as "little more than a desperate rearguard action to save the existence and indivisibility of the soul [p. 304]."

A more elaborate case for linking consciousness with the left cerebral hemisphere has been advanced by Jaynes (1976), who suggests that cerebral lateralization may have evolved within recorded human history. According to Jaynes, the human mind as depicted in the *Iliad* or the Old Testament lacked consciousness in the sense of self-awareness and of individual responsibility for action. People of that era were guided in their actions by hallucinations, which they interpreted as the voices of the gods. It was only through specialization of the left cerebral hemisphere that humans evolved the concept of self and came to govern their own behavior. The evolution of cerebral lateralization will be discussed in detail later, but it may be noted here that the evidence does not square easily with Jaynes's theory, elaborately documented though it is. In any event, it is extremely unlikely on a priori grounds that cerebral lateralization could have evolved over such a brief time span, a point that Jaynes himself recognized. Jaynes's theory, like Eccles's, seems to owe more to the desire to preserve the myth of human uniqueness than to the empirical evidence.

A more popular theme in contemporary views of cerebral lateralization is, not that one cerebral hemisphere is conscious and the other not, but rather that the two cerebral hemispheres mediate different kinds of consciousness. In this context, cerebral lateralization has taken over from handedness the role of substrate for those dichotomies that are paraded in popular philosophy—the symbolic potency of laterality has, literally, gone to our heads. Over a hundred years ago, it was discovered that, in most people, the left cerebral hemisphere is dominant for language (Broca, 1861; Dax, 1865). Until recently, it was generally supposed that the right cerebral hemisphere played a relatively unimportant role, and indeed it was often termed the "minor" hemisphere.

Some authors, however, had sought some more basic dichotomy that might characterize hemispheric asymmetry. For instance, Hughlings Jackson (1864) suggested that the left hemisphere might be generally dominant for expression and the right hemisphere for perception. Others proposed that the left hemisphere might normally be dominant for linguistic or propositional functions, while the right played the major role in visual or imaginative processes (e.g. Humphrey & Zangwill, 1951; Weisenberg & McBride, 1935). A. L. Anderson (1951) suggested that if the left hemisphere played the executive role, the right hemisphere might be specialized for storage, and in a similar vein, Bruner (1968) proposed that the left hemisphere was specialized for "operating" and the right hemisphere for "holding."

Speculation about the nature of hemisphere asymmetry took a more transcendental turn in the late 1960s and early 1970s with a series of articles by Bogen (1969a, 1969b; Bogen & Bogen, 1969), whose main themes were popularized by Ornstein (1972). Bogen saw in cerebral asymmetry a neurological basis for a fundamental dichotomy in human thought: Whereas the left hemisphere was rational, analytic, and logical, the right hemisphere was emotional, holistic, and intuitive. Bogen suggested the terms *propositional* and *appositional* to capture the two poles of this dichotomy. One might also discern here something of the male and female values more traditionally associated with the right and left hands, respectively. Notice that the neurological facts have forced a left–right reversal, with right-hand values now associated with the *left* hemisphere, and conversely. While this may have confused some commentators, it has worked to the advantage of those left-handers who like to wear T-shirts proclaiming themselves to be in their right minds.

Bogen also saw left-hemisphere attributes as typical of materialistic Western culture, whereas right-hemispheric values characterized the more spiritual Eastern culture. Following Bruner (1968), he also suggested that the right hemisphere might be the more creative, an idea that has been enthusiastically pursued by some educators, especially those involved in the teaching of art. In an article in the *Los Angeles Times,* for instance, an art teacher was quoted as saying that her aim was to teach people to "gain access to the right hemisphere and be able to use it for education in general ["The Art of Putting the Brain to Work," 1977, p. 20]." Again, Garrett (1976) deplores the overemphasis on left-hemispheric values in American schools and notes "the tragic lack of effort to develop our children's right brain strengths. That potential—a source of equally essential creative, artistic, and intellectual capacity—is at present largely unawakened in our schools [p. 244]."

The dichotomy envisaged by Bogen was not new but represented a recurrent distinction in philosophical writing. Bogen (1969b) himself recognized essentially the same dichotomy in the pre-Confucian Chinese concepts of *yin* and *yang,* in the Hindu notions of *buddhi* and *manas,* in Levi-Strauss's distinction between the *positive* and *mythic.* Bogen's contribution was to suggest that the neurological basis for this common dichotomy might lie in hemispheric specialization, although he was anticipated in this premonitory passage, attributed to Maurice Maeterlinck, and written over half a century ago:

The one produces here reason, and consciousness; the other secretes yonder intuition, religion, and subconsciousness. The one reflects only the infinite and the unknowable; the other is interested only in what it can limit, what it can hope to understand. They represent in an image that may be illusory, the struggle between the material and moral ideals of humanity. They have more than once tried to penetrate each other, to mingle, to work in harmony; but the Western lobe, at least over the most active part of the globe, has up to the present paralysed and almost destroyed the efforts of the other. We owe to it not only our extraordinary progress in all the material sciences but also catastrophes such as we are experiencing today, which, unless we take care, will not be the last or the worst [quoted in Massis, 1926, p. 487].

All that is lacking here is specific reference to left and right hemispheres, although Maeterlinck came uncannily close with his reference to Western and Oriental "lobes."

The dichotomy between so-called left-brain and right-brain styles of thinking is now thoroughly engrained in our folklore. It was accepted and further reinforced, for instance, by the eminent astronomer and writer of popular science, Carl Sagan, in his entertaining book *The Dragons of Eden* (1977). Sagan characterizes the right hemisphere as an intuitive pattern recognizer with a somewhat emotional, paranoid quality, often seeing patterns or conspiracies where they do not exist. In the pursuit of knowledge, the left hemisphere is required to submit proposed patterns to critical analysis. Where others have emphasized the conflict between the hemispheres, Sagan's characterization at least recognizes the collaborative aspect of interhemispheric relations:

> Our objective is to abstract patterns from Nature (right hemisphere thinking), but many proposed patterns do not in fact correspond to the data. Thus all proposed patterns must be subjected to the sieve of critical analysis (left hemisphere thinking). The search for patterns without critical analysis, and rigid skepticism without a search for patterns, are the antipodes of incomplete science. The effective pursuit of knowledge requires both functions [p.183].

The impact of so-called hemispheric duality has been so far-reaching that there is little point in documenting it further; it must surely be well known to all. H. Gardner (1978) summarizes with only a touch of exaggeration:

> It is becoming a familiar sight. Staring directly at the reader—frequently from a magazine cover—is an artist's rendition of the two halves of the brain. Surprinted athwart the left cerebral hemisphere (probably in stark blacks and greys) are such words as "logical," "analytical," and "Western rationality." More luridly etched across the right hemisphere (in rich orange or royal purple) are "intuitive," "artistic," or "Eastern consciousness." Regrettably, the picture says more about a current popular science vogue than it says about the brain [cited in Springer & Deutsch, 1981, p. 187].

This is not to say that I am totally opposed to what such authors as Bogen, Jaynes, and Sagan have to say. The distinctions they draw are useful and in many respects valid, and they help make sense of a variety of aspects of human thought and culture. The basic dichotomy between the rational and the intuitive has been so often described that it scarcely even needs the prop of hemispheric specialization to support it. It would be churlish to deny the advantages of teaching children to think visually as well as verbally, or of fostering the creative imagination as well as the more traditional critical and computational skills, although again one scarcely needs to refer to the cerebral hemispheres to make the point. De Bono (1967, 1970, 1976), for instance, has successfully promoted the teaching of "lateral thinking" without succumbing to the tyranny of the left–right metaphor.

Perhaps it would also be wrong to insist that the neuropsychological distinction proposed by Bogen and the others is totally in error. I do not of course wish to claim that cerebral lateralization is a myth (pace L. Goldstein, 1980); it is a fact of very considerable interest and importance, not least because of its potential for attracting mythical interpretation. Insofar as the cerebral hemispheres can be regarded as distinct entities, with distinct cognitive capacities, they may well lean somewhat in the directions suggested by Bogen. The main error, perhaps, is that of overdichotomization. It is, on the face of it, extremely unlikely that structures as alike as the two cerebral hemispheres could subserve cognitive functions as opposite as the poles of a dichotomy, and there is nothing in the neuropsychological evidence, at least to my knowledge, that contradicts this expectation. The discrepancy between functional asymmetry and structural symmetry remains a fairly striking and to some extent inexplicable one, but it has undoubtedly been exaggerated. Even the more conservative researchers have emphasized functional differences between the hemispheres at the expense of the considerable degree of functional overlap between them, a point made over a decade ago by Milner (1971).

A related error is that of personifying the hemispheres, treating each as though it were a separate person with a "mind" of its own (D. N. Robinson, 1976). This tendency was prompted mainly by the rather dramatic effects of the so-called split-brain operation, in which patients suffering intractable epilepsy underwent section of the commissures connecting the two cerebral hemispheres—Bogen, in fact, was one of the surgeons who performed this operation. The evidence will be reviewed in more detail later but showed in effect that information projected to one cerebral hemisphere of a split-brain patient remained inaccessible to the other. Each hemisphere could thus be shown to mediate different, independent, and even conflicting perceptions and decisions. It is often forgotten, however, that it took subtle techniques to demonstrate these effects, and in their everyday behavior the split-brain patients seem as integrated and single-minded as normal people (for a more extended discussion, see Marks, 1980). In any event, it is obviously wrong to draw inferences about dual consciousness in the normal brain on the basis of evidence from split-brains. It is scarcely surprising, except perhaps to an ardent dualist, that a person with a split brain should show some evidence for a split consciousness, but this need not tell us anything very important about the nature of consciousness in a normal person.

NEW MYTHS FOR OLD?

Although part of my aim in this book is to demythologize human laterality, the discerning reader will no doubt discover that I have substituted new myths for old. I make no apology for this. For one thing, the influence of myth in the interpretation of laterality has been so manifestly strong that I cannot possibly claim any special immunity from it. The best I can do is to recognize the problem and try to maintain a reasonably objective view. Second, myth has an important, even indispensable, role to play in science. *Chambers Twentieth Century Dictionary* (1972 edition) defines a myth as ''an ancient story of gods or heroes, especially one offering an explanation of some fact or phenomenon.'' Except for the word *ancient,* this might also do as a definition of science; our present-day gods include genes, quarks, and schedules of reinforcement. Scientific theories go beyond the facts in the attempt to discover coherence and structure, and they are therefore inevitably subject to human biases and preconceptions.

This book is therefore not simply a review of evidence about human laterality. It is written in the conviction that there is an underlying unity to its various manifestations, including handedness and the various aspects of cerebral asymmetry. Part of my purpose, then, is to characterize this underlying asymmetry and to document and speculate on how and why it evolved.

A second theme is that it is more appropriate to emphasize the continuity between humans and other species than to focus on human uniqueness. Although handedness and cerebral asymmetry are in certain respects peculiar to human beings, certain comparable asymmetries can be found in other species. The question of whether laterality in other species is homologous or merely analogous to human laterality (cf. Warren, 1978) is an elusive one, but in either case, it is often reasonable to assume that common principles underlie different manifestations of asymmetry in different species. I shall therefore draw from time to time on examples of asymmetry in other animals that may seem quite remote from the asymmetries that are observed in humans.

A final theme that underlies the book is that laterality should be viewed in the context of the overwhelming bilateral symmetry that characterizes the bodies and nervous systems of all animals, including human beings. It is probably safe to say that, for all but a tiny part of our evolutionary history, the evolutionary contingencies on the structure of the limbs and of the nervous system have favored bilateral symmetry rather than asymmetry (cf. Corballis & Beale, 1970). Human laterality may therefore be best understood as a property that has been superimposed on structures that are fundamentally symmetrical.

2 Human Handedness

Andrew Buchanan, writing in the *Proceedings of the Philosophical Society of Glasgow* of 1860–1864, made the following assertion:

> The use of the right hand in preference to the left must be regarded as a general characteristic of the family of man. There is no nation, race or tribe of men on the earth at the present day, among whom this preference does not obtain; while, in former times, it is shown to have existed, both by historical documents and by the still more ancient and authentic testimony of certain words, phrases, and modes of speaking, which are, I believe, to be found in every spoken language [Buchanan, 1862, quoted by Wilson, 1872, p. 198].

Now, more than a century later, the evidence still very largely supports this bold statement.

Occasionally, there has been a suggestion that some particular nation or culture may have been predominantly left-handed, but the evidence is usually indirect and invariably flimsy. In his classic monograph on handedness, for instance, Blau (1946) seemed to endorse an argument put forward by Erlenmayer in the 1880s that the ancient Hebrews may have been mostly left-handed because Hebrew is written from right to left. There is no reason to suppose, however, that the direction of script bears any strong relation to handedness. Although the average right-hander may feel that it is more "natural" to write from left to right, one can argue equally that in the early engraving of primitive symbols on stone tablets it was more natural to begin on the right, the side of

11

the dominant hand. Until about A.D. 1500, in fact, right-to-left scripts were about as common as left-to-right ones, and the gradual predominance of left-to-right scripts since that time can be attributed to historical influences rather than to considerations of handedness (Hewes, 1949). Among present-day Israelis, there appears to be no difference in handedness between those who read only from right to left (Hebrew and other Semitic languages) and those who also read from left to right (Indo-European languages); Israelis are also predominantly right-handed, although when compared to British and Taiwanese samples, there appeared to be more Israelis at the extremes of both left- and right-handedness (Silverberg, Obler, & Gordon, 1979).

Again, it has been suggested that the ancient Egyptians may have been predominantly left-handed because they usually depicted human and animal figures in right profile on their hieroglyphics and monuments, whereas it is generally considered more natural for the right-hander to draw left profiles. Discussing this argument, D. Wilson (1872) was inclined to reject it on the grounds that the direction of profile was often dictated by other artistic considerations. In a more convincing refutation, Erman (1894) noted that it was a general law of art that figures should present their right sides to the spectator, a law that in fact suggest that the ancient Egyptian were predominantly *right*-handed. Moreover, W. Dennis (1958) examined the frequencies of left- and right-handedness as depicted in paintings in the Egyptians tombs of Beni Hasan and Thebes, dating from about 2500 B.C., and observed a predominance of right-handedness comparable to that observed in modern societies.

Wilson, after discussing the evidence from the Egyptians and other early civilizations, came to the conclusion that the only evidence for a left-handed people that could not be dismissed on the basis of other considerations occurred in a passage in the eclogues of Stobaeus, the Macedonian, written about 600 A.D.: "Those on the south-west are sure-footed, and for the most part fight with the left hand; and as much force as others exert with their right side, they exert by application of their left [cited in D. Wilson, 1872, p. 225]." A similar curiosity occurs in John H. Tooke's *Diversions of Purley, 1786–1805,* published in 1840: "I remember to have read in a voyage of Da Gama's to Kalekut . . . that the people of Melinda, a polished and flourishing people, were all left-handed [cited in Wile, 1934, p. 20]."

Blau (1946) also drew attention to the 700 left-handed men in the army of Benjamin, referred to in the Old Testament (Judges 20:16), but neglected to mention that these were but a fraction of the total army of 26,700. Other observations of left-handed peoples, such as those of the previous paragraph, no doubt suffer from similar biases or misconceptions. In any event, these isolated and fragmented reports fade into insignificance when set against the weight of evidence from art, stories, folklore, and indeed words themselves, which overwhelmingly attest to the universal dominance of the right hand. In

Chapter 1, for instance, I cited examples from various cultures of polarities associated with left and right in which the association of the positive poles with the right is evidence for right-handedness itself; for fuller documentation, the reader is referred to the collection of readings edited by R. Needham (1973).

The Chinese appear to have been somewhat unique in bestowing special honor on the left hand, but other aspects of their culture attest to the prevalence of right-handedness (Granet, 1953). A modern survey of Chinese in Taiwan reveals the incidence of right-handedness there to be about the same as in Western societies, and even higher in the activities of writing and eating, due no doubt to cultural pressures (Teng, Lee, Yang, & Chang, 1976). The Chinese evidently go only so far in holding the left hand in high esteem.

The reference to the 700 left-handed men in the army of Benjamin appears to be the first written record of left-handedness. These represent 2.6% of the total army of 26,700; at first glance, this seems a rather low estimate of the percentage of left-handers, but of course, there is no evidence that the remaining 26,700 were all right-handed (Hardyck & Petrinovich, 1977)! Coren and Porac (1977) examined handedness as depicted in works of art dating back some 5000 years and discovered that the proportion of left-handers was remarkably constant at about 10% over the entire period. This is very close to present-day estimates and suggests that the relative proportions of left- and right-handers have remained more or less constant since the beginning of recorded history.

Despite this, there have been remarkable changes within the present century in the proportion of individuals using the left hand for writing. Figure 2.1 summarizes data from the United States (Levy, 1974) and from Australasia (Brackenridge, 1981). In each case, the increase is from about 2% to over 10% and is no doubt due to the lessening of educational or parental pressure to write with the right hand; it is of interest that the increase began earlier in Australia and New Zealand, reflecting the more advanced social attitudes of enlightened Antipodeans. Both curves reach asymptotes at 10–12%, suggesting that this is indeed the proportion of "natural" left-handers in human populations. It is also of note that the lower limit of 2%, which seems to be a lower asymptote, at least in the case of the Australasian sample, corresponds quite closely to the proportion of left-handed writers in present-day Taiwan, where the pressure to write with the right hand remains strong. This proportion may represent some hard core of natural left-handers who are resistant to change.

In the absence of clear evidence to the contrary, then, it seems safe to assume that the majority of humans have been right-handed at least since the beginning of recorded history, regardless of race or geography. This is one of the grounds for supposing that the basis of right-handedness is biological rather than cultural. Before exploring this proposition a little further, however, it is

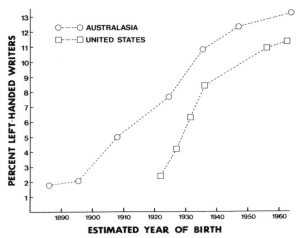

FIGURE 2.1. Percentage of left-handed writers plotted according to estimated year of birth, among samples from Australasia (after Brackenridge, 1981) and from the United States (after Levy, 1974).

pertinent to consider in more detail how handedness can be measured and what its main characteristics are.

THE MEASUREMENT OF HANDEDNESS

For the most part, there is little doubt in deciding whether a person is left- or right-handed, although some troublesome individuals are ambidextrous or use different hands for different activities. For some purposes, however, rough classification of individuals into categories does not capture all the information about a person's handedness. A number of more precise scales have been devised in which handedness is represented as a continuum rather than as a dichotomy or trichotomy. In measuring handedness, it may also be important to distinguish between measures based on *preference* and those based on actual *performance:* A person may prefer to use one hand for a certain task but may be more skillful with the other (e.g., Humphrey, 1951)—although this state of affairs is rare, at least among those who display strong handedness.

In measuring *preference,* the usual method is to select a number of different unimanual activities and inquire as to which is the preferred hand in each case. One widely used test is the Edinburgh Handedness Inventory, developed by Oldfield (1971) at Edinburgh University. The testee is simply asked to indicate the preferred hand in each of the following activities: writing; drawing; throwing; using scissors, toothbrush, knife (without fork), spoon, and broom (upper hand); striking a match; and opening a lid. These activities were carefully culled from a larger set to provide a reliable overall index and to exclude activities with an obvious cultural bias (such as playing baseball or cricket). The inventory, together with instructions for scoring, is shown in Figure 2.2. As explained there, it is possible to compute from the subject's responses a *laterality quotient*, ranging from −100 for extreme left-handedness, through 0 for complete ambidexterity, to +100 for extreme right-handedness.

When this inventory was administered to 394 men and 734 women undergraduates at Edinburgh University, 10% of the men and 6% of the women were found to have quotients of less than zero, indicating at least some degree of left-handedness. These percentages may not be representative of the population as a whole, but they do illustrate the common observation that a higher proportion of men than of women are left-handed (e.g., M. M. Clark, 1957; Hécaen & Ajuriaguerra, 1964; Teng *et al.*, 1976). On the basis of a survey of

---

The following is the short form of the inventory developed by Oldfield (1971) and standardized in Edinburgh. The instructions to the subject are as follows:

Please indicate your preferences in the use of the hands in the following activities by *putting + in the appropriate column*. Where the preference is so strong that you would never try to use the other hand unless absolutely forced to, *put + +*. If in any case you are really indifferent *put + in both columns*.

Some of these activities require both hands. In these cases the part of the task, or object, for which hand preference is wanted is indicated in brackets.

Please try to answer all the questions, and only leave a blank if you have no experience at all of the object or task.

	LEFT	RIGHT
1. Writing		
2. Drawing		
3. Throwing		
4. Scissors		
5. Toothbrush		
6. Knife (without fork)		
7. Spoon		
8. Broom (upper hand)		
9. Striking Match (match)		
10. Opening box (lid)		

To find the laterality quotient, add up the number of + signs in each column. Subtract the number under LEFT from the number under RIGHT, divide by the total number, and multiply by 100.

FIGURE 2.2. Edinburgh Handedness Inventory

undergraduates in a Canadian university, however, Bryden (1977) has argued that this difference between men and women may reflect a bias in reporting, with women more likely than men to claim extreme use of one hand, rather than a true difference in preference. Silverberg *et al.* (1979) found no sex differences in handedness among their sample of 1171 Israelis.

Factor analysis of the Edinburgh Handedness Inventory suggests that it does indeed measure a unitary handedness factor that is stable across sex and over a test–retest interval (McFarland & Anderson, 1980; K. White & Ashton, 1976). McFarland and Anderson (1980) also report that the item on the use of scissors is unreliable upon retest, perhaps because scissors are intrinsically for the right-handed, and that the items to do with using a knife or a broom and with opening the lid of a box do not load well on the handedness factor; they suggest that these items should be given less weight than the others. Bryden (1977) factor analyzed items from the Edinburgh Handedness Inventory and from a more extensive list of items from the inventory devised by Crovitz and Zener (1962), and also extracted a primary handedness factor. He recommended a shortened test based on just five items: writing, throwing, drawing, using scissors, and using a toothbrush.

Figure 2.3 shows the distribution of laterality quotients obtained by Oldfield (1971). It is clearly bimodal; that is, most people show a consistent preference for one or the other hand, and relatively few are ambidextrous or display even preference. For instance, about 50% of those with positive quotients have laterality quotients above 80, while 50% of those with negative quotients have quotients less than −76. The distribution is rather more even across the neg-

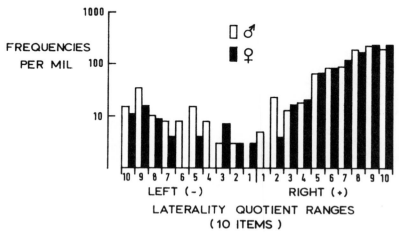

FIGURE 2.3. Distribution of laterality quotients in Edinburgh sample. [From Oldfield, 1971.]

ative values than across the positive ones; that is, right-handers are more right-handed, on the whole, than left-handers are left-handed. Because of this, some authors have preferred the label "non-right-handed" to "left-handed."

Measuring handedness in terms of differences in *performance* between the two hands is more complicated and time consuming, but it is in some respects more satisfactory than measuring preference because it does not rely on individual testimony. People do not always answer questionnaires reliably or honestly, and some, especially children, are in any case often confused about which is left and which is right (see Corballis & Beale, 1976, for review). One difficulty in using measures of differential skill, however, is that there are many different skills to choose from. In their classic study of the distribution of handedness, Woo and Pearson (1927) analyzed the data on intermanual differences in the strength of hand grip from 4948 of the cases recorded by Sir Francis Galton at the Health Exhibition of 1884. The distribution was bell shaped and displaced to the right of equality between the hands, meaning that the right hand was the stronger in the majority of cases. Woo and Pearson concluded that "dextrality and sinistrality are not opposed alternatives, but quantities capable of taking values of continuous intensity and passing one into the other [p. 199]."

Strength of grip may not be an altogether appropriate measure, however, if the aim is to discover a person's natural handedness, uncontaminated by experience or cultural pressures. A natural left-hander may conceivably have developed greater strength in the right hand through having been forced to write with that hand. Annett (1970, 1976) has devised a peg-moving task, in which the subject is timed while moving 10 pegs from one row of holes to another, and has claimed that this task is indeed relatively immune from experiential factors. For instance, she found that children became more adept with age, but the difference between the hands in the time taken to perform the task remained approximately constant over the age range from 3½ to 15 years (Annett, 1970). For the majority of children and adults, the right hand was the faster and the differences between hands were highly correlated with the subjects' preferences for one or the other hand (Annett, 1970, 1976).

The distribution of intermanual differences in the time to perform the peg-moving task, like the distribution of differences in the strength of grip, is unimodal and approximately normal, with a mean favoring faster performance with the right hand (Annett, 1972). In this, it differs markedly from the distribution of scores on measures of preference, which is bimodal (see Figure 2.3). One consequence of this is that the relation between hand preferences and intermanual differences is nonlinear, although monotonic; there is a gain factor such that handedness is expressed more strongly in preference than in differences between the hands in strength or skill. Annett (1972) also found that the mean intermanual difference in favor of the right hand in the peg-moving task was significantly higher among women and girls than among men and boys. This suggests, contrary to Bryden (1977), that the sex difference in handedness cannot be attributed entirely to differential bias in responding to questionnaires.

Similar results have been reported for intermanual differences in finger tapping. Peters and Durding (1978) had children tap as quickly as they could with the index finger of each hand in turn, in bursts of 10 sec. The differences in speed between the hands, where speed was defined as the mean interval between taps, were again distributed approximately normally, with a mean favoring the right hand. There was a strong correlation with hand preference. In a later study, Peters (1980) reported similar results among adults and showed that intermanual differences in finger tapping could not be attributed to different effects of fatigue in the two hands, or to differences in the separate upward or downward movements of the two index fingers, or to differential sensory feedback. Rather, the difference seemed to lie in the precision with which force was modulated in the two hands, and in a version of the task requiring more controlled movement, the difference was enhanced.

In a more global attempt to discover the dimensions of manual skill, Barnsley and Rabinovitch (1970) tested people with each hand in turn on a wide range of unimanual tasks. They factor analyzed the intercorrelations between tasks separately for preferred and nonpreferred hands, and they found essentially the same factor structure in each case. The most important factors were identified as reaction time, speed of arm movement, wrist–finger speed, arm–hand steadiness, arm movement steadiness, and aiming. In all except reaction time, subjects performed better with the preferred than the nonpreferred hand, a result replicated by Rigal (1974b). This again demonstrates the relation between measures based on preference and those based on performance.

Because unimanual skill is multidimensional, Barnsley and Rabinovitch (1970) suggest that tasks should be sampled from each factor in order to provide a global measure of handedness. Rigal (1974a) has suggested a specific procedure for doing this. The importance of selecting tasks from the different factors may well have been exaggerated, however, for although unimanual skill is multidimensional, it does not necessarily follow that handedness itself is multidimensional. That is, the differences between the hands on the various factors might well be intercorrelated and reveal a single common factor—the point has not to my knowledge been put to the test. In any event, it may well be more important to choose tests that are relatively free of the effects of learning than to choose tests representative of the range of manual skills, although this may in turn depend on one's reasons for measuring handedness in the first place.

There will no doubt always be anomalies in the measurement of handedness—minor discrepancies between preference for one or the other hand and intermanual differences in performance, or discrepancies between different tasks within these categories. One reason is that, as in virtually all psychological testing, it is probably impossible to produce a culture-fair test of handedness or to remove all the influences of education or environment. More generally, handedness probably has an intrinsically stochastic component. As Annett (1972) has pointed out, the conspicuous feature of the distribution of inter-manual differences in humans that distinguishes it from comparable distributions in animals is the right shift; among mice (Collins, 1970), rats (G. M. Peterson, 1934), monkeys, (Cole, 1957; Lehman, 1978), chimpanzees (Finch, 1941), and baboons (Trevarthen, 1978), the distribution of intermanual differences is centered on the point of equality. There is some evidence that cats, on the other hand (so to speak), display a small *left* shift (Cole, 1955), although this is by no means as striking as the right shift in humans. In people as in other animals, however, deviations from the mean must depend at least in part on the chance effects of a multitude of factors, environmental as well as constitutional, prenatal as well as postnatal. Collins (1975) has referred to this chance component in the expression of handedness as the "asymmetry lottery."

RIGHT-HANDEDNESS: BIOLOGICAL OR CULTURAL?

Perhaps the most salient issue in the history of ideas about handedness is whether this right shift is a biological or a cultural endowment. The issue actually goes back to Aristotle and Plato (Wile, 1934). Aristotle wrote that the organs of the right side of the body were more powerful than those of the left, but Plato argued against this, attributing any weakness of the left to "the folly of nurses and mothers." In particular, if a nurse or mother habitually carries an infant on one arm, then one side of the infant's body is cramped while the other is free to move. Discussing this issue, however, Baldwin (1906) observed that most right-handed nurses and mothers carried their infants on their left arms, leaving the child's *left* arm free; hence right-handed mothers should have left-handed children, and vice versa, which is not generally the case.

Nevertheless, the idea that handedness is imposed by child-rearing practices has been a recurrent one. In *Emile,* for instance, the eighteenth-century French philosopher Jean Jacques Rousseau wrote: "The only habit the child should be allowed to acquire is to contract none. He should not be carried on one arm more than the other or allowed to make use of one hand more than the other [translation in Boyd, 1956, p. 22]." The English novelist and propagandist Charles Reade was more severe; in a letter to *Harpers Weekly* of 2 March 1878, he wrote

> Six thousand years of lop-armed, lop-legged savages, some barbarous, some civilized,
> have not created a single lop-legged, lop-armed child, and never will. Every child is
> even and either handed till some grown fool interferes and mutilates it [p. 175].

There seems to have been a groundswell of propaganda in favor of ambi-
dexterity in England around the turn of the century, with the formation of the
Ambidextral Culture Society. Its founder was John Jackson, author of a tract,
influential at the time, called *Ambidexterity or Two-Handedness and Two-
Brainedness* (1905). Among its supporters was Lord Baden-Powell, the famous
British soldier who founded the Boy Scout Movement, and it was partly to
encourage ambidexterity that the Boy Scouts shake hands with the left hand
(L. J. Harris, 1980a). Hertz was another vigorous advocate of the idea that the
two hands possess equal potential for skilled action, and he tried to persuade
educators to develop programs to foster this potential. "One of the signs which
distinguish a well-brought-up child," he wrote, with irony, "is that its left
hand has become incapable of independent action [Hertz, 1909/1960, p. 92]."

Implicit in movements to foster ambidexterity is the assumption, or belief,
that handedness is shaped by culture, not by biology. One author who has
maintained this perspective is Collins (1970, 1975). Collins is not dogmatic on
the issue, however, as his argument is indirect. He makes two main points.
First, by examining the distribution of handedness among siblings, and in particular among twins, Collins (1970) argued that the direction of handedness
(i.e., left or right) is not under genetic control. I shall consider the inheritance
of handedness, and Collins's arguments in particular, in Chapter 7. Second,
Collins (1975) demonstrated that mice, placed in a "right-handed world,"
showed a predominant preference for the right paw. Collins measured paw
preference by placing food in a glass tube and observing which forepaw each
mouse used to extract the food. In the absence of environmental asymmetries,
individual mice typically show a clear preference for one or the other paw, and
the preferred paw is usually the one with the stronger grip (Collins, 1970).
When Collins moved the glass tube to the right so that is was more accessible
to the right paw than to the left, the majority of mice favored the right paw.
A stubborn minority of about 10%, however, persisted in reaching awkwardly
with the left paw—a proportion, Collins (1975) noted, "not unlike the proportion of left handers in human societies [p. 183]."

Yet the bulk of evidence suggests that our predominant right-handedness
is not shaped by culture, but rather that our "right-handed world" is a consequence of biological right-handedness. One argument mentioned earlier in
this chapter is simply that right-handedness appears to predominate in all human cultures, including those that have been geographically isolated from one
another for centuries, if not millennia. For all the vehemence of their advo-
cates, ambidexterity movements have not survived; even the Boy Scouts, I suspect, remain predominantly right-handed.

The other arguments have to do with aspects of handedness, and more generally of laterality, to be covered in subsequent chapters of this book. These aspects include the relation between handedness and other asymmetries, including cerebral lateralization (Chapters 3 and 4), the development of laterality (Chapter 5), the evolution of laterality (Chapter 6), and the inheritance of laterality (Chapter 7). The biological basis of laterality is indeed one of the major themes of the book.

LEFT-HANDEDNESS

Throughout history, left-handers have been singled out for special treatment, most of it no doubt unwanted and unwelcome. The negative qualities so readily attributed to left-handers are almost certainly due in part to mythic properties, described in Chapter 1, that are attached to the left and right hands. Wile (1934) notes, for instance, that there are some 80 references in the Bible to the right hand, ascribing to it honors, virtues, and powers, but that "there is not one honorable reference to the left hand [p. 340]." Even in the twentieth century, left-handers have been described in the most unflattering terms, as in the following extract from Burt (1937):

> They squint, they stammer, they shuffle and shamble, they flounder about like seals out of water. Awkward in the house, and clumsy in their games, they are fumblers and bunglers at whatever they do [p. 287].

To be sure, Burt recognized that not all left-handers conform to this pattern, noting such conspicuous exceptions as Leonardo da Vinci. Even so, his statement stands as a cruel caricature that bears little relation to the facts.

Nevertheless, it is a curious fact that left-handers should have constituted an apparently stable minority for as far back as the historical record takes us, and there has been considerable speculation as to what might explain it. Blau (1946), for instance, concluded that left-handedness was most commonly the result of "emotional negativism," meaning presumably a stubborn refusal to conform with the majority. Again, Bakan has argued that left-handedness may be due to minor brain injury caused by hypoxia at birth, noting that left-handedness occurs more frequently among firstborns and among those born fourth or later—birth orders known to put infants at higher medical risk than those in between (Bakan, 1971, 1977; Bakan, Dibb, & Reed, 1973). There is also a considerable literature relating left-handedness to other disorders, such as reading disability (e.g., Orton, 1937), stuttering (e.g., Orton & Travis, 1929), alcoholism (e.g., Bakan, 1973), and mental retardation (e.g., Burt, 1937). It has also been claimed that the incidence of left-handedness is higher in twins than in the singly born (e.g., Nagylaki & Levy, 1973; Springer & Deutsch, 1981), suggesting that it may be linked to the higher incidence of minor pathology in twins (Springer & Searleman, 1980).

Claims as to the pathological basis of left-handedness are exaggerated, at the very least. In one review, Hardyck and Petrinovitch (1977) conclude that "the data indicating that left-handedness is associated with deficits of various kinds is far from compelling [p. 394]." Other studies have failed to show any relation between handedness and birth order (Hicks, Evans, & Pellegrini, 1978; Hubbard, 1971; Schwartz, 1977), and McManus (1980), in a review of the literature, has argued that there is no convincing evidence for an increased incidence of left-handedness among twins. A large-scale study of high school students in California revealed essentially no difference in intelligence between left- and right-handers (Hardyck, Petrinovitch, & Goldman, 1976).

In large part, then, it seems that the negative qualities attributed to left-handers are as much a consequence of the abiding left–right myth as of the empirical evidence (cf. Corballis, 1980b). That said, however, I think it is possible that there is a small thread of truth in some of the assertions about left-handers: In Chapter 8, for instance, I review evidence that certain disorders of language, including reading disability, stuttering, and developmental dysphasia, may in some instances be associated with anomalies of lateralizaion, but the relation between these and left-handedness is indirect.

To some degree, the notion that left-handers belong in a special category is a consequence of dichotomization— the tendency to divide people categorically into left- and right-handers (with occasional concessions to the ambidextrous). This in turn is no doubt due to the fact that the hands are a pair, and the choice between them is a dichotomous choice. Nevertheless, we saw earlier that if differences in skill between the hands are considered, then handedness emerges as a continuous variable rather than a dichotomous one. The distribution of intermanual differences is approximately normal, but shifted to the right. It is quite possible, then, that left-handedness occurs simply through the accumulation of chance influences that override some congenital right-shift factor. Such influences may well include some that may be described as pathological (such as cerebral anoxia at birth), although there is no convincing evidence that these play more than a minor role. In other words, the right shift is not so strong as to guarantee that all individuals will be right-handed, and indeed it may well have been held in check by the advantages of at least some degree of ambidexterity; left-handedness may therefore be no more than an extreme expression of the natural variation underlying handedness.

Despite this simple argument, Annett (1972) argued that there is a minority of the human population who lack the right-shift factor. Among this minority, who represent perhaps 10–15% of the population, any culturally unbiased measure of handedness should yield equal numbers of left- and right-handers, although in practice there may be a slight preponderence of manifest right-handers due to environmental pressures. According to Annett, then, there are in effect two superimposed normal distributions underlying the distribution of intermanual differences, one (RS+) exhibiting the right shift and the other (RS−) centered on the point of equality between the hands. These hypothetical distributions are shown in Figure 2.4. According to this theory, many left-handers, perhaps the majority, belong to the RS− group, although some will be drawn from the leftward tail of the RS+ distribution.

It may be seen as a criticism of Annett's theory that, having gone to such pains to remove the dichotomy implicit in the very idea of handedness, she should at once replace it with another dichotomy. On the grounds of parsimony, there seems little point in postulating two distributions when one will do (cf. Corballis, 1980a). Yet on broader examination of the evidence, there are grounds for supposing that Annett's theory is at least a good approximation to the truth.

One line of argument has to do with asymmetries on measures other than measures of handedness. According to Annett's theory, left-handers are much more likely than are right-handers to be drawn from the RS− distribution. Now if the RS− subpopulation exhibits no consistent bias on variables other than handedness, then one would expect left-handers to be less lateralized than right-handers on all measures of laterality. In fact, left-handers show inconsistent laterality on virtually all indices, including eye dominance (Friedlander,

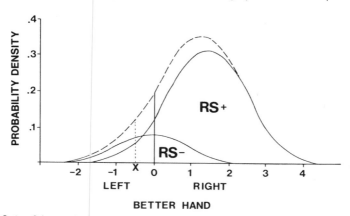

FIGURE 2.4.   Schematic representation of two distributions of intermanual skill hypothesized by Annett (1972). One distribution (RS+) represents those individuals inheriting the right-shift factor; the other (RS−) represents those without this factor. X represents the criterion for phenotypic expression of left- or right-handedness and may deviate from 0, the point of neutrality. [Reprinted by permission from M. Annett, The genetics of handedness, *Trends in Neurosciences*, 1981, *3*, 257.]

1971), footedness (Peters & Durding, 1979), and asymmetries of fingerprints (Rife, 1955), whereas the majority of right-handers are right-eyed, right-footed, and show clear asymmetries in fingerprints. During speaking, left-handers tend to gesture about equally often with either hand (Kimura, 1973b), whereas right-handers gesture almost exclusively with the right hand (Kimura, 1973a). Left-handers also show mixed patterns of laterality in both functional and structural measures of cerebral asymmetry, whereas right-handers show much more consistent asymmetries on these measures; evidence for this is documented in the following two chapters.

A second line of argument is genetic. Annett (1972, 1978, 1981) has argued that the presence or absence of the right-shift factor is governed in Mendelian fashion by a single gene locus. Of all genetic theories so far proposed, this one gives the most satisfactory account of the facts of the inheritance of handedness, and indeed of laterality generally. This topic is pursued in Chapter 7.

Annett's theory effectively shifts the emphasis from left-handers per se to that subgroup presumed to lack the right shift. Evidence about the characteristics of individuals in that subgroup must still come largely from left-handers, however, since the proportion of left-handers in the RS− group (about 50%) is assumed to be much larger than the proportion of left-handers in the RS+ group (perhaps 5%). Left-handers thus provide the main window, albeit a distorted one, on the hypothetical RS− population. For instance, given that the proportion of left-handers has remained more or less constant through the ages, one must suppose that the relative proportions of RS− and RS+ individuals has remained roughly constant. Again, one is led to wonder what evolutionary contingencies have led to this steady-state condition.

One must conclude, first, that there can have been no serious disadvantage, in terms of fitness or adaptation, in being left-handed, since this would have favored RS+ individuals at the expense of RS− ones. Given that handedness is related to genotype in probabilistic fashion in Annett's theory, any effects of natural selection might have been slow, but they should still have been discernible over the ages. In fact, no such effects are evident. This should be sufficient to rule out any suspicion that the RS− classification represents a throwback to our more symmetrical prehuman ancestors.

Hardyck and Petrinovich (1977) have argued that there may have been a slight adaptive *advantage* in bilaterality. In particular, they review evidence that the left-handed, and by implication those with more bilateral representation of function in the brain, are better protected from the lasting effects of brain injury. They comment as follows:

> Dobzhansky (1970) has shown that a trait that is present in a small proportion of the population and that affords only a slight selective advantage will be subject only to the effects of genetic drift. However, it is also possible that bilaterality of cerebral organ-

ization and associated left- or mixed-handedness may be increasing in frequency in the human race, but at such a slow rate that changes are difficult to detect [p. 399].

There are other respects in which RS— individuals may be at a slight advantage. Woo and Pearson (1927) suggested that it may have been better in primitive warfare to be able to throw stones rapidly with alternate hands than with just one hand, although the one-handed thrower could use the other hand as a magazine. There is evidence that left-handers are better than right-handers on tasks requiring the association of verbal with nonverbal symbols (Dimond & Beaumont, 1974), which might explain the supposedly high proportion of left-handers in architecture (J. M. Peterson & Lansky, 1974). Ambilateral subjects seem to excel in acoustic memory for pitch and perhaps in other musical skills as well (Deutsch, 1978).

Levy (1969) has proposed that the increased incidence of bilateral representation of language in left-handers may produce some impairment in nonverbal performance. She reported, in fact, that 10 left-handers among a group of 25 male graduate students scored significantly lower than their right-handed colleagues on the performance tests of the Wechsler Adult Intelligence Scale (WAIS), but that the two groups scored equally well on the verbal tests. Subsequent tests of Levy's hypothesis have produced extraordinarily mixed results. For instance, Burnett, Lane, and Dratt (1982) found that spatial visualization was highest among those of mixed handedness, and among those with left-handed relatives—that is, among those most likely to belong to Annett's RS— category. However, Sanders, Wilson, and Vandenberg (1982) reported that spatial visualization was higher among strongly left-handed males than strongly right-handed males, but that the reverse was true of females. Subjects of Japanese or Chinese ancestry yielded a different pattern of results, but again males and females showed opposite trends. These two recent studies include reviews of earlier evidence for those interested in unravelling this tangled web; for the present, there seems as much reason to suppose that left-handers, or more specifically those belonging to the RS— category, are superior in spatial abilities as to suppose that they are inferior.

It is scarcely rational, however, to insist too strongly on the advantages of bilaterality, given that one of the conspicuous characteristics that has distinguished human evolution is lateralization. There must have been at least some adaptive advantage in being right-handed, or in having asymmetrical representation of functions in the brain. In Chapter 8, however, I argue that RS— individuals may be slightly more susceptible to disorders of language than are RS+ individuals, which would not be surprising if the evolutionary advantages of asymmetry have particularly to do with the representation of language.

I suspect, therefore, that the relative advantages of bilaterality and lateralization are in a state of balance. It would clearly be to our great disadvantage

if laterality were to so invade our bodies and nervous systems that we were to
become essentially one-armed, one-legged, one-eyed, although just this possibility was foreseen by none other than Plato. In *The Symposium,* he had
Zeus speak as follows:

> I think I have a scheme whereby men may exist yet stop their licentiousness; we'll
> debilitate them. We'll slice each of them in two, he said, and they shall both be weak-
> ened and more useful to us, through increase in numbers. And if their wantonness
> seems to continue and they refuse to buckle under, why, he went on, I'll slice them
> in two again! They can go round on one foot, hoppity-hop [translation in Groden,
> 1970, p. 63]!

The relative advantages associated with bilaterality may depend in part on
RS− individuals remaining in the minority. From the left-handed men of the
army of Benjamin through to such modern left-handed warriors as Jimmy Con-
nors, Rod Laver, Martina Navratilova, and John McEnroe, part of the advantage
of being left-handed lies in its surprise value, although some underlying ambilaterality may confer an extra benefit as well. Again, it is possible that representation of function in the RS− brain is more variable and thus less
predictable than representation in the RS+ brain, since it is not subject to the
lateralizing influence that stamps a uniformity on the RS+ brain. This may
result in a *cognitive* surprise, a measure of creativity or ability to see relations
that might escape the more conventional. Leonardo da Vinci, Charles Chaplin,
and Benjamin Franklin are examples of left-handers who in different ways have
demonstrated remarkable creativity (Fincher, 1977).

SUMMARY

In this chapter, I have reviewed the main characteristics of handedness and
introduced some of the issues to be pursued in the following chapters. Right-
handedness appears to be uniquely but universally human. On close examination, however, human handedness appears to be continuous rather than
dichotomous, with a distribution that spans the range from left- to right-
handedness but that is centered to the right of the point of equality.

There are two main questions to be asked about the distribution of handedness: First, why is the distribution shifted to the right? And second, why are
some individuals left-handed? I suggested that the right shift is fundamentally
biological rather than cultural. I also suggested that variations in handedness
are in large part stochastic and in fact derived from two distributions, one
(RS+) shifted to the right the other (RS−) centered on equality between the

hands. Both themes will be pursued in the following chapters, but in the larger context of laterality generally.

In order to establish this larger context, it is necessary now to introduce the second strikingly asymmetrical aspect of the human nervous system—the asymmetry of the human brain.

3 Functional Asymmetry of the Human Brain

In the great majority of people, perhaps 95%, language is represented primarily in the left cerebral hemisphere, whereas certain nonverbal functions are represented more strongly in the right hemisphere. The concern of this chapter is to document and characterize this typical pattern of asymmetry. A minority of individuals show systematic departures from this pattern, and these will be considered in the following chapter, in which cerebral lateralization is related to handedness and other asymmetries.

LATERALIZED REPRESENTATION OF LANGUAGE

Lesion Studies

The discovery that language is represented predominantly in the left side of the brain in most people is usually attributed to Marc Dax, an obscure general practitioner whose one and only contribution to science was a short paper read in 1836 at a medical society in Montpelier, France. Dax observed that in more than 40 patients suffering from disturbances of speech there were signs of damage to the left cerebral hemisphere. He could find not a single case in which there was evidence of damage to the right hemisphere only. Dax concluded that speech is controlled by the left cerebral hemisphere.

Dax's historic insight initially made no impact, and indeed it might not have been recognized at all had it not been for the efforts of his son nearly 30 years later. Anxious to establish his father's priority, Gustav Dax located the text of the original talk and arranged for it to be published in 1865 (Springer & Deutsch, 1981). In the meantime, in 1861, Paul Broca had read a case study to the Anatomical Society of Paris in which he described the results of a post mortem examination of the brain of an aphasic patient known as "Tan," so called because this was the only articulate sound he could make. Broca attributed Tan's aphasia to a lesion in the frontal lobe of the left hemisphere, in a specific area now known as Broca's area (see Figure 3.1).

Although Tan had lost the ability to talk, he could write normally and showed no impairment in comprehension of written or oral language. He seemed to suffer no paralysis of the lips or tongue, and indeed he could move his tongue to the left or right on command. The deficit seemed to be restricted to the movements of articulated speech. Broca coined the term *aphemia* (*aphémie*) to refer to this disorder. In 1864, however, Trousseau introduced the more general term *aphasia* to refer to language disorders not attributable

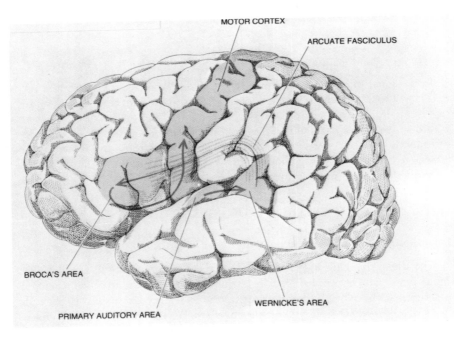

FIGURE 3.1. Representation of the left hemisphere of the human brain illustrating the principal language-mediating areas. The arrows indicate the presumed flow of information involved in hearing, comprehending, and then speaking a word. [Reprinted by permission from Specializations of the Human Brain by Norman Geschwind. Copyright © 1979 by Scientific American, Inc. All rights reserved.]

to dysfunction of the musculature or the peripheral sensory system, or to general mental deficiency, and this term eventually won acceptance (Critchley, 1967). The condition described by Broca is an example of *motor aphasia,* since the impairment is one of expression rather than of comprehension. It is also sometimes called *Broca's aphasia* to distinguish it from other kinds of motor aphasia.

In 1874 Carl Wernicke described a type of aphasia sometimes called *sensory aphasia,* in which the pattern of deficits is essentially the converse of that in Broca's aphasia; comprehension is grossly impaired, but the patient is capable of fluent, even garrulous speech. Sensory aphasia typically occurs as a consequence of lesions in an area in the upper, posterior part of the temporal lobe, known as Wernicke's area. Although the utterances of the sensory aphasic are apparently meaningless, their grammatical structure remains more or less intact—perhaps it was a brief lapse into sensory aphasia that produced Chomsky's (1957) famous sentence "Colorless green ideas sleep furiously." This impairment is also sometimes known as *jargon aphasia,* since the victim's speech is typically characterized by jargon and neologisms, as the following real-life example illustrates: "I think that there's an awful lot of mung, but I think I've a lot of net and tunged it a little wheaten duhvayden [from Buckingham & Kertesz, 1974]." Geschwind (1969) has characterized this kind of speech as "the running on of the relatively isolated Broca's area [p. 111]." This may be something of an oversimplification, since the patient evidently retains access to knowledge about grammar.

Wernicke also recognized another kind of aphasia, known as *conduction aphasia* or *central aphasia,* which apparently results from lesions between Wernicke's and Broca's areas—or, more specifically, from lesions in the arcuate fasciculus, a tract of fibers that normally relays information from the auditory areas to the motor speech areas (Benson, Sheramata, Bouchard, Segarra, Price, & Geschwind, 1973). The patient is able to comprehend speech and can produce speech that is fluent except for an excess of circumlocution and what are called *paraphasic errors,* in which phonemes are substituted or otherwise incorrectly rendered (e.g., "fots of fun" for "lots of fun"—see Buckingham & Kertesz, 1974, for further examples and analysis). But the most striking symptom is an impairment in the ability to repeat what someone else has just said. Strub and Gardner (1974) have shown that this deficit is not one of short-term memory, but rather it is a linguistic deficiency in the processing and ordering of phonemes.

In contrast with conduction aphasia, *transcortical aphasia* is characterized by a compulsive but apparently meaningless repetition of what is said by another person—a symptom known as *echolalia.* Transcortical motor aphasia results from damage to the frontal lobe marginal to Broca's area; the patient retains good comprehension, and may be able to read aloud or name objects, but exhibits a severe loss of spontaneous speech (Rubens, 1976). Transcortical sensory aphasia is a consequence of damage to the posterior parietal lobe and may result from disconnection of Wernicke's area from parietal association areas. The patient exhibits extremely poor comprehension and an inability to name objects (Buckingham & Kertesz, 1974). The echolalic utterances produced by transcortical aphasics are not entirely parrot-like, since even in the case of transcortical sensory aphasia, where comprehension is minimal, the patient often corrects minor errors of syntax in the original utterance (e.g., L. Davis, Foldi, Gardner, & Zurif, 1978; Whitaker, 1976). For instance, in one study the sentence "The boy gave she a present" was repeated as "The boy gave her a present" by all three transcortical aphasics who were tested (Davis et al., 1978).

This brief review has of course oversimplified matters somewhat. For instance, there is considerable dispute even today over the exact nature of Broca's aphasia, despite the fact that it was first described over 100 years ago. Zurif and Caramazza (1976) have shown that it is not exclusively a deficit of production but includes some impairment in syntactic aspects of comprehension, thus raising doubts as to any clear-cut distinction between motor and sensory aphasias. There is even doubt as to whether Broca's aphasia is due to lesions in Broca's area! In a review of evidence, Mohr (1976) argues that the deficit described by Broca actually requires damage to an area that far exceeds Broca's area and includes most of the operculum, insula, and underlying white matter. According to Mohr, Broca's area is simply part of the preassociation respiratory system and has little to do with language per se. It is clear that there is still some way to go in accurately characterizing the deficits involved in different kinds of aphasia and in precisely identifying the brain areas involved.

There is a deeper problem, however, in "locating" language functions in the brain. Historically, there has been disagreement between those, such as Broca, who have argued for the localization of specific functions in particular areas of the brain and "holists," such as Head (1926) and K. Goldstein (1948) who have argued that the brain acts as a unitary whole. Hughlings Jackson long ago warned that "to locate the damage which destroys speech and to locate speech are two different things [J. Taylor, 1958, p. 130]." D. Caplan (1981), in a careful review of the logical and empirical issues involved, similarly notes that the localization of symptoms is "clinically invaluable" but that inferences about the localization of normal functions are beset with difficulties. Following Klein (1978), he lists the conditions that should be met if such inferences are to be drawn, and he suggests that these have seldom been met in practice.

We need not dwell on questions of detail about localization of function, however, since these have mainly to do with localization within hemispheres, whereas the primary concern of this chapter is rather with differences between hemispheres. For the most part, it is clear that aphasia results from damage to the left hemisphere rather than to the right, and it is reasonable to conclude that language is mediated primarily by the left hemisphere. There is some question, however, as to whether the right cerebral hemishere possesses any capacity at all for language. In many cases of aphasia following unilateral left-hemispheric lesions, the disturbance of language, whether of production or of comprehension, seems so complete as to suggest that the right cerebral hemisphere is virtually incapable of mediating language.

On the other hand, there is some evidence that patients with unilateral right-hemisphere lesions may be impaired relative to normal controls on certain tests of language. For example, Lesser (1974) reported such an impairment on a semantic test involving comprehension of spoken words but not on a phonological or a syntactic test. Although there is some evidence that this impairment may have been due in part to deficits in spatial perception or to general deterioration (Gainotti, Caltagirone, & Miceli, 1979), there is evidence for a residual deficit even when these factors are ruled out (Gainotti, Caltagirone, Miceli, & Masullo, 1981). Gainotti *et al.* (1981) observed some deficit in the comprehension of written as well as of spoken words, but it was most marked in the case of spoken words. Since they used a large sample of right-handed patients, it is unlikely that their results were contaminated to any significant extent by subjects who were right-hemisphere dominant for language. Gainotti *et al.* suggest that the right cerebral hemisphere does possess some competence in certain restricted aspects of linguistic processing, and perhaps especially in the comprehension of spoken words. In this limited respect, then, the right hemisphere might contribute in supplementary fashion to the normal processing of language.

Hemidecortication

An interesting case arises when an entire cerebral cortex is removed. Hemidecortication is sometimes carried out to treat incurable and otherwise fatal tumors. St. James-Roberts (1981) has provided a valuable summary of the published evidence of the six cases reported to have undergone left hemidecortication when over 13 years of age,[1] all predictably showed disturbances of language. What is surprising, however, is that the disturbances were much less profound than one would expect on the basis of the effects of more circumscribed lesions. Although all patients showed deficits in the productions of speech, none seemed to exhibit any marked impairment in comprehension.

[1] Evidence on hemidecortication carried out on children and infants will be reviewed in Chapter 5.

The majority were (perhaps understandably) able to swear and to utter other automatic phrases (Searleman, 1977). One patient could sing entire songs and could express herself much better in song than in normal speech (Gott, 1973). Some patients were even capable of limited propositional speech (e.g., A. Smith, 1966; Zaidel, 1973; Zangwill, 1976). The 25 patients who underwent right hemidecortication after age 13 were all assessed as normal or better in both the production and comprehension of speech.

The surprisingly high degree of linguistic competence in cases of left hemidecortication patients contrasts with the profound deficits of both production and comprehension of speech that result from lesions to specific areas of the left hemisphere. One might conclude from this that language is represented in both cerebral hemispheres but that the left hemisphere normally exerts an inhibitory influence over the right. Only when the left cortex is removed can the full linguistic capabilities of the right hemisphere be revealed. An alternative possibility is that the six patients with left hemidecortication do not constitute a representative sample for the assessment of language representation in the normal brain. All these patients had suffered for some time prior to the operation from tumors infiltrating the left hemisphere, and this might well have led to some earlier reallocation of language representation to the right hemisphere. The extent to which language is represented in the normal right hemisphere remains a matter of some controversy.

Commissurotomy

Further evidence on the nature of hemispheric specialization comes from studies of patients who have undergone section of the commissures linking the two hemispheres of the brain. This operation was first performed by William Van Wagenen in the 1940s on some two dozen patients for the relief of epilepsy (Van Wagenen & Herren, 1940), but this series was later discontinued because the operation seemed to have little beneficial effect. Psychological testing of the patients after surgery also revealed surprisingly little in the way of perceptual or motor deficits (Akelaitis, 1941, 1944).

In the early 1960s, two surgeons in California, Philip J. Vogel and Joseph E. Bogen, suggested that the earlier work may have failed because Van Wagenen's patients did not undergo complete section of the commissures. Van Wagenen's procedures varied, but he usually sectioned the anterior portion of the corpus callosum and in one or two cases the anterior commissure as well. Bogen and Vogel therefore undertook to carry out complete commissurotomy on a series of patients with severe epilepsy, and this operation has proved medically successful beyond expectations, even preventing seizures altogether in some cases (Bogen & Vogel, 1963). These patients also became the focus of intense psychological scrutiny, especially from those interested in hemispheric specialization, because it became possible to study the functional capacities of each cerebral hemisphere in isolation from the other. It should be noted, however, that in their everyday behavior and discourse the "split-brained" patients appear quite normal, and it has taken subtle testing to reveal the dramatic effects of the commissurotomy.

The left-hemisphere superiority in language was clearly demonstrated in these patients. They were easily able to name words or pictures of objects flashed tachistoscopically to the right visual hemifield, which projects to the left cerebral hemisphere, but they could not name words or pictures flashed to the left hemifield. Similarly, they could name objects felt with the right hand but hidden from view, but they could not name objects felt with the left hand (Gazzaniga, 1970; Gazzaniga & Sperry, 1967). These observations implied that the right cerebral hemisphere was incapable of the production of speech, at least in the context of naming things.

It could be demonstrated, however, that the right hemisphere was capable of verbal comprehension. For instance, the patients could correctly point with the left hand to an object named by a word in the left visual field, a task that must be mediated by the right cerebral hemisphere. They could also pick out objects with the left hand on the basis of quite sophisticated comprehension. One patient, for instance, was asked to pick out with his left hand the one object among 15 that "makes things look bigger," and he correctly chose a magnifying glass (Nebes & Sperry, 1971). Early studies of the split-brained patients suggested that comprehension in the right hemisphere was restricted to concrete nouns and that the isolated right hemisphere could not process tachistoscopically presented verbs (Gazzaniga, Bogen, & Sperry, 1967). Levy (1970) showed that the deficit was largely restricted to the case in which the patients had to perform the action named by the verb (e.g., tap, wave), although performance was also rather poor when they had to pick out pictures of the named actions. However, they could easily pick out objects associated with verbs, such as a toy chair for the word *sit*. This rather peculiar deficit may have to do with an inability of the right hemisphere to initiate and organize sequential actions, or it may reflect some limitation in the use of tachistoscopic tests of hemispheric specialization.

Zaidel (1973, 1975) has developed a technique for presenting visual input to a single hemisphere of a split-brained patient for minutes at a time, thereby overcoming one of the major limitations of tachistoscopic presentation. One eye is covered and the other fitted with a contact lens with a small screen on it; half the screen is opaque, blocking out vision in half the visual field. The patient can look around freely but can see only things to one or the other side of fixation. Zaidel asks the patient oral questions about visually presented information, with either the left or right hemifield blocked out. Although both hemispheres receive the question, only one hemisphere can act upon it, since the other hemisphere does not receive the relevant information. Zaidel was therefore able to test each hemisphere separately for its ability to comprehend oral questions. The right hemisphere proved somewhat deficient when compared with the left, but the differences seemed more quantitative than qualitative. The right hemispheres of adult patients achieved the vocabulary of a child between about 12 and 18 years of age, could understand both nouns and verbs, and could understand sentences of different syntactic construction, including both active and passive sentences (Zaidel, 1976). The left hemisphere could cope with longer sentences and was less affected by variations in word order.

Zaidel (1981) has also shown that the visual vocabulary of the disconnected right hemisphere is considerably less than the auditory vocabulary, being equivalent only to that of a normal child between about 6.5 and 10.5 years of age. This depleted visual vocabulary may come about because the right hemisphere reads ideographically rather than by mapping graphemes onto phonemes. Zaidel and Peters (1981) showed that the right hemisphere of one split-brained patient was capable of "evoking the sound image" of a word by matching pictures with homonymous names, such as a flying *bat* and a baseball *bat,* and by matching pictures with rhyming names, such as *bat* and *hat.* The disconnected right hemisphere could not name these words, however, and could not translate print into sounds by matching a printed word with a picture with a rhyming name, or by matching words that rhyme but are orthographically dissimilar, such as *pea* and *key.* These interesting results suggest that the disconnected right hemisphere reads in ideographic fashion, treating printed words as wholes rather than as assemblages of graphemes.

When words are presented dichotically—that is, in simultaneous pairs, one to each ear—split-brained patients can report back those presented to the right ear but can tell little or nothing of what is presented to the left ear, again suggesting a dominance of the left cerebral hemisphere (Milner, Taylor, & Sperry, 1968; Sparks & Geschwind, 1968; Zaidel, 1973). It appears that dichotic presentation induces a strong prepotency of the contralateral over the ipsilateral connections between ears and cerebral hemispheres (Kimura, 1961a, 1961b), although the precise reason for this is still not fully understood (Mononen & Seitz, 1977; Studdert-Kennedy, 1975). The split-brained patient can obey dichotic commands presented to either ear, however, even though unable to state the commands presented to the left ear (H. W. Gordon, 1973). This finding corroborates Zaidel's evidence that the right hemisphere can mediate understanding of verbs as well as of nouns, at least when they are presented orally.

In only one case, described by Gazzaniga, Volpe, Smylie, Wilson, and LeDoux (1979), has there been evidence of the production of speech mediated by the right hemisphere of a split-brained patient. This young man was operated on at 15 years of age, and for some years after the operation could name words directed to the left hemisphere but not to the right. He did appear, however, to show unusually sophisticated comprehension of verbal information directed to the right hemisphere and could spell words by choosing letters with his left hand. Between 26 and 36 months after the operation, however, he showed a marked change in his ability to describe orally information directed to the right hemisphere; he could name words and pictures flased to the left visual field and produce verbal responses about scenes projected in the left visual field. These verbal responses were not entirely accurate. For instance, when asked to produce a word describing the scene followed by more detailed explanation, the word was usually correct but the subsequent explanation was often astray. Gazzaniga *et al.* argue that this patient's new-found ability represents the acquisition of a capacity for verbal expression by the isolated right hemisphere.

Overall, evidence from commissurotomized patients confirms the impressions gained from studies of hemispherectomized patients. The representation of language is lateralized toward the left cerebral hemisphere and is much more pronounced with respect to production of speech than with respect to comprehension. With a sole exception, the right hemisphere of the split-brained patients appears to be essentially mute, while capable of comprehending language to a level that differs only quantitatively from the level achieved by the left hemisphere. The right hemisphere, however, does seem to be more proficient in the processing of spoken than of written language.

Electrical Stimulation of the Brain

It should be noted that studies of split-brained patients may again overestimate the language functions of the normal right hemisphere. Since these patients have a history of intractable epilepsy, it is likely that they present an abnormal picture of language representation in the brain. A report by Ojemann and Whitaker (1978) gives some indication of the high variability in language representation among epileptic patients. These authors studied patients undergoing surgical removal of brain tissue containing epileptic foci, adapting a technique pioneered by Wilder Penfield and his colleagues at the Montreal Neurological Institute (Penfield & Jasper, 1954; Penfield & Roberts, 1959). The patient is conscious but mildly sedated during the operation and is given the task of naming drawings of objects while a weak electrical current is applied to localized areas of exposed cerebral cortex. Impairment in naming is taken as evidence that the stimulated area lies close to, or overlaps, an area that mediates language. In most patients, stimulation of a specific region of the Rolandic cortex (part of the motor cortex) produced disturbances of speech, presumed to be due to motor disruption rather than to inhibition of a language-mediating area. Stimulation of other areas typically produced disturbances of naming but not of speech per se. These language-mediating areas were widely distributed throughout an area overlapping the frontal, parietal, and temporal lobes, but there was also marked variation among the 11 patients tested. Indeed, no one area was common to all patients, and some language areas were unique to individual patients. Although there is no clear way to tell whether a similar degree of variability is present among normal people, it seems likely that the variability noted by Ojemann and Whitaker reflects in part the rearrangement of language representation due to the effects of early epileptic seizures.

In one patient shown to be left-cerebrally dominant for language, the epileptic focus was in the *right* cerebral hemisphere. Stimulation of the Rolandic cortex produced an arrest of speech, but outside of this area, stimulation of 26 different sites failed to produce any disruption in the naming task. There was no evidence for *any* language representation in the right hemisphere of this patient. A single case does not prove a rule, but it remains a possibility that this is also the state of affairs among the majority of normal people.

It has also been possible to demonstrate the lateralization of speech functions at a subcortical level by the use of electrical stimulation. In order to relieve a condition known as dyskinesia, small surgical lesions are sometimes made in the nuclei of the thalamus, and in particular in the ventrolateral nucleus that projects to the frontal cortex. These lesions sometimes result in deficits in verbal fluency or in the rate and quality of speech itself, and they are more likely to do so when the lesion is on the left than on the right (e.g., Bell, 1968; Darley, Brown, & Swenson, 1975; Laitinen & Vilkki, 1977). Ojemann and Ward (1971) stimulated the ventrolateral nuclei prior to surgery and found that stimulation of the left nucleus was more likely than stimulation of the right nucleus to produce deficits of naming, although stimulation hardly ever produced total arrest of speech. Similarly, Mateer (1978) reported that stimulation of the left nucleus, but not stimulation of the right, produced an increase in the duration of a naming response and also tended to result in slurring and articulatory distortions.

Studies of Normal Subjects

There are several techniques for studying cerebral lateralization in normal subjects, including the tachistoscopic and dichotic-listening procedures discribed earlier. The evidence for lateralization tends to be less dramatic than in the case of split-brained patients because the commissures allow transfer of information between hemispheres, but consistent interhemispheric differences do emerge when laterality measures are averaged over trials and over subjects. For instance, most people identify words or letters more accurately if they are flashed in the right than in the left visual field (e.g., McKeever & Huling, 1971; Orbach, 1953). This is generally accepted as evidence that the left hemisphere is the more specialized for processing verbal information, although such artifacts as eye movements, directional scanning habits, and faulty fixation can influence the results (M. J. White, 1969, 1972). Of course normal subjects, unlike split-brained patients, *can* name words or letters in the left visual field, presumably because the right hemisphere does have access, via the commissures, to the speech mechanisms of the left.

Similarly, with dichotic listening, most people are slightly more accurate in indentifying or recalling speech sounds presented to the right ear than those presented to the left ear. This right-ear advantage has been demonstrated with a variety of speech sounds, including spoken digits (e.g., Kimura, 1961b, 1967), meaningful as well as nonsense words (Kimura & Folb, 1968), prose passages (Treisman & Geffen, 1968), vowels (Godfrey, 1974; Weiss & House, 1973), and even, although perhaps less certainly, the prosodic and syntactic aspects of ordinary speech (Zurif, 1974). In most of these studies, the right-ear advantage has been measured in terms of accuracy of performance, but it has also been shown that there is a right-ear advantage in terms of speed of identification (e.g., Springer, 1971, and indeed a right-ear speed advantage has been demonstrated with monaural as well as with dichotic presentation (Fry, 1974; Haydon & Spellacy, 1973; Morais & Darwin, 1974).

There is also evidence for left-hemispheric dominance in the control of the tongue and jaw in movements that do not involve speech. Sussman (1971) has developed a technique in which the subject tries to match a target tone presented to one ear with a reference tone of varying pitch presented to the other ear. In one experiment, the subjects controlled the pitch of the target tones by moving their tongues laterally; the arrangement was such that movements in one direction increased the pitch and movements in the other direction decreased it. Matching was more accurate when the target tone was presented to the right ear. Sussman and his colleagues (Sussman & MacNeilage, 1975b; Sussman, MacNeilage, & Lumbley, 1975) also reported a right-ear advantage when the target tone was controlled by movements of the jaw, but not when it was controlled by arm movements. Although these tasks do not involve speech, Sussman and his colleagues argue that the precise motor control required resembles that required in speech, in which vocal output must be continuously modulated to match some internal representation. Their data suggest that left-hemispheric specialization is tied not only to the production of speech per se but also to a closed-loop monitoring system that allows precise regulation of the articulators. It is an open question, however, as to whether this system is acquired through learning to speak or whether it is a prerequisite for speech.

Studies of normal subjects do not provide a clear answer to the question of whether there is any representation of language in the right hemispheres of those who are left-cerebrally dominant for language, although there has been some speculation on the matter. Moscovitch (1973, 1976) has argued that the dominant left hemisphere normally inhibits the right hemisphere's language skills, so that verbal information projected to the right hemisphere is relayed via the commissures to the left hemisphere for processing. This explains why verbal information is processed with shorter latency when projected directly to the left hemisphere. Moscovitch suggests, however, that when the commissures are sectioned the inhibition of the right hemisphere is lifted and the right hemisphere is then capable of verbal comprehension. There are difficulties with this interpretation. One is that the representation of language in the right hemispheres of split-brained patients may be due to the pathological effects of early epileptic seizures rather than to the cessation of interhemispheric inhibition. Another is that the difference in latency between hemispheres in normal subjects may have nothing to do with interhemispheric transfer; it may simply mean that the right hemisphere processes verbal information more slowly than does the left hemisphere.

Day (1977) has argued that the right hemisphere can process concrete words but not abstract ones. Abstract words projected in the right visual field were processed, on average, about 35 msec faster than abstract words projected to the left visual field, in right-handed subjects. This time differential remained roughly constant across different experimental tasks, suggesting that it was due to interhemispheric transfer rather than to different speeds of processing within the hemispheres; that is, abstract words projected to the right hemisphere were relayed via the commissures to the left hemisphere for verbal analysis, and this interhemispheric transmission took about 35 msec. With concrete words, however, there was no significant difference in latency of processing between the two visual fields. But can we legitimately infer from this that concrete words were processed in the right hemisphere? Statistically speaking, it is dangerous to base conclusions on lack of a significant difference, especially when there are large individual differences. Moreover Day's subjects made quite a lot of errors, more than 30% under some conditions, and they were generally slightly more accurate even with concrete words when these were presented in the right rather than in the left visual field. This raises the possibility that equal latencies in the two fields may have been achieved at the expense of accuracy in the left field. Nevertheless, Day's results and conclusions again conform to the general outcome of clinical studies—namely, that the right hemisphere is capable of at least some language processing, but at a lower level of sophistication than is the left hemisphere.

Conclusions

The evidence shows compellingly that in most people language is represented primarily in the left cerebral hemisphere. In general, lateralization seems to be more pronounced with respect to the expressive components of language than with respect to its perception or comprehension, although at least some of the clinical evidence probably overestimates the degree of language representation in the right hemisphere in normal people. Moreover, although lateralization may be a matter of degree, the left hemisphere is generally dominant for all aspects of language—from perception of individual phonemes to the processing of syntax, semantics, and prosody; from control of simple nonverbal movements involving the articulators to the complex organization of propositional speech. For the great majority of individuals, therefore, it is reasonable to speak of the left hemisphere as the hemisphere that is dominant for language.

LEFT-HEMISPHERIC SPECIALIZATION FOR NONVERBAL FUNCTIONS

In studies of left-hemispheric specialization, the major emphasis has been on that hemisphere's dominance for the representation of language. We have already seen, however, in the work of Sussman and his colleagues, that left-hemispheric specialization may go beyond language per se and include specialized control over fine movements of the tongue and other articulators. Indeed, the very phenomenon of right-handedness may be taken to imply a left-hemispheric superiority in motor skill, since the right hand is in most people the more skilled and is controlled primarily by the left cerebral hemisphere. I now consider further evidence that the left hemisphere plays a specialized role in the production and perception of sequences.

Apraxia

It has long been known that lesions of the left hemisphere may give rise to a class of disorders known as the *apraxias,* which are disorders of skilled, voluntary movement that cannot be attributed to such factors as weakness, tremor, intellectual impairment, incomprehension, or uncooperativeness (Heilman, 1979a). Jackson had described patients with disorders of this type as early as 1866 (J. Taylor, 1958), but it was Liepmann, just after the turn of the century, who offered the first insights into the neurological bases of apraxia. For instance, Liepmann and Maas (1907) described a patient with lesions in the left frontal cortex and anterior corpus callosum. This patient suffered right hemiplegia (paralysis of the right side) due to the left cortical lesion, but he was also unable to carry out verbal commands with his left hand or to imitate skilled movements or use objects correctly with his left hand. Failure to carry out verbal commands might have been due in part to the callosal lesion, which would have disconnected the language centers of the left hemisphere from the motor centers of the right. Liepmann and Maas realized that this would not explain the patient's failure to imitate or to use an object, however, and concluded that the motor programs controlling purposive skilled actions are mediated by the left hemisphere.

It has since been confirmed that, in right-handed patients, almost all cases of apraxia are due to lesions of the left cerebral hemisphere (see Heilman, 1979a, for a review). This means that apraxia is often accompanied by aphasia, which may create difficulties in diagnosis. In a well-controlled study, however, Goodglass and Kaplan (1963) compared aphasic patients with and without apraxia on their ability to gesture and to copy simple and complex actions. Although the two groups were matched on Performance IQ, the apraxic subjects performed more ineptly on these motor skills. Moreover, the degree of apraxia did not seem to be correlated with the degree of aphasia, suggesting that the two disorders are somewhat independent.

Reviewing the evidence, Heilman (1979a) argues that "visuokinesthetic motor engrams" for the programming of skilled acts are stored in the left parietal lobe. Apraxia may result either from destruction of this area or disconnection of this area from the motor association area, which has a more direct role in actual execution of movements. The various neural circuits involved in Heilman's schema are illustrated in Figure 3.2. According to this schema, it should be possible to distinguish different kinds of apraxia. Those with disconnected or lesioned motor association areas should exhibit deficits of performance, but they should be able to correctly recognize skilled movements. Lesions of the parietal area should produce failures of recognition as well. Heilman cites unpublished work by Valenstein and Heilman showing that some patients with apraxia do exhibit deficits in recognition of pantomimed acts shown on film. It is of interest that in apraxia, as in aphasia, deficits may occur in comprehension as well as in production.

Apraxics may be defective in a variety of sequential skills, including manual skills and buccofacial skills (e.g., sticking out the tongue or blowing a kiss), and including meaningful as well as meaningless actions (Heilman, 1979a). Although some authors, such as K. Goldstein (1948) and Geschwind (1975) have characterized the deficit as one of "symbolization," Kimura and Archibald (1974) have suggested that sequencing is a critical ingredient; they note, for instance, that apraxic patients can copy static positions of the hand and arm but cannot copy movements. Precise characterization of the apraxic defect may have been hampered by the lack of an adequate model of motor control. Most authors have tacitly assumed a hierarchical model in which motor commands are initiated in some higher center and transmitted in linear fashion through various lower centers down to the limbs. For a discussion of the shortcomings of this approach, and a sketch of an alternative, more flexible model, the reader is referred to Kelso and Tuller (1981).

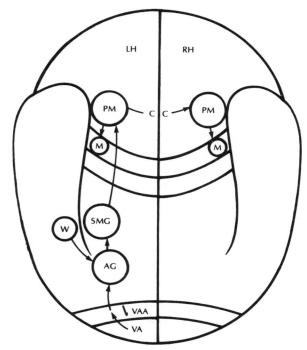

FIGURE 3.2. Heilman's model of brain areas involved in imitating skilled actions or in using objects. The brain is depicted as viewed from the top, and the legend is as follows: W = Wernicke's area; VA = primary visual area; VAA = visual association area; AG = angular gyrus; SMG = supramarginal gyrus; PM = premotor area (motor association cortex); M = motor cortex; CC = corpus callosum; LH = left hemisphere; RH = right hemisphere. Disruption of the circuit shown may lead to apraxia. [Reprinted by permission from K. M. Heilman, Apraxia, in *Clinical Neuropsychology*, edited by K. M. Heilman & E. Valenstein (Oxford: Oxford University Press, 1979).]

Rhythmic Dominance

There is evidence that the right hand is more proficient than the left in tapping rhythms, a phenomenon that may well relate to the specialized left-hemispheric mechanisms inferred from studies of apraxia. For example, P. H. Wolff, Hurwitz, and Moss (1977) found no difference between the hands in the ability to tap in time to a metronome, but the right hand proved the more proficient in tapping a simple rhythm. This was true of the majority of left-handers as well as of right-handers, suggesting that it was not a simple manifestation of handedness per se.

Rhythmic dominance appears to be especially pronounced when both hands are involved. Ibbotson and Morton (1981) tested the ability of subjects to tap a simple rhythm (such as dah-dah-dit-dit-dah) with one hand while tapping the beat with the other. For most subjects, this was easy when the right hand tapped the rhythm and the left hand the beat, but virtually impossible the other way round. (The interested reader should try it.) Similarly, the hands dominated the feet. Only serious musicians seemed able to cope with any combination of limbs, whereas most of the remainder of subjects showed clear dominance effects. Since 60% of left-handers displayed a dominance of the *right* hand, Ibbotson and Morton concluded that the effect was not related to handedness per se, and they suggested that it was linked to cerebral dominance for language.

The left-cerebral dominance for rhythm may apply to the perception as well as to the production of rhythmic sequences. G. M. Robinson and Solomon (1974) presented different rhythmic sequences of 900-Hz pulses simultaneously to each ear of right-handed subjects and recorded a right-ear advantage on a test of recognition, implying left-cerebral dominance. None of the subjects was familiar with Morse code, suggesting that the asymmetry was not due to verbal coding. However, Milner (1962) found no difference between patients with unilateral lesions of left and right hemispheres on the rhythm subtest of the Seashore Measures of Musical Talents, although the patients with *right*-sided lesions were disadvantaged on the time, loudness, timbre, and tonal memory subtests.

There is evidence for left-hemispheric specialization on a number of other tasks involving the processing of temporal information. One of the most striking examples involves a curious auditory illusion discovered by Deutsch (1974). Subjects heard sequences of tones, alternating in frequency between 400 Hz and 800 Hz. Each tone was presented for 250 msec and immediately succeeded the previous one. The sequences were presented dichotically and were exactly out of phase; that is, while one ear received the higher tone, the other received the lower. Most subjects heard only the sequence that was presented to the right ear, although the perceived *location* of the tones seemed to alternate between ears, with the higher tone on the right and the lower tone seemingly (and incorrectly) located on the left. This is illustrated in Figure 3.3 and suggests a dissociation between perception of pattern and perception of location. But with respect to the perception of temporal pattern, it clearly implies a left-hemisphere advantage.

Deutsch inferred that this effect was related to cerebral dominance, since the right-ear dominance was more marked for right-handers than for left-handers, who showed much more varied perceptual reactions. In a similar paradigm, in which subjects heard pairs of tones that were out of phase to each ear, Efron and Yund (1976) and Christensen and Gregory (1977) failed to

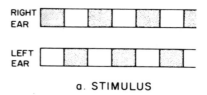

a. STIMULUS

FIGURE 3.3. Schematic representation of auditory illusion discovered by Deutsch: (a) Representation of stimulus pattern; (b) representation of illusory percept most commonly reported by right-handed listeners. The pattern was presented for 20 sec without pause. [From D. Deutsch, The octave illusion and the what-where connection, in R. S. Nickerson (Ed.), *Attention and Performance, VIII* (Hillsdale, N.J.: Erlbaum, 1980).]

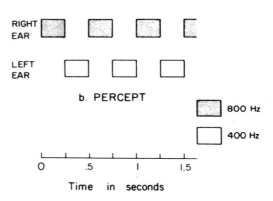

b. PERCEPT

observe a consistent advantage of one or the other ear, and also failed to observe any consistent relation to handedness. Reviewing the evidence, Craig (1979) argued that the dominance effect is contingent upon receiving a long sequence of tones and is thus related to left-cerebral dominance for rhythm.

There is evidence for left-hemispheric superiority in judgments about the simultaneity and temporal order of tones (Bosshardt & Hörmann, 1975; Efron, 1963a, 1963b, 1963c). Such authors have observed that patients with left-hemispheric lesions perform more poorly on discrimination of the duration of tones than do those with right-hemispheric lesions (M. C. Gordon, 1967; E. C. Needham & Black, 1970; Van Allen, Benton, & Gordon, 1966), although others have obtained just the opposite result (Chase, 1967; Milner, 1962). In any event, left-hemispheric specialization may go beyond the perception of rhythm per se and extend to other discriminations requiring precise temporal judgments (see Gates & Bradshaw, 1977, for a review).

Conclusions

There can be little doubt that the specialization of the left hemisphere is not restricted to language but extends to nonverbal tasks involving sequential processing. There is also some suggestion that this specialization, like that for language, is more pronounced for the production than for the perception of sequences. It is, of course, true that language, especially in its oral form, is fundamentally sequential, which suggests that the left-hemispheric specialization for language may have its origins in some more basic specialization for sequencing and fine temporal programming. This theme will be pursued at the end of this chapter and expanded in the remaining chapters of this book.

RIGHT-HEMISPHERIC SPECIALIZATION

For nearly a century following the momentous 1860s, when the discoveries of Dax and Broca about left-cerebral dominance for language were made known, little importance was attached to the right hemisphere. To be sure, the perspicacious Hughlings Jackson (1864) had speculated that if "expression" resided in one hemisphere, then one might raise the question of whether "perception—its corresponding opposite," might reside in the other. Yet Jackson himself used the term *leading hemisphere* to refer to the hemisphere dominant for language. The left hemisphere was also termed the *dominant* or *major* hemisphere, while the right was the *nondominant* or *minor* one—terms that are often still used. As late as 1962, the eminent zoologist J. Z. Young wondered if the right hemisphere was merely a "vestige" but prudently allowed that he would rather keep his than lose it.

Perceptual Skills

Some years after his speculation about right-hemispheric specialization or perception, Jackson (1876) described the case of a patient with a tumor in the right hemisphere who suffered from what Jackson called "imperception," which included failure to recognize familiar people and places, spatial disorientation, and failure to dress properly. This case was largely ignored, however. Oddly enough, a great deal more attention was paid to Munk's (1881) demonstration that bilateral removal of the upper surface of the occipital lobe resulted in a peculiar visual disturbance—in dogs! This disturbance was actually not unlike that described by Jackson and was referred to by Munk as "mindblindness"; the dogs could move about freely and avoid obstacles, but they seemed not to recognize objects that should have been familiar. Similar symptoms were later observed in human cases (e.g., Badal, 1888; Dunn, 1895; Lissauer, 1890; Wilbrand, 1887), leading to a great deal of discussion about the nature and taxonomy of the disorder. Freud (1891) introduced the term *agnosia* in place of *mindblindness* to refer to the various disorders of recognition, discrimination, and spatial orientation. A useful review of the various agnosias and their relation to cerebral function is provided by Rubens (1979).

In spite of Jackson's early insight and of the early interest in agnosias, it was really not until after World War II that disturbances of perception were related to hemispheric specialization. Many of these disturbances are associated with right-hemispheric lesions and seem to involve quite elementary perceptual functions. In the visual domain, patients with unilateral lesions of the right hemisphere perform more poorly than patients with comparable left-hemispheric lesions on test of figure–ground differentiation (e.g., Russo & Vignolo, 1967; Teuber & Weinstein, 1956), visual synthesis (e.g., Scotti & Spinnler, 1970), visual localization (e.g., Hannay, Varney, & Benton, 1976), judgments of the direction of lines (Benton, Hannay, & Varney, 1975), stereopsis (Carmon & Bechtold, 1969), memory for familiar environments (Hécaen & Angelergues, 1963), visuoconstructive ability (Benton, 1967), mental rotation (Ratcliff, 1979), and learning spatial mazes (Milner, 1965). (For further details and discussion, see Benton, 1979.) A similar list can be compiled from studies of hemifield differences in tachistoscopic perception in normal human subjects. For instance there is a left-field advantage, implying right-hemispheric specialization, in perception of nonsense shapes (Hellige, 1978), patterns of dots (Kimura, 1966), curvature of lines (Longden, Ellis, & Iversen, 1976), orientation of lines (Atkinson & Egeth, 1973), facelike stimuli (K. Patterson & Bradshaw, 1975), and localization of dots (Bryden, 1976), and even in such elementary tasks as judging depth (Durnford & Kimura, 1971), color (Davidoff, 1975), and lightness (Davidoff, 1976).

Cases of auditory agnosia for nonspeech sounds are rarely reported, but one study does suggest a critical role for the right cerebral hemisphere. Spreen, Benton, and Fincham (1965) described the case of a right-handed man with a specific deficit in recognizing common sounds, although the perception of speech was normal. This patient was shown on post-mortem examination to have lesions restricted to the right hemisphere. Studies of dichotic-listening in normal subjects have revealed a left-ear advantage, and thus right-hemispheric specialization, in perception of environmental sounds (Curry, 1967), sonar sounds (Chaney & Webster, 1966), vocal nonverbal sounds (King & Kimura, 1972), melodies (Kimura, 1964), musical pitch (Blumstein & Cooper, 1974), timbre (Kallman & Corballis, 1975), and harmony (H. W. Gordon, 1970).

Experiments on hemispheric asymmetries tend to focus on interhemispheric differences at the expense of interhemispheric cooperation. In some tasks, both hemispheres play important but different roles. This appears to be so in the perception of faces. Bodamer (1941) drew attention to a specific form of agnosia for familiar faces, which he termed *prosopagnosia*. He argued that perception of familiar faces was subserved by specific neural mechanisms represented bilaterally in the parieto-occipital region. Other evidence has been conflicting; for instance, Marzi and Berlucchi (1977) reported a right-visual-field superiority in the recognition of famous faces presented tachistoscopically, implying a left-hemispheric superiority, whereas others have reported evidence for a specific right-hemispheric involvement (e.g., Geffen, Bradshaw, & Wallace, 1971: Milner, 1968; Tzavaras, Hécaen, & Le Bras, 1970). In a review, Benton (1980) argues that there is a fundamental difference between the identification of familiar faces and the identification of unfamiliar ones. He suggests that the right hemisphere plays a primary role in both but that the left hemisphere is also critically involved when there is a strong memory component. In a more recent review, Sergent and Bindra (1981) suggest rather that the relative roles of one or the other hemisphere depend on the task. The right hemisphere plays the major role if holistic perceptual judgments are required, whereas the left is the more crucial if the task allows more analytic judgments.

Musical perception may also involve specialized contributions from both hemispheres. We have seen that there is a right-hemispheric advantage in the perception of melody, pitch, timbre, and harmony, but a left-hemispheric advantage in the perception of rhythm. Thus, H. W. Gordon (1978b) found a right-ear advantage in the identification of dichotically presented melodies differing only in rhythm, no difference between ears in identification of melodies differing only in pitch, and a left-ear advantage in identification of chords. In another experiment, however, he found the right-hemispheric (left-ear) advantage in the identification of chords to be restricted to those subjects with musical training (H. W. Gordon, 1978a). Other experiments have suggested that experienced musicians show a *left*-hemispheric advantage in recognition of melodies, whereas musically naive listeners display a *right*-hemispheric advantage (Bever & Chiarello, 1974; Wagner & Hannon, 1981). Yet there have been reports of composers who have retained their musical skills despite damage to the left hemisphere severe enough to cause aphasia. Maurice Ravel, for instance, suffered sensory aphasia following an automobile accident at age 57, but he could still recognize tunes and identify musical errors with high accuracy (Alajouanine, 1948). The Russian composer V. G. Shebalin also suffered severe sensory aphasia following a vascular lesion to the left hemisphere at age 51, but his musical skills remained intact and he even continued to compose some notable pieces of music (Luria, Tsvetkova, & Futer, 1965). Brust (1980), however, has drawn attention to two right-handed professional musicians with left-hemispheric lesions who were impaired in the ability to read and write music, although in other respects their musical ability remained normal.

Even so verbal a task as reading may call upon the specialized skills of the right hemisphere if the spatial component is sufficiently complex. In Japanese script, for instance, there are two kinds of script: *Kanji,* which are Chinese logographs in which each word is represented by a single symbol, and *Kana,* in which the symbols correspond to syllables. Tachistoscopic studies have shown a right-visual-field (left-hemispheric) advantage in recognition of *Kana* symbols and a left-visual-field (right-hemispheric) advantage in recognition of *Kanji* symbols (Hatta, 1977; Sasanuma, Itoh, Mori, & Kobayashi, 1977). Since the reading of *Kanji* must be ideographic rather than phonemic, one is reminded here of the results of Zaidel and Peters (1981) showing that the disconnected right hemisphere reads English words in ideographic fashion. Yet it is probably an oversimplification to suppose that *Kanji* processing is exclusively the preserve of the right hemisphere. Evidence from Japanese aphasics suggests a more complex pattern of representation, and Hung and Tzeng (1981), reviewing the evidence, suggest that the right-hemispheric advantage for *Kanji* depends in part on a holistic mode of processing rather than on the localization of representations.

Even in the identification of single, English letters, the left or right hemisphere may prevail, depending on spatial complexity. In an unpublished study, Lee Brooks of McMaster University has claimed a left-visual-field advantage in the recognition of handwritten words, but a right-visual-field advantage for typed words. Bryden and Allard (1976) have shown that the degree of left-hemispheric (i.e., right-visual-field) superiority in the identification of tachistoscopically presented letters depends on the typeface and that the more complex, scriptlike typefaces may give rise to a right-hemispheric advantage. Finally, it is noteworthy that most readers of Braille prefer to use the left hand to identify the symbols, implying a right-hemispheric advantage (L. J. Harris, 1980c). Presumably, this is again because of the superior spatial skill of that hemisphere.

Manipulospatial Skill

Perhaps the most extreme example of right-hemispheric specialization has been the observation that split-brained patients are much better able to carry out certain manipulospatial tasks with their left hands than with their right hands (Gazzaniga, Bogen, & Sperry, 1962, 1967; LeDoux, Wilson, & Gazzaniga, 1977). In one such task, the subject must arrange four patterned blocks to match a sample design. Split-brained patients prove adept at this with the left hand, but with the right hand, they are so inept that the left hand often has to be physically restrained from helping! Similarly split-brained patients, even though normally right-handed for drawing, cannot draw a representation of a three- dimensional object, such as a cube, with the right hand but have relatively little difficulty with the left hand. Examples are shown in Figure 3.4.

LeDoux *et al.* (1977) have shown that the sharp lateralization of such tasks is not dependent simply on perceptual lateralization. The split-brained patient in their study could easily recognize a design presented to either the left or the right visual field, even though he could not arrange blocks with his right hand to match that design. The same patient could readily select a match-stick model of a cube in response to the word *cube* flashed in the right visual field, showing

P.S.   3/6/76

FIGURE 3.4. Examples of a commissurotomized patient's attempts to draw a cube, with left and right hands. [Reprinted by permission from *Neuropsychologia, 15,* J. E. LeDoux, D. H. Wilson, &
M. S. Gazzaniga, Manipulo-spatial aspects of cerebral lateralization: Clues to the origin of lateralization. Copyright 1977, Perga-
mon Press, Ltd.]

that the left hemisphere could mediate perception of a cube even if it could
not direct the right hand to draw one. LeDoux *et al.* argue, however, that the
critical component in lateralization of these tasks is not the manipulative one,
since the *right* hand is normally dominant for manipulation and drawing.
Rather, the critical right-hemispheric component is the mapping between spatial and motor representation. Puccetti (1981) has taken issue with this interpretation and suggested (rather obscurely, in my view) that the critical
ingredient is a right-hemispheric advantage in constructive visualization.

However, evidence from studies of unilateral brain lesions does not seem
entirely consistent with these findings. Kleist (1923) drew attention to a defect
known as *constructional apraxia,* which includes impairment·in such tasks as
block design, three-dimension construction with blocks, copying line drawings,
or drawing figures or pictures in response to verbal commands—the sorts of
skills, in fact, that split-brained patients seem unable to process with their left
hemispheres. Yet Kleist identified this defect with lesions in the posterior
parietal lobe of the left hemisphere. In a review of evidence, Benton (1979)
points out that, although some evidence supports the role of the left hemisphere, cases of more severe or more frequent constructional disability occur with damage to the right hemisphere (e.g., Benton, 1967, 1968; De
Renzi & Faglioni, 1967), although some investigators have not found interhemispheric differences (e.g., Benton, 1973; Warrington, James, & Kinsbourne, 1966). LeDoux *et al.*(1977) note, however, that in many of these
studies only the patients' right hands were tested, suggesting that some of the
deficits observed following left-hemispheric lesions may not have been evident
had the patients been allowed to use their left hands.

Representation of Space

One rather curious manifestation of hemispheric asymmetry in spatial representation has to do with a phenomenon known as *hemineglect,* in which
patients with unilateral brain lesions tend to ignore one side of space. The
patient may fail to observe objects to one side of the midline, or may neglect
to dress one side of the body, or if asked to draw a clock may produce only
one side of it. Examples are shown in Figure 3.5. What is interesting is that

these symptoms nearly always affect the left side of the body or of visual space, and are due to lesions of the right cerebral hemisphere; damage to the left hemisphere only rarely produces a neglect of the right side (Battersby, Bender, Pollack, & Kahn, 1956; Critchley, 1953; De Renzi, 1978).

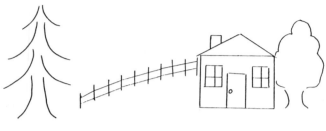

COPY THIS DRAWING IN THE SPACE BELOW

DRAW IN THE
NUMBERS ON
THE CLOCK
FACE

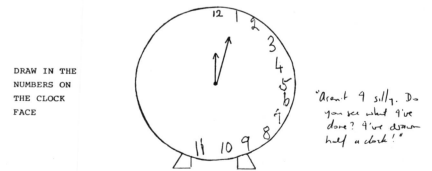

FIGURE 3.5. Examples of left hemineglect, taken from records of patients studied at University of Auckland by J. A. Ogden.

that the right cerebral hemisphere plays the more prominent role in mediating emotion.

Emotion

The phenomenon of hemineglect is in some respects reminiscent of the symptoms of the hysterical neuroses, now no longer so prevalent as they were earlier in the century. The hysteric, although apparently free of organic defects, may be unable to see, hear, feel, or move, and in some cases, the symptoms are restricted to one side of the body. Janet (1907) observed that, among those of his patients with lateralized lesions, twice as many were afflicted on the left side as on the right. It might perhaps be argued that right-handed patients are unwilling to let their right hands fall victim to their neuroses and that this explains the asymmetry, but the evidence is rather against this interpretation. Only a small proportion of patients suffered paralysis of the hands or arms, and the bias was anyway no more marked in these cases than in the cases of those with hysterical symptoms in other parts of the body. It is therefore not unreasonable to suppose that the left-sided bias reflects a greater involvement of the right hemisphere in emotion.

Disturbances of right-hemispheric functioning, whether of neurological or psychological origin, often result in neglect, denial, and a general loss of emotion—or what Janet called *"la belle indifférence."* Conversely, damage to the left hemisphere may induce what has been termed the "catastrophic reaction," which includes weeping, swearing, expressions of despair and guilt, and aggression (Gainotti, 1972). Different emotions typically follow injections of sodium amytal to one or the other side of the brain, a technique used to determine which hemisphere is dominant for speech (Wada & Rasmussen, 1960). Following a left-sided injection, which temporarily incapacitates the left hemisphere, the patient typically exhibits a catastrophic reaction, whereas a right-sided injection induces denial that anything is the matter, sometimes amounting to mania or euphoria—the patient laughs, jokes, and expresses positive well-being (Terzian, 1964). Of course, it is possible that these reactions are secondary consequences of the effect of the injection on speech. Left-sided injections may induce despair because the patient cannot speak, whereas right-sided injections induce relief that speech is not impaired.

Other studies suggest a more fundamental basis for interhemispheric differences in emotion, however. There is evidence that lesions of the right hemisphere produce selective disturbances in the recall of emotionally charged narratives (Wechsler, 1973) and in the comprehension of affective aspects of speech (Heilman, Scholes, & Watson, 1975). Studies of differences between the ears in dichotic listening in normal subjects have shown a left-ear advantage in the identification of emotional intonation in speech (Haggard & Parkinson,

1971) and in the identification of nonverbal emotional sounds, such as laughing and crying (Carmon & Nachshon, 1973). Safer and Leventhal (1977) had subjects rate the emotionality of monaural passages and found that those who listened with the right ear tended to use cues from the content of the passages, whereas those who listened with the left ear tended to base their ratings on the tone of voice. Suberi and McKeever (1977) found that the left-field advantage in recognition of tachistoscopically presented faces was enhanced when the faces expressed emotion compared with when they were neutral. Several other investigators have argued that the right-hemispheric advantage in the perception of facial emotion is distinct from the right-hemispheric advantage in the perception of faces themselves (Ley & Bryden, 1979; McKeever & Dixon, 1981; Strauss & Moscovitch, 1981).

Interhemispheric differences in emotional expression may be manifest in differences in expressivity between the two sides of the face. Most people, even though right-handed, are "left-faced," in that they have better control over the facial muscles on the left than on the right (Chaurasia & Goswami, 1975; Sackeim & Gur, 1978); the reader might like to check this by winking, grimacing, or trying to smile as broadly as possible with each side of the face in turn. Aside from the matter of facial control, there is evidence that emotions are expressed more intensely on the left side than on the right (Borod & Caron, 1980; Campbell, 1978). These observations suggest that the right hemisphere is generally dominant in the expression of facial emotion.

There is some contradiction in the literature as to whether emotion is mediated predominantly by the right cerebral hemisphere or whether the two hemispheres play complementary roles. We saw earlier that disruption of the right hemisphere may induce euphoria, whereas impairment of the left induces a catastrophic reaction, suggestion that the left hemisphere may mediate positive emotions and the right hemisphere negative ones. Reuter-Lorenz and Davidson (1981), in an investigation of reaction time to identify emotional expressions of faces presented tachistoscopically, found a left-field advantage for sad faces and a right-field advantage for happy ones. Similarly, Dimond and Farrington (1977) used a contact-lens technique to restrict visual input to one visual hemifield at a time, and found that heart rate was greater when an unpleasant film was shown to the left visual field than to the right, whereas the reverse was true of a humorous film. Dimond and Farrington nevertheless concluded that the right hemisphere bears "responsibility for 'emotion' viewed in the broadest sense [p. 259]."

Others have failed to find evidence for a left-hemispheric specialization for positive emotion. Thus, Borod and Caron (1980) found that both positive and negative emotions were expressed more intensely on the left than on the right side of the face. Others who have studied hemifield differences in responses to emotional faces have observed left-field advantages for both positive and negative emotions (Ladavas, Umilta, & Ricci-Bitti, 1980; Ley & Bryden, 1979; Strauss & Moscovitch, 1981).

It seems likely, in any case, that the lateralization of emotional representation is not absolute. In one study, for instance, patients with unilateral brain lesions were shown emotionally charged pictures (e.g., a woman in a bikini, a cut hand), and their arousal was measured by means of the galvanic skin response (GSR) and respiration rate (Morrow, Vrtunski, Kim, & Boller, 1981). Patients with right-hemispheric lesions showed virtually no arousal by the GSR, but patients with left-hemispheric lesions also showed a reduced GSR compared with normal controls. As in the case with asymmetries in perceptual skills, the degree and even the direction of asymmetry in emotional representation may depend on such factors as the subject's sex, the nature of the stimuli, and perhaps the subject's degree of familiarity with the materials.

Conclusions

This review has been by no means exhaustive, but it should be sufficient to illustrate the great variety of functions that are lateralized toward the right cerebral hemisphere. One is tempted to conclude that some degree of right-hemispheric specialization exists for all functions that are not concerned with language or with the specialized involvement of the left hemisphere in sequencing or rhythm. It is noteworthy that so-called right-hemispheric skills include quite elementary perceptual functions, such as the judgment of depth, color, and lightness.

It is also clear that right-hemispheric specialization is relative rather than absolute. In the more complex tasks, such as the perception of music or of faces, or even in reading, lateral asymmetries may even change direction, depending on quite subtle aspects of the task. In most cases, then, we can suppose that both cerebral hemispheres are involved, and the interhemispheric differences are slight compared with the cooperation that exists between them.

OVERVIEW

We have seen that a wide range of functions are lateralized, at least to some extent, toward one or the other cerebral hemisphere. Indeed, one might be hard pressed to discover any perceptual, cognitive, or motor task that does not exhibit some degree of lateral asymmetry, given a sufficiently sensitive measure. The question now is whether lateralization follows any coherent pattern. Certainly, the assignment of functions to one or the other hemisphere, although seldom absolute, does not appear to be merely random. On the other hand, it is difficult to discover any single principle that might underlie it.

We can reject the idea, implicit in much of the earlier writing on the topic, that the basic distinction is that the left hemisphere is primarily verbal and the right hemisphere nonverbal. This does not account for such findings as the left-hemispheric advantage in motor sequencing or in the perception of rhythm, neither does it square with the evidence that the disconnected right hemisphere is capable of quite sophisticated verbal comprehension. We can also rule out the view that only the left hemisphere is conscious (cf. Jaynes, 1976; Popper & Eccles, 1977). We have seen that split-brained patients can respond intelligently, if not vocally, to pictures, words, and even sentences presented to the right hemisphere. There is also evidence that patients remain aware during incapacitation of the left hemisphere by injection of sodium amytal (Rossi & Rosadini, 1967). On the strength of evidence that the disconnected right hemisphere can mediate consciousness of self (Sperry, Zaidel, & Zaidel, 1979), even Eccles (1981) has admitted that "the minor hemisphere has a limited self-consciousness [p. 105]," although he goes on to question whether it can worry about the future or make decisions based on a value system! Geschwind (1981), on the other hand, has argued that the right hemisphere has a *superior* consciousness, on the grounds that right-hemispheric lesions are more likely than left-hemispheric lesions to produce hemineglect. Clearly, there is little basis for hemispheric asymmetry in the presence of or absence of consciousness, and no consensus as to a basis in relative degree of consciousness. There might perhaps be a basis for lateralization in the *quality* of consciousness, but this merely returns us to the original question.

The idea that the left hemisphere is an analytic processor whereas the right hemisphere is a holistic processor has a popular currency, and indeed some genuine appeal, if only because it transcends the verbal–nonverbal distinction and helps explain some of the shifts in perceptual asymmetry that occur when certain parameters are varied. As noted earlier, for instance, Sergent and Bindra (1981) explained many of the inconsistencies in the lateralization of facial recognition in terms of variations in stimulus and task conditions that would have altered the relative importance of analytic and holistic processing. Nebes (1978) has argued more generally that the right hemisphere is the better able to mediate perception of the relations between parts and wholes, and to construct whole information from parts (e.g., to construct an impression of a circle from an arc of the circle). Again we saw from experiments on split-brained patients that right-hemispheric comprehension of words is limited to a global appreciation of each word, with little or no appreciation of its phonemic structure.

Yet on closer examination, the distinction between analytic and holistic processing has an ill-defined, post hoc quality. This can be illustrated by an example from Cooper (1981). He cites evidence that patients with left-hemispheric damage are often impaired in the timing of speech but maintain normal control over intonation, whereas those with right-hemispheric damage have difficulty with intonation but not with timing. At first glance, and in retrospect, this seems compatible with the idea of the left hemisphere as the more analytic and the right as the more holistic. Yet Cooper (1981) wonders if one would have predicted this result:

> In fact, the programming of fundamental frequency contours [intonation] can be viewed at least in part, as a time-dependent sequential process, rendering it suitable for specialization in the left hemisphere according to the analytic/holistic hypothesis. And conversely, the programming of word durations seems to require a sort of global processing [p. 69].

The distinction between analytic and holistic processing in any event seems to apply more obviously to perception than to motor functions, yet it is with respect to motor functions that lateralization seems most pronounced, at least in the context of language and of manipulospatial skill. But even in the perceptual domain, it is not always clear what is analytic and what is holistic. One can arrange conditions in a laboratory so that a given perceptual task is more or less analytic, less or more holistic, but it is difficult to divide up the real world in this way. M. J. Morgan (1981) gives the example of "aperture viewing," in which an object drawn behind a narrow slit is perceived as a spatially extended whole. He asks: "Is this serial or parallel? Analytic or holistic? Left or right hemisphere [p. 75]?" Who knows? But perhaps the most damning indictment of the analytic versus holistic dichotomy is that it does not really tell us anything interesting about the development, evolution, or biology of lateralization; it is not a *theory*. In terms of heuristic value, one might as well assign "the left hemisphere to Apollo, the right to Dionysus [Studdert-Kennedy, 1981, p. 76]."

And so it goes for related dichotomies—that the left hemisphere is rational and the right intuitive, or that the left is propositional and the right appositional (Bogen, 1969b). The definition is imprecise, the fit loose, the heuristic value negligible. Consider, for instance, the question of how we decide whether a mental representation is propositional. Few would deny that language is fundamentally propositional in character, and indeed language is represented primarily in the left cerebral hemisphere. Spatial imagery is typically associated with the right rather than the left hemisphere, and it is commonly suggested that imagery is essentially nonpropositional in nature (e.g., Kosslyn & Pomerantz, 1977; Paivio, 1976). So far so good. However, Pylyshyn (1973, 1978) has vigorously maintained that even spatial imagery is fundamentally propositional, despite its subjectively pictorial quality. In a careful analysis, J. R. Anderson (1978) has concluded that it is actually not possible to decide, on the basis of psychological evidence, whether a given representation is propositional or not. He notes also that evidence on cerebral lateralization does little to resolve the issue. And even if it were true that left-hemispheric processing was in some respects more analytic, rational, or propositional than right-hemi-spheric processing, we would still want to know whether these qualities derive simply from the left-hemispheric dominance for language or whether they are antecedent to it. Labels do not substitute for theory.

What, then, can we conclude about hemispheric specialization? In the fol-lowing section, I shall suggest a number of general conclusions that might be drawn from the evidence reviewed in this chapter. These conclusions are them-selves rather tentative and might perhaps be considered as vulnerable as the various dichotomies I have already criticized. Part of my purpose, however, is to steer speculation away from the search for elusive dichotomies and toward a framework that might lend itself more readily to a more functional, biological analysis.

General Conclusions

The first and perhaps most obvious point is that cerebral lateralization is relative rather than absolute. This point has been reiterated many times, but it is apt to be forgotten in the enthusiastic search for hemispheric asymmetries. The similarities between the two hemispheres are of course obvious structurally from the high degree of bilateral symmetry of the brain. They are also clear functionally from the careful experiments of Milner (1971, 1978) and her col-leagues, who have compared and contrasted the effects of opposite lesions in the temporal and frontal lobes on the two sides. Milner (1971) summarizes as follows:

> The data indicate that homologous areas in the two hemispheres play somewhat similar behavioral roles, so that both the side and the locus of a lesion determine the quality of the deficits seen. This fact helps bridge the gap between man and lower primates, where numerous studies have shown that bilaterally symmetrical lesions are needed in order to demonstrate the functional significance of a given cortical area. It would be strange if, with the emergence of hemispheric asymmetry, this bilateral cerebral organization were totally superseded in man [p. 276].

She goes on to note evidence, reviewed earlier in this chapter, that the right cerebral hemisphere is capable of verbal comprehension, just as the left hemi-sphere has some role in spatial functions.

The relative nature of hemispheric specialization was also emphasized by Zangwill (1960), as well as by Bradshaw and Nettleton (1981) in their review. It is clear from the evidence reviewed earlier that both hemispheres make im-portant contributions to such everyday activities as recognizing faces, perceiving music, and even reading. Moreover, it takes subtle techniques, such as tach-istoscopic presentation or dichotic listening, and sensitive measures to register perceptual asymmetries at all. In ordinary perception, it makes little difference which visual field, ear, or hand we use.

The second conclusion is that left-hemispheric specialization is essentially superimposed on a brain that would otherwise be bilaterally symmetrical. Right-hemispheric specialization is therefore achieved by default (cf. Corballis & Beale, 1976; Corballis & Morgan, 1978; Jaynes, 1976; LeDoux *et al.*, 1977). Some will see this theory as a reaffirmation of the traditional view that the left hemisphere is the dominant one, and it may therefore not find favor with those who argue that the hemispheres are essentially equal but complementary. However, the idea that left-hemispheric specialization is superimposed need not imply total dominance or even superiority. Even if right-hemispheric specialization is achieved only by default, it may still constitute a dominance of that hemisphere on various nonverbal or perceptual tasks. The present view need not imply either that the right hemisphere is the more primitive in its functions. Even if evolution brought about specializations superimposed on the left hemisphere, this need not imply that the right hemisphere did not itself continue to evolve or that right-hemispheric functions lack complexity or subtlety.

There are several arguments in favor of this theory, some of which will be amplified in later chapters. One is simply the argument of parsimony; it is simpler to suppose that hemispheric asymmetry evolved through changes in the functioning of a single hemisphere than to suppose that both hemispheres changed in complementary ways. Another argument is that left-hemispheric specialization seems more coherent and definable than right-hemispheric specialization. Even in the popular characterizations of hemispheric asymmetry, to which we should not deny some measure of truth, the labels attached to the left hemisphere are more explicit than the complementary labels attached to the right; it is easier to define the terms *analytic, rational,* and *propositional* than it is to define *holistic, intuitive,* and *appositional.* Hence so-called right-hemispheric functions are more easily defined by negation or exclusion than by reference to common properties.

As we have seen, the range of functions for which there is a right-hemispheric advantage is broad and includes perceptual functions that seem quite elementary. It is difficult to believe, for instance, that mechanisms evolved specifically in the right hemisphere for the perception of depth, lightness, or color, or even for the expression and perception of emotion. These are functions that are performed bilaterally in other species, and there seems no compelling reason why they should be lateralized in humans. Indeed, one might argue quite the reverse, that perceptual functions should be symmetrically represented because the world is itself without systematic left–right bias, at least in the manner in which it impinges on our sense organs. It is this fact that presumably explains the predominant bilateral symmetry of the body, and especially of the limbs, sense organs, and nervous system (Corballis & Beale, 1970, 1976; Weyl, 1952). That bilateral symmetry should be sacrificed, albeit only to a minor degree, suggests the influence of an invading asymmetry.

Evidence for an invading specialization in the left hemisphere also comes from comparisons between humans and other primates. For instance, Lynch (1980) has observed that contralateral hemineglect following unilateral lesions to either hemisphere in monkeys is markedly less profound than is hemineglect following right-hemispheric lesions in humans. He also documents electro-physiological evidence that there are single cells in the parietal lobes of the monkey that seem to signal attention to visual stimuli. Most of these are more active when the target is in the contralateral hemifield, but there are some that respond when the target is in the ipsilateral hemifield (Heilman, Watson, Valenstein, & Bowers, 1980; D. L. Robinson, Goldberg, & Stanton, 1978). In these respects, both hemispheres of the monkey seem to resemble the right hemisphere of the human, whereas the left hemisphere of the human seems mainly restricted to the representation of the contralateral side of space. This is consistent with the view that spatial representation in the left hemisphere is diminished because of that hemisphere's involvement with language and motor skill.

LeDoux *et al.* (1977), discussing the right-hemispheric specialization for manipulospatial functions, also cite evidence that similar functions are represented in both hemispheres in nonhuman primates (Hyvarinen & Poranen, 1974; Mountcastle, Lynch, Georgopoulos, Sakata, & Acuna, 1975). Their conclusion is precisely the one I am advocating here:

> These comparative observations suggest to us that with the evolution of man and the emergence of language, synaptic space devoted to body-space functions in the left hemisphere of preverbal primates was sacrificed. As a consequence, we feel that the superior performance of the right hemisphere of split-brain patients on a variety of manipulospatial tasks may not reflect the overall cognitive style and evolutionary specialization, but instead may represent localized processing inefficiencies in the left parieto-temporal junction due to the presence of language [p. 746].

Yet it is with respect to the right-hemispheric specialization for manipulospatial skills that the "default" argument might seem most vulnerable. This is perhaps the one right-hemispheric advantage that rivals the left-hemispheric advantage for speech in degree of lateralization. LeDoux *et al.* explain this in terms of the fact that the critical areas in the right parietotemporal junction are homologous to a principle language-mediating area in the left cerebral hemisphere. In this case, then, the invasion of the corresponding area in the left hemisphere is virtually complete. By the same token, however, one could argue that the right-hemispheric specialization is superimposed on an area that would otherwise have been dedicated to language representation. The argument against this is simply that language representation is, in the evolutionary sense, the more obviously "superimposed." The conspicuous differences between humans and other primates are, first, that humans possess a sophisticated form of propositional language and, second, that hemispheric specialization is much more pronounced in humans than in other primates. Evidence on these points will be reviewed in more detail in Chapter 6.

The final question that demands a general answer is: What is the nature of the specialization superimposed on the left cerebral hemisphere? Historically, the most conspicuous aspect of left-hemispheric specialization is that hemisphere's dominance for language, and especially for the production of language. However, there is also a left-hemispheric dominance in certain nonverbal praxic skills, involving the initiation and execution of sequences of action (Kimura, 1979). The left hemisphere also appears to be dominant for the perception and comprehension of language, as well as for the perception of rhythm, simultaneity, and the temporal order of events that occur in rapid succession.

It seems likely that the origins of left-hemispheric specialization are motor rather than perceptual. Handedness itself is most obviously a motor phenomenon, evident in such activities as writing, throwing, or eating rather than in sensitivity of touch. Handedness has been apparent for thousands if not tens of thousands of years, whereas perceptual asymmetries have been documented only with the advent of such devices as the tachistoscope and tape recorder. Again, the left-cerebral dominance for language appears to hold more strongly for the expression than for the perception or comprehension of language.

The common ingredient underlying speech and the dominant praxic functions of the left cerebral hemisphere appears to be fine control over sequences of acts. Speaking, writing, throwing, and actions commonly described as "manipulative" all require precise temporal coordination. Moreover, all are purposive, in the sense that they are internally generated; they are not merely reactions to the environment. As long ago as 1908, Liepmann wrote that the left hemisphere was primarily concerned with the control of "purposive movements, that is, those learned connections of elementary muscle actions [p. 19]." Nearly 70 years later, Zangwill (1976) reached much the same conclusion. "There seems little doubt," he wrote, "that purposive motor activity proceeds for the most part under left hemispheric control [p. 305]."

Some further qualification may be necessary to pin down precisely what are the critical dimensions that call for left-hemispheric specialization. Certainly, the right hemisphere is not incapable of directing purposeful actions. As we have seen, the left hand of the split-brained patient can point to objects on the basis of information supplied to the right hemisphere, and it is actually better than the right hand at certain manipulospatial tasks. Similarly, the right hemisphere evidently has more sophisticated control over the facial muscles and emotional expression on the left side of the face than the left hemisphere has over the right side. In defining a left-hemispheric specializaton for sequencing, we perhaps still need a more precise characterization if we are to explain why there is a left-hemispheric advantage for rhythm but a right-hemispheric advantage in the perception of melody. Kim, Royer, Bonstelle, and Boller (1980) have even claimed that the right hemisphere is the more specialized for temporal sequencing of nonverbal material and that the left-hemispheric advantage is restricted to the sequencing of verbal information.

This claim, however, overlooks a strong spatial component in the tests used to measure nonverbal sequencing. These tests were the Knox Cube Test and the Block Sequencing Test. In both cases, an array of blocks is displayed in front of the testee, and the tester taps them in random sequence. The testee must then tap them in the same order. The critical right-hemispheric component may well be the mapping between spatial and motor representations, which is precisely the component identified by LeDoux *et al.* (1977) in the right-hemispheric superiority for manipulospatial functions. Moreover, the temporal component in these block-tapping tasks is fairly undemanding, since the tester taps the blocks at a steady rate of only one per second. One might contrast this with the temporal demands imposed by the production and perception of rhythm, which yield left-hemispheric advantages.

Studdert-Kennedy (1980) has argued that language was drawn to the left cerebral hemisphere because that hemisphere already possessed the neural circuitry for coordination of the two hands, which in turn was associated with the evolution of manipulative skills. Unilateral control over bilateral musculature was precisely what was needed for control of the vocal apparatus in speech. Given the requirements for temporal precision, bilateral control would presumably be too inefficient, and likely to lead to interhemispheric conflict (Corballis & Beale, 1976; Levy, 1969. Nottebohm (1970) states the argument as follows:

> A behavioral sequence has to commence, and unless it is rigidly programmed, it must incorporate a continuous decision-making process. Control of the commencement of behavior and decision making might be inefficient under equipotent and simultaneous bilateral representation [p. 953].

I shall pursue discussion of the evolution of left-hemispheric control over sequential actions in Chapter 6, and in Chapter 8 review evidence that stuttering may in certain cases result from a failure to establish dominant unilateral control over speech.

Given the left-hemispheric dominance for motor sequencing, and thus for the control of speech, it is not surprising that equivalent perceptual and cognitive processes should be lateralized toward the left hemisphere as well. These processes include the perception of rhythm, temporal order, and simultaneity, and the perception and comprehension of language, both oral and written. Some have suggested that the perception of speech depends on essentially the same mechanisms as does the production of speech (e.g., Liberman, Cooper, Shankweiler, & Studdert-Kennedy, 1967), and Studdert-Kennedy and Shankweiler (1970) have suggested that only the left hemisphere is specialized for the extraction of linguistic features from the speech signal. This implies that the capacity of the right hemisphere to respond to speech is not true speech perception at all, but depends on repeated association of a relatively crude auditory analysis with the outcome of the left hemisphere's linguistic analysis (Levy, 1974; Studdert-Kennedy, 1981; Zaidel, 1978). This would explain the holistic character of the perception of speech by the right hemisphere, documented earlier.

In summary, I have tried to relate cerebral lateralization in the first instance to a left-hemispheric specialization for the precise temporal control over motor sequences. This in turn may have been a consequence of the evolution of an upright stance, which would have freed the forelimbs from direct involvement in locomotion and permitted the development of manipulative skills. A left-hemispheric specialization for sequencing would also have provided a natural vehicle for the evolution of speech; it is not clear, however, whether the critical ingredient was temporal precision or unilateral control over bilateral musculature, or whether both ingredients were critical. Perceptual skills related to these activities would also tend to be lateralized toward the same hemisphere, especially in cases where perceptual and motor sequencing share common neural substrates (as has been claimed for speech).

And so, what is left to the right? The answer, roughly, is everything else, although the degree of right-hemispheric specialization will vary depending on the extent to which different cortical areas in the left-hemisphere are invaded by specialized circuitry devoted to language and sequencing. I believe that this "default" argument provides the most parsimonious explanation for why right-hemispheric advantages apply to such a broad range of functions, why many of these functions appear to be of an elementary nature, and why they are functions that appear to be represented bilaterally in nonhuman primates.

4 Relations between Handedness and Cerebral Lateralization

The previous chapter was an elaborate portrayal of that worthy denizen of the silent majority, the right-hander with language represented predominantly in the left cerebral hemisphere. Much of the contemporary myth of the duality of the brain, with its Eastern and Western lobes, is based on this individual, who is in truth not so much an individual as a statistical aggregate, compiled very largely from college students, epileptics, and those unfortunate enough to have sustained unilateral brain injury. I have already argued that the interpretation of hemispheric asymmetry based on these "normative" data suffer from what has been termed "dichotomania" (McKeever, 1981)—the tendency to overpolarize and overdramatize the functional differences between the two sides of the brain.

A further corrective to this tendency is contained in the simple fact that individuals differ. Not every person is right-handed, and not everyone is left-cerebrally dominant for language. In this chapter, I examine variations in cerebral lateralization, in particular relation to variations in handedness. I shall focus mainly on cerebral dominance for language. One reason for this is simply that the bulk of evidence between handedness and cerebral lateralization deals only with this particular aspect of hemispheric specialization. In the previous chapter, moreover, I argued that right-hemispheric specialization is secondary to left-hemispheric specialization, at least among those who are in fact left-cerebrally dominant for language and for manipulative skills. As a first approximation, then, it seems reasonable to suppose that the relation between handedness and cerebral dominance for language would very largely dictate the overall pattern of lateralization in the human brain.

We have seen that handedness varies between individuals in continuous rather than dichotomous fashion, and it is reasonable to suppose that the same is true of cerebral lateralization. For instance, Zangwill (1960) writes that hemispheric asymmetry in the control of speech is a "graded characteristic, varying in scope and completeness from individual to individual [p. 27]." Little is known, however, of the psychometric properties of cerebral lateralization, of its distribution or factorial structure, and in the following review, I shall be reduced to classifying individuals in terms of whether language is represented predominantly in the left cerebral hemisphere, bilaterally, or predominantly in the right hemisphere. In cross-classifying cerebral lateralization for language with handedness, moreover, the majority of investigators have similarly lumped variations in handedness into categories. Indeed, they often treat left- and mixed-handers in the same category, and I shall follow the same scheme. Even this rather simplified portrayal of the relations between handedness and cerebral lateralization will lead to a reasonably coherent view of the underlying nature of human laterality.

HISTORICAL BACKGROUND

As soon as it became clear that language was represented predominantly in the left cerebral hemisphere, it seemed natural to link this phenomenon with right handedness. Perhaps the first to do so was Bouillaud; in discussion at the Académie Impériale de Médecine in Paris in 1865, he attributed both phenomena to a general dominance of the left cerebral hemisphere (Riese, 1947). A few weeks later, Broca (1865) suggested that the left hemisphere was responsible for writing, drawing, and other fine movements, as well as for speech.

Broca also described the case of a left-handed woman who had suffered right hemiparesis since infancy, but who showed no impairment in speech. He concluded that this woman had speech represented in the *right* cerebral hemisphere, and, influenced perhaps by Bouillaud, he suggested that this would always be the case among left-handers. He overgeneralized, however, for it soon became clear that there was far from a perfect correlation between handedess and cerebral lateralization for language. As early as 1868, Hughlings Jackson remarked on the case of an aphasic with left hemiplegia who was a natural right-hander—evidently a case of a right-handed person with speech lateralized in the right cerebral hemisphere. Similar cases of so-called crossed aphasia have since appeared frequently in the literature; Penfield and Roberts (1959) cite reports of 53 cases of right-handers with aphasia following right-hemispheric lesions, and 66 cases of left-handers or "predominantly left-handers" with aphasia involving the left hemisphere.

Kennedy (1916) tried to account for crossed aphasia in terms of what he called "stock-brainedness," arguing that handedness and cerebral lateralization were independently determined, although both were subject to a strong lateralizing influence. It now seems reasonably clear, however, that handedness and cerebral lateralization for language are to some extent correlated, although the correlation is not perfect. We now have a reasonably coherent picture of the nature of its correlation, although it has not been easy to obtain data that are at once reliable and representative. The most reliable methods for determining which cerebral hemisphere is dominant for language are generally reserved for testing neurological patients and are not suitable for testing the population at large. Consequently, there is a risk that the data are nonrepresentative. Conversely, those measures of cerebral lateralization that are appropriate for testing normal subjects, such as asymmetries in dichotic listening or tachistoscopic perception, are typically rather unreliable, although there are recent signs that the technology may be improving.

SODIUM AMYTAL TEST

One technique for assessing cerebral lateralization for speech that is generally considered reliable is the sodium amytal test (Wada & Rasmussen, 1960), already briefly alluded to in the previous chapter. Injection of sodium amytal into the carotid artery on one side causes a temporary inhibition of function on that same side of the brain. The patient is asked questions following injections to each side in turn, and if the injection to a given side produces suppression of the patient's verbal responses, it can be inferred that language is represented on that side. Data on the relation between handedness and cerebral lateralization as measured by this technique have been collected by Milner (1975) and by Rossi and Rosadini (1967), and are summarized in Table 4.1. Milner (1975) observed no systematic differences between left- and mixed-handers, and pooled their results. They are also pooled in Table 4.1.

Use of the sodium amytal test is limited to patients about to undergo surgery for chronic epilepsy, and such patients are scarcely representative of the population at large. One might expect a higher incidence of language representation in the right hemisphere due to the pathological effects of left-temporal-lobe epilepsy. Note, however, that the incidence of language representation in the right hemisphere in these studies is extremely low, especially among right-handers, suggesting that any pathological influence on cerebral lateralization was minimal. Moreover, Milner (1975) excluded from her sample any patients with evidence of early injury to the left hemisphere,

TABLE 4.1

Percentages of Right-Handers and of Left- and Mixed-Handers with Speech Represented Predominantly in the Left Hemisphere, Bilaterally, or in the Right Hemisphere, According to Different Tests

Test	Right-handers				Left- and mixed-handers			
			Hemisphere				Hemisphere	
	N	Left	Bilateral	Right	N	Left	Bilateral	Right
Sodium amytal test								
Milner (1975)	140	96	0	4	122	70	15	15
Rossi and Rosadini (1967)	74	99	1	0	10	40	10	50
ECT test								
Pratt and Warrington (1972)	55	99	0	1				
Warrington and Pratt (1973)					30	70	7	23
Geffen, Traub, and Stierman (1978)	24	92	0	8	9	67	0	33
Unilateral lesion studies								
Carter, Hohenegger, and Satz (1980)								
Studies 1–12[a]	1356	95	0	5	313	24	76	0
Studies 8, 9, 11[a]					155	51	36	12
Dichotic monitoring								
Geffen and Traub (1979)	43	84	9	7	62	61	15	24

[a] See Table 4.2.

and among these patients, the incidence of language representation in the right hemisphere was indeed higher.

ELECTROCONVULSIVE THERAPY STUDIES

Another technique is to test verbal functions following unilateral electro-convulsive therapy (ECT), which is sometimes used in the treatment of severe depression. An electric current is passed through the brain by means of elec-trodes attached to the scalp and induces convulsions, which are thought to be of therapeutic value. Until quite recently, the general practice has been to apply current to both sides of the brain at once, but evidence now suggests that the risks of memory loss is lessened if ECT is delivered only to one side. The procedure adopted at the National Hospital in Queen Square, London, has been to deliver ECT to each side of the head on separate days. Simple tests of language comprehension are given as soon as the patient has recovered suf-ficiently to tell the questioner his or her name. Data based on this test are also shown in Table 4.1 (Pratt & Warrington, 1972; Warrington & Pratt, 1973). Of course, depressed patients are also not representative of the general pop-ulation, but there seems no compelling a priori reason to suppose that they differ with respect to the lateralized representation of language. In any event, Table 4.1 shows that the data based on the ECT test are in remarkable con-formity with those based on the sodium amytal test.

EFFECTS OF UNILATERAL LESIONS

Evidence on the relation between handedness and cerebral lateralization for language is also yielded by studies of aphasia following unilateral lesions of the brain. Carter, Hohenegger, and Satz (1980) have provided a useful com-pilation of data from virtually all reports published between 1935 and 1973, and this is reproduced in Table 4.2. Notice that the proportion of right-handers with crossed aphasia following right-hemispheric lesions is very low, ranging from 0 to 6% in different studies. Left-handers again show a mixed pattern, with a somewhat higher probability of aphasia following left-hemispheric le-sions than following right-hemispheric lesions. Overall, these probabilities are 0.65 and 0.48, respectively. The fact that these probabilities sum to a value greater than unity implies that some left-handers, at least 13% in fact, must have bilateral representation of language.

These data do not lend themselves to unambiguous estimates of the pro-

TABLE 4.2

Observed Incidence of Aphasia in Left- and Mixed-Handers and in Right-Handers from a Unilateral Lesion to the Left or Right Hemisphere[a]

Studies[b]	Cases	Left-sided lesions		Right-sided lesions		
		Aphasia (%)	No aphasia (%)	Aphasia (%)	No aphasia (%)	Total aphasia (%)
Left- and mixed-handers						
1	8	4 (67)	2 (33)	2 (100)	0 (0)	75
2	12	5 (83)	1 (17)	6 (100)	0 (0)	9
3	20	5 (50)	5 (50)	5 (50)	5 (50)	50
4	10	5 (100)	0 (0)	4 (80)	1 (20)	90
5	9	6 (86)	1 (14)	2 (100)	0 (0)	89
6	14	7 (58)	5 (42)	0 (0)	2 (100)	50
7	13	5 (83)	1 (17)	5 (71)	2 (29)	77
8	33	13 (72)	5 (28)	1 (7)	14 (93)	42
9	63	11 (37)	19 (63)	8 (24)	25 (76)	30
10	58	28 (85)	5 (15)	20 (80)	5 (20)	83
11	59	22 (59)	15 (41)	11 (50)	11 (50)	56
12	14	2 (50)	2 (50)	3 (30)	7 (70)	36
Totals	313	113	61	67	72	
Right-handers						
8	353	115 (73)	42 (27)	1 (0.5)	195 (99.5)	33
9	704	218 (56)	170 (44)	19 (6)	297 (94)	34
10	650	—	—	—	—	36
11	299	81 (50)	82 (50)	0 (0)	136 (100)	27
12	200	—	—	—	—	34
Totals	2206	414	294	20	628	

[a]After Carter, Hohenegger, and Satz (1980).

[b]Studies: 1 = Weisenberg and McBride (1935), 2 = Chesher (1936), 3 = Conrad (1949), 4 = Humphrey and Zangwill (1952), 5 = Zangwill (1954), 6 = Critchley (1954), 7 = Goodglass and Quadfasel (1954), 8 = Penfield and Roberts (1959), 9 = Newcombe and Ratcliff (1966), 10 = Gloning and Quatember (1966), 11 = Hécaen and Ajuriaguerra (1964), 12 = Bingley (1958).

portions of left-hemispheric, right-hemispheric, and bilateral representation of language in left- and right-handers, since certain critical parameters are unknown. In particular, we do not know the probability that a patient will become aphasic following a lesion to the language-dominant hemisphere, or whether this probability depends on which hemisphere mediates language or on whether language is unilaterally or bilaterally represented, or indeed on whether the patient is left-or right-handed. Carter *et al.* have provided estimates based on the assumptions that right-handers have unilateral representation of language and that the probability of aphasia following a lesion to the language-dominant hemisphere is independent both of which hemisphere(s) mediates language and of handedness. These estimates are also shown in Figure 4.1. They are again broadly in line with those based on sodium amytal and ECT tests. The most obvious discrepancy is that the estimated proportion of left-handers with language represented unilaterally in the right cerebral hemisphere is zero, whereas the estimate even for right-handers is 5% (although this is to some extent a forced estimate, since Carter *et al.* assumed that right-handers do not have bilateral representation of language).

This anomaly might be due in part to differential bias in the samples of left-and right-handers. For instance, if we restrict the left-handed samples to Studies 8, 9, and 11, which are the studies that yielded the right-handed samples, we obtain lower estimates of the incidence of aphasia. In this restricted group of studies, the proportions of left-handers exhibiting aphasic symptoms are only 0.54 and 0.40 following left- and right-hemispheric lesions, respectively. Applying Carter *et al.*'s procedure to these figures, we obtain the second row of estimates shown in Table 4.1. Notice that 12% of left-handers are now estimated to have language represented in the right cerebral hemisphere. Neither set of figures has any prior claim to represent the true state of affairs. The point is simply that the estimates themselves vary considerably depending on which studies one includes in the sample, due no doubt to variations in the criteria used to identify aphasic symptoms and to variations in the severity of lesions.

Even allowing for such variations, it is clear that left-handers are more likely than right-handers to suffer aphasia following unilateral lesions. However, they are also more likely to recover. The combined data of Luria (1947) and Subirana (1958) show that the proportion of residual aphasias following left-hemispheric lesions was 0.95 in right-handers but only 0.32 in left-handers—that is, nearly all right-handers who become aphasic following left-hemispheric lesions remain so, whereas fewer than half of left-handers in this category remain aphasic. This is due, no doubt, to the higher proportion of left-handers with bilateral representation of language, so that there is built-in compensation if one side of the brain is lesioned.

ANATOMICAL ASYMMETRIES

Although the overriding impression of the human brain is one of bilateral symmetry, it is now known that there are anatomical asymmetries that appear to bear some systematic relation to functional asymmetries. For instance, Geschwind and Levitsky (1968) observed in 100 adult brains that the temporal planum was larger on the left than on the right in 65% of cases. The planum was approximately equal on the two sides in 24% and larger on the right in 11%. The difference is in some cases quite striking. Geschwind and Levitsky claim that the left planum may be up to five times larger than the right planum, and Wada, Clarke, and Hamm (1975) have reported instances where the right temporal planum is absent altogether. Since the left temporal planum is one of the language-mediating areas, overlapping Wernicke's area, it is reasonable to suppose that this anatomical asymmetry is related to the left-hemispheric specialization for language.

I know of no evidence directly relating the asymmetry of the temporal planum to handedness, although such evidence does exist for a related asymmetry of the Sylvian fissure. Cunningham (1892) long ago observed that in most human brains the Sylvian fissure is longer and more horizontally oriented on the left, whereas the right Sylvian fissure is angled more sharply upward.

TABLE 4.3
Percentages of Anatomical Asymmetries among Right-Handers and among Left- and Mixed-Handers

Asymmetry	Right-handers			Left- and mixed-handers		
	Yes	Equal	Reverse	Yes	Equal	Reverse
Sylvian fissure higher on right (Galaburda, LeMay, Kemper, & Geschwind, 1978)	67	25	8	20	70	10
Occipital horn of lateral ventrical longer on left (McRae, Branch, & Milner, 1968)	60	30	10	38	31	31
Frontal lobe wider on right (LeMay, 1977)	61	20	19	40	33	27
Occipital lobe wider on left (LeMay, 1977)	66	24	10	36	48	26
Frontal lobe protrudes on right (LeMay, 1977)	66	20	14	35	30	35
Occipital lobe protrudes on left (LeMay, 1977)	77	10.5	12.5	35	30	35

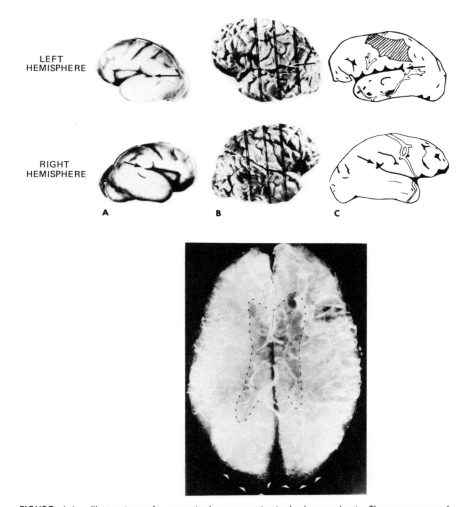

FIGURE 4.1. Illustrations of anatomical asymmetries in the human brain. The upper part of the figure shows the left and right hemispheres of (A) a 16-week-old fetus; (B) an adult human; and (C) drawings made from the endocranial cast of the Neanderthal cast found at La Chapelle-aux-Saints. In all three, the tip of the Sylvian fissure, indicated by the arrows, is higher on the right than on the left. [From LeMay & Culebras, 1972, reprinted by permission of *The New England Journal of Medicine*.] The lower part of the figure shows an X-ray of a brain in which the blood vessels were injected post-mortem with an opaque substance. The tips of the occipital lobe are shown by white arrowheads, and the ventricles are outlined by a dashed line. This figure shows both the counterclockwise torque described in the text and the asymmetry of the ventricles. [From LeMay, 1976, reprinted by permission of the New York Academy of Sciences.]

This is illustrated in Figure 4.1. Galaburda, LeMay, Kemper, and Geschwind (1978) have reported data based on carotid angiography showing that the asymmetry is more common among right-handers than among left-handers. These data are summarized in Table 4.3.

At least two other anatomical asymmetries of the human brain appear to be related to handedness. LeMay (1977) has observed that most brains, when viewed from the top, exhibit a counterclockwise torque, such that the frontal lobe is wider and protrudes further forward on the right, while the occipital lobe is wider and extends further to the rear on the left (see Figure 4.1). Computerized transaxial tomography reveals that this asymmetry is more common among right-handers than among left-handers. An asymmetry of the occipital horns of the lateral ventrical exhibits a similar pattern (McRae, Branch, & Milner, 1968). Among the majoriy of right-handers, the horn on the left is the longer, whereas among left-handers, the two sides are evenly balanced. The data relating these two asymmetries to handedness are also summarized in Table 4.3.

PERCEPTUAL ASYMMETRIES IN NORMAL SUBJECTS

With one possible exception to be discussed later, indices of cerebral lateralization based on dichotic listening in normal subjects are too unreliable to yield useful estimates of the proportions of left- and right-handers with language represented in one or the other hemisphere. Estimates of the test–retest reliability of differences between ears, expressed as product-moment correlations, range from 0.21 to 0.86 (Blumstein, Goodglass, &Tartter, 1975; Hines & Satz, 1974; Studdert-Kennedy, 1975), and the percentage of right-handers showing the expected right-ear advantage typically ranges from 75 to 87% (Blumstein *et al.*, 1975), which is appreciably below the estimates of left-hemispheric dominance for speech among right-handers derived from more stringent techniques (see Table 4.1). Blumstein *et al.* also reported that no fewer than 29% of their right-handed subjects showed a reversal of asymmetry between test and retest, on the most reliable of their three tests. Nevertheless, several dichotic-listening studies have confirmed the basic finding that the majority of both right- and left-handers show a left-hemispheric advantage (as inferred from a right-ear advantage) for verbal materials, but that the proportion is higher among the right-handed than among the left-handed (Bryden, 1965; Curry, 1967; Curry & Rutherford, 1967; Hines & Satz, 1974; Kimura, 1961a; Satz, Achenbach, Pattishall, & Fennell, 1965).

The exception is the dichotic-monitoring test developed by Geffen, Traub, and Stierman (1978). The subject hears a long sequence of dichotic pairs of words and presses a button when she or he detects a particular target word (e.g., *dog*) in one or the other ear. Classification of subjects is based in the first instance on differences in accuracy between the ears, and if this fails to discriminate significantly, it is then based on differences in reaction time. Geffen *et al.* applied this procedure to 29 patients whose lateral dominance for speech had also been assessed following unilateral ECT, and to a further 4 patients who had been assessed by the sodium amytal test. Only in one case did the dichotic-monitoring test fail to agree with the other tests. Geffen and Traub (1979) have used dichotic monitoring to classify cerebral lateralization among 105 normal subjects of varying handedness, and these data, along with those of Geffen *et al.*'s (1978) study, are tabulated in Table 4.1. It should be noted that four right-handers could not be classified even on the basis of reaction time and that the proportion of right-handers showing evidence of left-hemispheric dominance for language on the dichotic-monitoring test is still somewhat below that expected on the basis of such invasive techniques as the sodium amytal or ECT test. Dichotic monitoring might be slightly more equivocal than these other tests because lateralization is less pronounced for perception than for production of speech.

The reliability of indices of laterality based on hemifield differences in tachistoscopic perception appears to be even lower than that of indices based on dichotic listening. Hines and Satz (1974), for instance, report a reliability of only 0.46 in a tachistoscopic test, whereas their dichotic-listening test gave a reliability of 0.86. Even so, this study confirms that left-cerebral dominance for language, even as estimated by hemifield, is more frequent among right-handers than among left-handers. A further point to emerge from this interesting study is that there was a positive correlation between ear differences and hemifield differences for right-handers, but no correlation between these measures for left-handers. This confirms that left-handers, on the whole, do not exhibit the consistent pattern of asymmetry that right-handers do.

It is apposite to conclude this survey on a mythical note. Levy and Reid (1976, 1978) have claimed that the hemisphere dominant for language can be inferred from the way a person holds a pen when writing. Some individuals, especially left-handers, adopt an inverted style sometimes known as "hook" writing (Barsley, 1970) in which the hand is held above the line of script and the pen points toward the bottom of the page. Levy and Reid proposed that those who adopt this writing posture have language represented in the hemisphere ipsilateral to the writing hand, whereas those who write normally have language represented in the contralateral hemisphere. This proposal is not without appeal. Hook writing is common among left-handers, as is left-cerebral dominance for language, whereas among right-handers both hook writing and right-cerebral dominance are rare, although not unheard of. It is often suggested that left-handers adopt the hook posture in order to avoid obscuring and possibly smudging the script as they write. In the case of a right-to-left script, such as Hebrew, this should apply to right-handers rather than to left-handers. Shanon (1978) has shown that even in Israel the hook posture is more common among left-handers than among right-handers, and although this trend is less pronounced than it is for Americans, it does suggest that the explanation for hook writing is at least partially neurological. Finally, Levy and Reid (1976, 1978) claim to have developed a reliable measure of cerebral lateralization based on hemifield differences in tachistoscopic perception, and in 70 out of 73 subjects the direction of lateralization on this measure was correctly predicted by their hypothesis.

Despite this claim, Levy and Reid's hypothesis appears to be invalid. In a careful review of the surprisingly voluminous literature that has already appeared on the matter, Weber and Bradshaw (1981) conclude that there is no evidence for any systematic relation between writing posture and cerebral lateralization, except of course for the evidence reported by Levy and Reid themselves. Several authors have failed to confirm the hypothesis, using various measures of cerebral lateralization, some more convincing than the measure devised by Levy and Reid. Weber and Bradshaw also point out that at least some of the variation in writing posture is due to factors unrelated to cerebral lateralization and that the incidence of the hook style does not in fact correspond closely to the incidence of language representation in the ipsilateral hemisphere. They nevertheless conclude that some unknown neurological factor probably does exert some influence over hand posture in writing and urge further investigation of the issue.

SUMMARY AND INTERPRETATION

The data reviewed in this chapter are in many respects far from ideal. Not all authors were meticulous in the measurement of handedness, and the criteria for assigning individuals to different categories of handedness undoubtedly varied from study to study. Classification of cerebral lateralization must also have varied. In particular, the criteria for determining that representation of language was bilateral, or that the two sides of the brain were equal, would surely depend in part on the measuring technique or on the individual investigators. In several cases, the samples were biased: The sodium amytal test is restricted to epileptics, the ECT test to depressives, and the dichotic-listening and tachistoscopic tests very largely to college students. On the whole, investigators did not take sex differences in cerebral lateralization into account (see McGlone, 1980, and the following chapter).

Despite these deficiencies, the data reveal a remarkably consistent pattern. The great majority of right-handers are left-cerebrally dominant for language and display a consistent pattern of cerebral asymmetry. Left- and mixed-handers also show a tendency toward left-cerebral dominance for language, but this is less marked than it is among right-handers. They are also much more likely than right-handers to have language represented bilaterally or to fail to exhibit anatomical asymmetries where such asymmetries are clearly evident in right-handers. There is little evidence that left-handers differ from mixed-handers in these respects.

In broad outline, these results conform well to the theory developed by Annett (1972, 1978, 1981) and introduced in Chapter 2. According to this theory, the great majority of right-handers inherit what Annett calls the right-shift factor (RS+) and accordingly are predominantly right-handed, right-footed, right-eyed, and so forth. We now observe that they are predominantly left-cerebrally dominant for language. Indeed, we may suppose that the right shift is more truly a *left* shift and that it is a dominance of the left hemisphere in both language and in certain aspects of motor control that gives rise to a dominance of limbs and sense organs on the right side of the body.

Some individuals are assumed to lack the right shift (RS−), and these constitute a much higher proportion of left-handers than of right-handers. This explains why left- and mixed-handers show a lesser degree of cerebral lateralization than do right-handers, and why they show a more varied pattern of lateralization. Indeed, among RS− individuals, different aspects of language might be lateralized toward different hemispheres—recall, for instance, that Hines and Satz (1974) found no correlation between visual and auditory indices of cerebral lateralization among left-handers, but a positive correlation among right-handers. In an electroencephalographic study of cerebral asymmetry in left- and right-handers, Herron, Galin, Johnstone, and Ornstein (1979) make the same point:

> Language is not a unitary function. In left-handers, or groups such as learning-disabled or stutterers whose cerebral organization is alleged to be less lateralized than typical right-handers, it may be only particular components of language that are lateralized differently. The concept of a language hemisphere may be most useful when describing typical right-handers in whom all these behaviors are lateralized fairly consistently to the left hemisphere; it may be misleading when applied to left-handers or ambidextrous persons whose patterns of specialization might differ for specific aspects of language [p. 1289].

For a more quantitative appraisal of Annett's theory, we need to distill the evidence reviewed in this chapter in order to obtain precise estimates of the distribution of hemispheric asymmetry in left- and right-handers. It seems clear that the most reliable estimates are those from the sodium amytal and ECT studies. Estimates from lesion studies involve too many unknowns, those based on perceptual asymmetries are too unreliable, and it is not yet clear how anatomical asymmetries of the brain relate to functional ones. I have therefore pooled the evidence from the sodium amytal and ECT studies summarized in Table 4.1 to yield the estimates shown in Table 4.4. These figures probably indicate the distribution of cerebral lateralization for speech production rather than for other aspects of language.

To estimate the proportion of RS— individuals among the left- and mixed-handers, we assume that the RS— group as a whole exhibits no overall asymmetry. We therefore add 19% with *left*-cerebral representation of speech to match the 19% with right-cerebral representation, include the 12% with bilateral representation, and sum to give a total of 50%. That is, exactly half of the left- and mixed-handers are assumed to inherit no consistent lateralizing influence, so that cerebral lateralization is allocated at random, with a relatively high proportion showing bilateral representation of speech. The remaining 50% of left- and mixed-handers are assumed to be RS+ individuals who are nonetheless left-handed, possibly because of pathology associated with birth stress (Bakan, 1977) or perhaps simply because of environmental influences not associated with pathology (such as a left-handed parent or sibling). This estimated percentage may be somewhat higher than the percentage in the general left-handed population, since it is based on samples with histories of pathology.

Using the same logic, we may estimate the proportion of RS— individuals in the right-handed sample to be 6%. The 6% among right-handers and 50% among left-handers are in almost exactly the ratio one might expect, given that about 12% of the population are left-handed. That is, in terms of *absolute* numbers, RS— individuals are divided equally into left- and right-handers, as Annett's theory predicts—although of course RS— individuals comprise a higher *proportion* of left-handers than of right-handers. Pooling these estimates suggests that about 11% of the total population lacks the right-shift factor.

The only aspect of the data that does not square easily with Annett's theory is that only 1 of the 10 right-handers without left-cerebral dominance for speech showed bilateral representation of speech, whereas the equivalent proportion for left- and mixed-handers was 21 out of 54. This difference is statistically

TABLE 4.4

Percentages of Right-Handers and of Left- and Mixed-Handers with Speech Represented in the Left Hemisphere, Bilaterally, and in the Right Hemisphere, Based on Pooled Data from Sodium Amytal and ECT Studies[a]

Handedness	Hemisphere		
	Left	Bilateral	Right
Right	97	0	3
Left and mixed	68	12	19

[a] See Table 4.1.

significant according to a chi-square test ($\chi^2 = 8.85$, $df = 1$, $p < .01$). There is no a priori reason to expect left- and right- handed RS— individuals to differ in this respect. One might argue a posteriori that some of the right-handers were right-cerebrally dominant for speech because of some pathological influence. In any event, the point need not be a matter of concern at this stage, since there may have been variations in the criteria used to classify a subject as possessing bilateral representation of speech, and the number of critical right-handed subjects is small.

In conclusion, the data again conform reasonably well to Annett's theory. Although this theory implies an underlying dichotomy, the reader is reminded that the phenotypic expression of laterality is continuous rather than dichotomous. Among RS+ individuals, there is an overall bias favoring left-cerebral dominance for language and manipulative skill, and no doubt a secondary right-cerebral bias for other spatial and perceptual functions, but the extent to which this bias is expressed in individuals must vary depending on environmental (including pathological) influences. This bias is expressed more strongly in cerebral lateralization for speech than in handedness, perhaps because minor cerebral pathology is more likely to influence handedness than cerebral dominance for speech (Satz, 1972). It is also expressed more strongly in cerebral lateralization for the production than for the reception of language, and perhaps more strongly in functional than in anatomical measures of cerebral asymmetry—although this may be a reflection of the measures themselves rather than of the true state of affairs. Among RS— individuals, by contrast, there is no overall bias affecting cerebral or manual asymmetry, but random environmental influences nonetheless operate to produce asymmetries ranging from right- to left-handedness or from left- to right-cerebral representation of language. However, different manifestations of asymmetry appear to be somewhat independent of one another, even within the domain of language.

RS— individuals are therefore not the homogeneous products that RS+ individuals are. This variability may well underlie some of the special talents that many left-handers and ambidextrous individuals seem to display (see Chapter 2), but it may perhaps in some cases produce difficulties in language or in manipulation. The question of whether left-handers are more prone than right-handers to difficulties in manipulation or sequencing is also a contentious one. Certainly, folklore has it that left-handers tend to be clumsy; Benjamin Franklin, a left-hander of considerable genius, wrote bitterly that ''more than once I have been beaten for being awkward, and wanting a graceful manner [cited in Barsley, 1976, pp. 129–130].'' Levy (1969) argued that left-handers should be on the whole worse than right-handers on performance measures, on the grounds that language is more likely to be bilaterally represented and so invade neurological ''processing space'' in the right cerebral hemisphere. She reported evidence that left-handers were indeed inferior to right-handers on the measure of Performance IQ on the Wechsler Adult Intelligence Scale (WAIS). The evidence on this point is far from unequivocal, however (see Bradshaw, 1980, for a review). Bradshaw, Nettleton, and Taylor (1981) have found that the deficit in Performance IQ is restricted to left-handers with some familial history of left-handedness, which is indeed what one might expect in terms of Annett's theory.

On the other hand, so to speak, we must of course be on guard against the age-old tyranny against left-handers for being different. Those left-handers who excel in such competitive sports as cricket, baseball, and tennis certainly dispel any notion that all left-handers are clumsy or deficient in skill requiring precise timing. Moreover, the impression of clumsiness must surely be reinforced by the fact that many implements, such as scissors and corkscrews, are made for the convenience of right-handers but the despair of left-handers. For a definitive statement on the manipulative abilities of left-handers, we must await more controlled tests.

5 Development of Laterality

Perhaps the most fundamental question that can be asked about human laterality is whether it is organic or whether it is a product of the environment. With respect to handedness, the question goes back to Plato and Aristotle; as we have seen, Plato attributed right-handedness to early experience, whereas Aristotle believed it to be a manifestation of the fundamental superiority of the right side of the body. The argument has persisted throughout history, but until recently, there has been curiously little attempt to resolve the issue by examining the development of laterality in children. As long ago as 1646, the English physician Thomas Browne argued that right-handedness was culturally imposed, but called for systematic observations of children to settle the matter. Such observations were slow to appear. Even by 1902 one reviewer, D. J. Cunningham, could find only one observational study, that of Baldwin (1890), and even that study was based on a single infant. Cunningham (1902) remarked that "It is a matter of regret . . . that this ready means of investigation has not been more fully taken advantage of [p. 280]."

There were, however, two earlier observations that Cunningham might have noted. In 1877, Charles Darwin wrote that his own son had displayed a preference for the right hand when about 2½ months old but had subsequently proved to be left-handed. He thought that the boy's left-handedness was inherited, since his grandfather, mother, and a brother were also left-handed. The reverse switch in handedness was noted by Hall (1891), who observed that two infants who showed an initial preference for the left hand later settled down to become right-handed. Woolley (1910) also reported that her own daughter at 8 months would wave "bye-bye" only with the left hand, but at 15 months was clearly right-handed. Woolley attributed the child's early left-handedness to the fact that the nurse always carried her on her left arm, leaving the child's left arm free. Yet another author to remark on an early phase of left-handedness in the first year of life was Meyer (1913). He wrote that it was

> plausible to assume that during the first months of life hand movements are predominantly controlled by the right hemisphere which serves simpler functions and probably matures at an earlier time. General left-handedness in infancy would be the consequence as naturally as general right-handedness in adult life [p. 53].

As we shall see, some more recent studies have also documented this early switch in handedness, although it is by no means a universal observation. Before pursuing this issue, however, I shall review evidence on two asymmetries to be observed in newborn infants that may well be precursors to handedness.

NEONATAL REFLEXES

Tonic Neck Reflex

One of the first clear manifestations of functional asymmetry in the developing child is the so-called tonic neck reflex, in which the head is turned to one side, the arm and leg on that side are extended, and the opposite arm and leg are flexed—a posture sometimes described as a "fencer's posture" (Coryell & Michel, 1978). This reflex may be observed in the fetal infant as early as the twenty- eighth week after conception but has usually disappeared by age 20 weeks after birth (Gesell & Ames, 1947). The great majority of infants exhibit a right tonic neck reflex, in which the head is turned to the right and the right arm and leg are extended. Furthermore, whether or not they exhibit the full-fledged reflex, most infants tend to lie with their heads turned to the right, a fact that is easily verified by a visit to a ward of healthy, newborn babies (Turkewitz, Gordon, & Birch, 1965).

There is some evidence that the direction of the tonic neck reflex is related to the subsequent handedness of a child. Gesell and Ames (1947) followed up 19 children—7 with a right tonic neck reflex, 9 with a left tonic neck reflex, and 3 with no consistent bias. The children with right tonic neck reflexes were all right-handed by age 10 years, although one had showed some ambilateral tendencies prior to that age. Of the 9 with left reflexes, 4 subsequently became left-handed and 5 right-handed, although these last all showed some evidence of ambilaterality. The 3 children with bidirectional reflexes also showed some ambilaterality but were predominantly right-handed. It is worth noting that these data correspond rather well to what one might predict from Annett's (1972, 1978) theory, elaborated earlier. Those with right reflexes would consist largely of those inheriting the right shift (RS +) and should therefore emerge as right-handed. Those with left reflexes or bidirectional reflexes would consist of those lacking the right shift (RS −) and would thus be approximately evenly divided into right- and left-handers and would include some with ambidextral tendencies.

Michel (1981) reported that 65% of a sample of 150 newborn infants preferred to lie with their heads to the right, whereas only 15% showed a clear preference for the left. Among a sample of 10 with a right preference and 10 with a left preference, he also showed a significant correlation between head-orientation preference and hand preference in reaching at 16 and 22 weeks of age. Eight of the 10 children with right head-orientation preference reached with their right hands, compared with only 2 of the 10 with left head-orientation preference.

Michel suggested that hand preference might be directly influenced by head orientation, since an infant whose head is turned to one side would be able to see only the arm on that same side, giving that arm the advantage in visually guided reaching (see also Coryell & Michel, 1978). It is also known that most infants are more sensitive to sounds on the right, and to touches on the right side of the face, than to comparable stimulation on the left, perhaps because the right side of the head is more often exposed to the external environment (Turkewitz, 1977). These effects may well be transient, however, and even the hand preference reported by Michel may not be a true indication of a child's subsequent handedness. Michel also recognized that both head-orientation preference and handedness might be influenced by the same underlying factor, and indeed suggested that the data were broadly consistent with Annett's theory. Certainly, this would help explain why the relation between the two asymmetries is not perfect.

The bias in head orientation is not restricted to posture. Liederman and Kinsbourne (1980b) have shown that most infants have a bias toward turning their heads to the right in response to stimulation, whether aversive or non-aversive. They also demonstrated that this right-turning bias is motor and does not depend on any difference in sensitivity to sight, touch, or taste between the two sides of the head. Liederman and Kinsbourne (1980a) have also shown that the rightward bias is more frequent among the children of two right-handed parents than among children with one non-right-handed parent. This further suggests a link with handedness and also that the direction of bias may have a genetic basis. Finally, J. Gardner, Lewkowicz, and Turkewitz (1977) have reported that the rightward postural bias was equally prevalent among premature and full-term infants. These observations suggest that the rightward bias is biologically rather than environmentally determined.

Although postnatal influences can almost certainly be ruled out, however, it might still be argued that the prenatal environment may play some role. In fact, there is a predominant asymmetry in the presentation of the infant at birth and in the positioning of the fetus prior to birth. The French physician A. J. Comte (1828, cited in Harris, 1980a, 1980b) long ago suggested that this might play a direct role in the determination of handedness. The great majority of infants are born head first in the so-called vertex presentation, and most of these are in left presentation, with the head slanted to the left (i.e., with the back of the head toward the left rear and the forehead toward the right front of the mother). Comte observed from a large sample that the ratio of left to right presentations was approximately nine to one, which is about the ratio of right- to left-handers. He argued that those born in left presentation would have been positioned in the womb with the left arm pinned against the mother's back and the right arm against the more yielding abdomen. This would permit a greater flow of arterial blood to the right arm, encouraging right-handedness. The opposite argument would apply to those born in the right presentation. Essentially the same theory has been proposed, apparently independently, by Moss (1929) and by Kopell (1971).

The idea that fetal position or birth presentation might underlie handedness had been largely ignored (L. J. Harris, 1980c), although one published abstract suggests that there is no correlation between the two (Overstreet, 1938). Moreover, more recent evidence suggests that the proportion of left to right presentations among vertex births is not so extreme as Comte's figures indicate; Kopell (1971) states that about two-thirds are in left presentation, whereas Steel and Javert (1942) give figures of 53% and 34% for left and right vertex presentations, respectively. Michel and Goodwin (1979) have found an association between postural head-orientation asymmetry and birth presentation, however, and their data are summarized in Table 5.1. The association is far from perfect, though, and suggests that there is no direct causal relation between positional asymmetry in the womb and head-orientation preference after birth. Both asymmetries might well be linked to some common, underlying factor.

Stepping Reflex

Another reflex that is present at birth, and that shows a striking asymmetry, is the stepping reflex. It is observed if the infant is lowered onto a flat surface so that the feet make contact. When contact occurs, the legs make coordinated stepping movements, with alternate flexion and extension of each leg. The reflex is more easily elicited if the infant is tilted slightly forward. Peters and Petrie (1979) tested for consistent asymmetry of the stepping reflex in 24 infants at ages 17, 51, 82, and 105 days. Each infant was tested three times at each age, and the foot that led two or three times out of the three trials was

TABLE 5.1

Distribution of Supine Head-Position Preferences of 109 Newborn Infants, Related to Birth Presentation[a]

	Preference (z) index[b]		
Birth presentation	Significantly right	Between + 1.96 and −1.96	Significantly left
Right	35	21	2
Left	12	31	8

[a] From Michel and Goodwin (1979).

[b] Defined as $(R - L) / \sqrt{R + L}$, where R and L are frequencies of observations of right and left preferences, respectively.

designated the leading foot. The majority of infants led with the right foot—the actual numbers who did so were 18, 19, 19, and 16, respectively, at the four different ages.

More dramatically, Melekian (1981) tested normal full-term babies at birth (i.e., during the first day of life), as well as 1 week later. Of 205 infants given a single trial at birth, some 88% led with the right leg—a percentage that is remarkably close to the percentage of right-handed adults. A smaller group of 108 were given three consecutive trials at birth, and 70.4% led with the right leg on all three trials, where as 26.9% were mixed and 2.8% consistently led with the left leg. Testing at 1 week produced essentially the same results.

The stepping reflex is not obviously related to the tonic neck reflex, at least in any mechanical sense. For one thing, the stepping reflex involves flexion of the leading leg, usually the right one, whereas the tonic neck reflex involves extension of the leg on the "preferred" side. It is not known, however, whether the two are correlated or whether the stepping reflex is correlated with subsequent handedness or footedness. There are certainly some common elements with footedness. Right-handed adults tend to kick with the right foot (Annett & Turner, 1974), and the right leg also typically leads in mounting a bicycle or horse (Peters & Durding, 1979). Despite the lack of explicit evidence relating the stepping reflex to other asymmetries, Melekian expresses the opinion that it is likely to prove the most satisfactory test of early lateralization. He cites evidence that it is less susceptible to environmental influences than is head-orientation preference and may thus be a more valid index of organically based lateralization.

HANDEDNESS

One of the most extensive investigations of the development of handedness itself was that carried out by Gesell and Ames (1947). They took records on moving film of children ranging in age from 8 weeks to 10 years. The numbers in each age group ranged from 12 to 45. The children were filmed in situations contrived to secure responses to various objects, such as pencils, paper, blocks, and construction toys. The first clear preference to emerge in the majority of children was for the left hand, at 16–20 weeks, corroborating the earlier observation of Hall and Woolley, described previously. However, there were shifts between left-handedness, bilaterality, and right-handedness during the first year of life, and indeed cyclic fluctuations persisted to some degree until about age 8 years. The cycles were increasingly dominated by right-handedness, however, after the first year of life. Similarly, Seth (1973) observed the development of hand preference in nine infants, and he also found that left-handedness prevailed during the first 9 months but gave way thereafter to right-handedness.

In these studies, handedness was defined principally in terms of reaching. G. Young (1977) has argued that this may not provide a sensitive index of handedness. For instance, Cohen (1966) studied reaching in 100 8-month-old infants and found that 74 preferred the right hand and 26 the left hand, which is a less extreme split than one would expect on the basis of data from adults. It is of course possible that these proportions were contaminated by the reversal observed by Gesell and Ames and by Seth, although Young argued in turn that the initial left-handed bias reported by these authors was not statistically reliable. In an attempt to overcome any problems with reaching as an index of handedness, Ramsay (1980c) has measured handedness in the way infants actually make contact with and use various toys, such as a rattle ball or a toy telephone. On measures of unimanual handedness, there was no evidence for any bias toward either the left or right hand at 5 months of age, but a clear right-handed bias was present at 7 months and persisted at 9 months. Handedness in bimanual operations, however, in which the preferred hand assumes an active role and the nonpreferred hand a passive, supportive role, did not emerge until toward the end of the first year (cf. Ramsay, 1979; Ramsay, Campos, & Fenson, 1979) and in the majority of infants was correctly predicted by unimanual preference.

The work of Ramsay and his colleagues also suggests that there may be a systematic relation between the onset of handedness and the development of speech. The onset of bimanual handedness appears to coincide with the infant's first two-syllable utterances, such as "doggie" or "thank you," toward the end of the first year of life (Ramsay, 1980a; Ramsay, Campos, & Fenson, 1979). Similarly, unimanual handedness, at least as measured in terms of contact and manipulation, does not seem to emerge until the child begins what Ramsay calls repetitive babbling at about 6 months of age (Ramsay, 1980b). In repetitive babbling, the child repeats the same syllable, as in "da-da" or "be-be," which Ramsay likens to the repetitive banging that infants indulge in when unimanual manipulation develops.

Ramsay (1980b) did note some anomalies, however. There was some tendency for girls to show a preference for the left hand in the month following repetitive babbling, although they later became predominantly right-handed. Boys tended to show some preference first for the right hand, then for the left hand, while later becoming predominantly right-handed. These trends may well prove unreliable upon further examination, but they do suggest that the chapter on early left-hand preferences in right-handed children may not yet be closed.

The evidence reviewed so far suggests that handedness is first manifest at around age 6 months. However, this conclusion applies principally to handedness as measured by preference. Other evidence suggests that handedness can be detected at a much earlier age if it is defined in terms of strength or endurance. P. J. Caplan and Kinsbourne (1976) reported that 2-month-old infants held a rattle longer, on average, in the right hand than in the left hand, a result corroborated by Hawn and Harris (1979). In a more extensive investigation, Petrie and Peters (1980) found that the majority of infants produced a stronger grasp with the right hand than with the left and also held a rattle longer in the right than in the left hand. The tests commenced at an average age of 17 days, with follow-up tests at 51, 82, and 108 days. The right-hand advantage, especially in strength of grasp, was clearly evident at all these ages.

It might be noted that there is no evidence in these studies of the left-hand advantage observed in some of the studies of hand preferences in reaching. Witelson (1977b) has pointed out that it might be precisely because the left hand is preferred in reaching for new objects that it drops the rattle first! If nothing else, this suggestion draws attention to the potential difficulties and artifacts involved in measuring handedness in infants.

The anatomical basis of handedness may well be present even before birth. In about 80% of human brains, adult as well as fetal, there are more pyramidal fibers from the forebrain to the right hand than to the left hand; this is true both of contralateral and of ipsilateral pathways. Moreover, the contralateral pyramidal tract from the left hemisphere to the right hand crosses at a higher level in the medulla than does the tract from the right hemisphere to the left hand (Yakovlev, 1972; Yakovlev & Rakic, 1966). Since the right hand receives the greater amount of innervation, it seems plausible to suppose that this asymmetry might underlie right-handedness. Curiously enough, however, the little evidence that is available suggests that variations in handedness are not correlated with asymmetry of the pyramidal tracts. Yakovlev (1972) observed that four left-handers all showed the usual right-sided bias, while Kertesz and Geschwind (1971) reported that the higher crossing of left-to-right contralateral fibers was present in six of seven non-right-handers. There must therefore be some question as to whether the asymmetries of the pyramidal tract have any true bearing on handedness.

Although handedness appears to be established functionally in the first year of life, it probably continues to show some development during childhood. Gesell and Ames (1947), it will be recalled, observed that hand preference did not stabilize until about age 8 years, and Coren, Porac, and Duncan (1981) reported a higher incidence of mixed responses to items on hand preference and a correspondingly lower incidence of consistently right-handed responses, among preschoolers than among young adults. Coren *et al.* also found that the proportions preferring the right foot, eye, and ear were higher in the older group and that the congruence between these different preferences increased with age. Yet it might also be recalled from Chapter 2 that Annett (1970) found the right-hand advantage on a peg-moving task to be approximately constant between ages 3½ and 15 years. Preference for one or the other hand may well show more fluctuation than do differences in actual performance between the hands. Be that as it may, the pattern of handedness is clearly established very early on, if not before birth, and any changes that occur after the first year or two of life are relatively minor.

In their classic study of the development of handedness, Gesell and Ames (1947) concluded that "handedness is a product of growth [p. 175]." They were impressed with the orderly way in which handedness emerges, and with its relation to an inborn asymmetry in the tonic neck reflex. That conclusion is surely reinforced by the evidence that has accumulated since. Asymmetries favoring the right side appear in both the tonic neck reflex and the stepping reflex, both of which are present at birth. Right-handedness itself appears to be detectable at least as early as age 17 days, and possibly even at birth. Different manifestations of handedness emerge in orderly fashion during infancy and appear to be related systematically to developments in speech. It is surely extremely unlikely, therefore, that the predominance of right-handedness can be attributed to any direct influence of our right-handed culture to any but the smallest degree. We must suppose instead that right-handedness is an inborn, biological predisposition that is possessed by the majority of humans.

CEREBRAL LATERALIZATION

Lateralization in Early Infancy

In the previous chapter, it was noted that in the majority of people the temporal planum, an area of the temporal lobe in the vicinity of Wernicke's area, is larger on the left than on the right (Geschwind & Levitsky, 1968). This anatomical asymmetry is present also in newborns (Wada, Clarke, & Hamm, 1975; Witelson & Pallie, 1973) and indeed can be detected in the fetus as early as the thirty-first week of pregnancy (Chi, Dooling, & Gilles, 1977). There are often additional gyri on one or the other temporal lobe, more often on the left than on the right, and this asymmetry is also present both in human fetuses and in adults (Chi *et al.*, 1977). Since these asymmetries appear to involve language-mediating areas, they suggest that the anatomical basis of cerebral lateralization for language is present even before birth.

There is evidence that functional asymmetries of the brain may also be present in early infancy, if not at birth. Molfese, Freeman, and Palermo (1975) found that evoked electrical responses to speech sounds, including meaningless syllables, were larger when recorded over the left than over the right temporal lobe. This was true of a group of infants ranging in age from 1 week to 10 months, as well as of older children and adults. In more recent studies, Molfese and his co-workers have complicated their analytic procedures somewhat, first normalizing the evoked responses, then subjecting them to principal-components analysis, then rotating the solutions, then applying analysis of variance to the component scores. I am a little skeptical as to whether the data can meaningfully survive such an onslaught, but it is perhaps worth summarizing the main conclusions claimed by Molfese's group. First, it is claimed that the *right* hemisphere responds in categorical fashion to the distinction between voiced and unvoiced consonants (as in *ba* versus *pa*) in adults (Molfese, 1978), preschoolers (Molfese & Hess, 1978), 2-to-4-month-old infants (Molfese & Molfese, 1979b), but not in newborns (Molfese & Molfese, 1979b). On the other hand, the *left* hemisphere seems to discriminate consonants that differ in place of articulation (as in *bae* versus *gae*) in both adults and newborns (Molfese & Molfese, 1979a).

Whether or not these results are a true indication of the nature of interhemispheric differences in infants, there are other psychophysiological studies that indicate at least that such differences exist. Gardiner and Walter (1977) took electroencephalographic recordings from the left and right sides of the scalps of four 6-month-old infants while they were presented with natural speech or music. In all four infants, there was a systematic interhemispheric difference between speech and music in terms of the distribution of power within a frequency band centered at 4.0 Hz. In adults, a comparable difference is to be found for a frequency band centered on the alpha rhythm, at around 10.0 Hz (e.g., Doyle, Ornstein, & Galin, 1973). A. E. Davis and Wada (1977) carried out a spectral analysis of evoked potentials to clicks and flashes of light in 16 infants whose mean age was only 5 weeks, and found that the higher amplitude, more localized and coherent centers of activity were in the left hemisphere for clicks and in the right hemisphere for flashes. They argue that the click is the more temporally structured event and so calls upon the specialized resources of the left hemisphere in fine temporal analysis (see Chapter 3).

Entus (1977) has claimed evidence for functional lateralization in infancy using a dichotic-listening paradigm. She presented dichotic pairs of sounds to infants, aged from 3 to 20 weeks, whenever they sucked on an artificial nipple. When sucking to a particular pair had habituated to a prescribed level, she changed the sound in one ear only and measured the increase in the rate of sucking. When the sounds were consonant–vowel syllables distinguished only by the consonant (*ba, da, ga, ma*), the increase was greater when the change occurred in the right ear than when it occurred in the left ear, but when they were musical sounds differing in timbre (the note A played on different instruments), the increase was greater when the change was in the left ear. Using the same paradigm, and a more automated procedure designed to lessen the possibility of the experimenter influencing the results, Vargha-Khadem and Corballis (1979) failed to replicate the left-hemispheric advantage for speech sounds.

Entus's findings nevertheless receive some support from a study by Glanville, Best, and Levenson (1977). Their study was very similar to Entus's, except that they measured heart rate instead of sucking. Their subjects were 12 3-month-old infants. Following habituation to dichotically presented syllables (either *ba-da* or *pa-ta*), increase in heart rate was greater after a change in the right ear than in the left ear, whereas the reverse was true of musical stimuli (notes played on organ, string, and flute).

Segalowitz and Chapman (1980) have claimed evidence for left-hemispheric specialization for the reception of speech in premature infants tested only 5 weeks after birth. They measured tremor in the arms and legs during exposure to speech, during exposure to orchestral music, and in the absence of any patterned stimulation. During speech, there was a greater reduction in tremor in the right than in the left limbs, implying greater cortical activity in the left cerebral hemisphere. There was no such asymmetry in response to music.

Infants are in some respects the Rorschach plates of psychology; we see in them what we want to see and impose on them our biased conceptions of the human mind. Nevertheless, there now seems little doubt that functional cerebral lateralization can be measured early in the first year of life and that its anatomical basis is present at birth. It may come as a surprise that cerebral lateralization for language should be manifest long before a child can understand or produce language. For more than a decade, however, research has indicated that infants can discriminate elementary speech sounds in very much the same way that adults do (see Morse, 1979, for a review), suggesting that there are innate mechanisms for the perception of speech. It need not be altogether surprising, therefore, that these mechanisms are localized primarily in the left cerebral hemisphere, even in newborn infants.

Does Lateralization Develop beyond Infancy?

Although it is now fairly well accepted that cerebral lateralization is present in early infancy, there is some dispute as to whether it continues to develop during childhood. Despite the evidence for early cerebral lateralization, there are some indications that children below about age 5 years are more likely to become aphasic following damage to the right hemisphere than are older children or adults (e.g, Hécaen, 1976; Krashen, 1972). This has been interpreted to mean that there is at least some degree of bilateral representation of language in early childhood and that this gives way to a progressive lateralization in the left cerebral hemisphere (e.g., Lenneberg, 1967). Kinsbourne and Hiscock (1977) have attacked both the evidence and the interpretation. The evidence, they claim, is likely to be biased in favor of reports of aphasia following right-hemispheric damage in children, and some of the evidence is in any event weak. In Hécaen's (1976) study, for instance, only two out of six children with right-sided lesions showed symptoms of aphasia, but one of these was left-handed and the other had had a history of cranial trauma. Kinsbourne and Hiscock cite evidence of their own that suggests that degree of lateralization in normal children remains approximately constant between the ages of about 3 and 11 years. Adding this to the evidence of cerebral lateralization in infants leads them firmly to the conclusion that lateralization does not develop, but is essentially fixed from birth.

Witelson (1977b) has reached much the same conclusion. In an exhaustive review, she found very little evidence that the degree of lateralization increases with age. In 36 experiments on dichotic listening in children, 30 yielded a right-ear advantage for verbal stimuli even in the youngest groups tested, and all yielded a right-ear advantage at least in the older groups. The few studies suggesting an increase in lateralization may have been contaminated by methodological difficulties involved in testing young children. In more recent studies on the development of lateralization in dichotic listening, Geffen and her colleagues have reported evidence that variations in lateralization reflect differences in the ability of children of different ages to attend to one or the other ear, but that underlying lateralization remains constant (Geffen, 1976, 1978; Geffen & Sexton, 1978; Geffen & Wale, 1979). Witelson (1977b) also reviewed evidence from tachistoscopic studies of differences between the visual hemifields, and although some of these do suggest that some asymmetries do not emerge until later in childhood, Witelson concludes that "not one tachistoscopic study of left-hemispheric specialization in children is free of methodological difficulty or provides unequivocal results [p. 236]."

Witelson's review may also serve to dispel the widely held view that cerebral lateralization for language emerges earlier in girls than in boys. Kimura's work on development of the right-ear advantage in dichotic listening is often cited as evidence for this, but in fact the evidence appears in only one of three studies reported by Kimura (1967). In another study, she found evidence for earlier development of language in girls than in boys, but no difference in degree of lateralization (Kimura, 1963). Over the entire assemblage of dichotic-listening experiments reviewed by Witelson, there was no consistent evidence for sex differences in degree or onset of lateralization; if anything, the evidence suggests a slightly higher degree of lateralization in boys than in girls. Among adults, however, there is fairly clear evidence that men are more highly lateralized, both with respect to language and with respect to so-called right-hemispheric functions, than are women (McGlone, 1980).

Eling, Marshall, and van Galen (1981) have also found essentially constant right-ear advantages in dichotic monitoring between age 8 years and adulthood. Although this result essentially confirms the results of Geffen and her colleagues, Eling *et al.* have some reservation as to its meaning. They use two kinds of monitoring—one requiring subjects to monitor the dichotic lists for words of a given category (e.g., *fruits*), the other requiring them to monitor for words rhyming with a particular word (e.g., *table*). They hoped to demonstrate different patterns of development for these different monitoring tasks, but instead both tasks yielded the same degree of lateralization at all ages. They suggest that lateralization had little to do with the nature of the task but may simply have reflected an attentional bias induced by the fact that the stimuli were verbal (cf. Kinsbourne, 1975). If this is so, then dichotic-listening studies may reveal little of the qualitative changes that may occur in the development of lateralization.

Studies of the development of laterality are fraught with methodological difficulties. There is a general problem in developmental research of ensuring that tests are equivalent, or tap the same abilities, in children of different ages. The measurement of difference creates special psychometric problems, whether in the context of laterality (e.g., Bryden & Sprott, 1981; Richardson, 1976) or of change (e.g., C. W. Harris, 1963)—and in the study of development of laterality, both contexts are involved.

In any event, it is surely not the case that all lateralized functions are lateralized from birth, or even from the first year of life, since many functions simply do not emerge until much later in development—although the neural substrates for subsequent lateralization may be present from birth. For instance, there is evidence that young children process unfamiliar faces in terms of a piecemeal representation of features and do not develop a more elaborate, configurational representation until about age 9 or 10 years (Carey & Diamond, 1977; Reynolds & Jeeves, 1978). Correspondingly, Leehey (1976) has found that a left-visual-field advantage in identification of unfamiliar faces was present in 10-year-olds but not in 8-year-olds. Phippard (1977), however, found a left-field advantage in recognition of faces by young adults but not by 10-year-olds. Witelson (1976) has also reported evidence that right-hemispheric specialization for tactile spatial processing develops much later in girls than in boys and that, in girls at least, it develops well after left-hemispheric specialization for verbal processing.

It should not be concluded from these examples that right-hemispheric specialization necessarily develops later than does left-hemispheric specialization, although there may be a trend in this direction. We have already seen that there is evidence for a right-hemispheric advantage early in infancy in the processing of musical sounds (Entus, 1977; Gardiner & Walter, 1977; Glanville *et al.*, 1977; Molfese, Freeman, & Palermo, 1975) and in the processing of flashes of light (Davis & Wada, 1977). Conversely, there is evidence that left-hemispheric specialization for some functions may not develop until adolescence (Bryden & Allard, 1978). For instance, Tomlinson-Keasey, Kelly, and Burton (1978) have observed a left-hemispheric advantage in the matching of words and of symbols that is present in adults and 13-year-olds, but not in 9-year-olds.

Environmental Influences

The evidence reviewed so far reinforces the view that the origin of lateralization is organic rather than cultural or environmental. Lateralization of some functions may not occur until those functions actually emerge in development, but once established, lateralization for a particular function probably does not undergo any appreciable change. Although lateralization is thus seen to emerge in programmed fashion, according to some biologically determined blueprint, this should not be taken to mean that the environment plays no part. Development in general is as dependent on environmental stimulation as it is on the processes of growth, and it would be surprising if this were not true of the development of lateralization. A dramatic example, although one that rests on a single case, is provided by a child known as "Genie," who was raised in virtual isolation from about age 20 months to nearly 14 years. She was thus deprived of exposure to language during the years in which children normally learn the skills of language. Genie has made some progress toward learning language since removed from her predicament, but it is of interest that her language skills appear to be mediated by the *right* cerebral hemisphere (Fromkin, Krashen, Curtiss, Rigler, & Rigler, 1974). It is not entirely clear what explains this curious anomaly, but it does at least suggest that abnormal environmental conditions may influence, and in this case even reverse, cerebral lateralization for language.

There is some evidence that cerebral lateralization may develop earlier, or may be less extreme, among children of low socioeconomic status than among those of middle socioeconomic status, perhaps reflecting an environment that is less verbally sophisticated. Geffner and Hochberg (1971) tested reports of dichotically presented digits in children aged from 4 to 7 years and found a right-ear advantage among all age groups of children in a middle socioeconomic sample. Since the majority of low socioeconomic children were black and the majority of middle socioeconomic children were white, it is conceivable that the result was due to ethnic origin rather than socioeconomic status per se. In a more systematic study, however, Borowy and Goebel (1976) found a larger right-ear advantage among children of middle than of low socioeconomic class, but there was no difference between black and white children in the latter group. There was apparently no difference in lateralization between ages 5 and 11 years, however, for either socioeconomic class, although the data are analyzed and presented in a way that makes it difficult to be sure of this. Although these data suggest that socioeconomic class may be important, they are difficult to reconcile with other evidence, reviewed earlier, that lateralization in dichotic listening remains constant from early infancy.

It has been suggested that left-hemispheric lesions are less likely to produce aphasia in illiterates than in educated people (Cameron, Currier, & Haeper, 1971). This is disputed, however, by Damasio, Castro-Caldas, Grosso, and Ferro (1976), who claim that there are neither qualitative nor quantitative differences between the aphasias of literate and illiterate patients. Tzavaras, Kaprinis, and Gatzoyas (1981) tested illiterate and educated adults in Epirus, a region in the northwest of Greece, and observed a smaller right-ear advantage in recall of dichotically presented digits among the literates than among the illiterates. Since the literates scored better overall, their right-ear advantages may have been restricted by a ceiling effect. In any event, the result suggests that literacy does not play a significant role in the development of cerebral lateralization, at least in the perception of oral speech. This result is also difficult to reconcile with the results described in the previous paragraph, since the illiterates were presumably of lower socioeconomic status than were the literate subjects.

Another source of environmental deprivation is deafness, and it is therefore pertinent to enquire about cerebral lateralization in the congenitally deaf. In North America, most deaf people use some variant of American Sign Language, in which each movement of the hand corresponds roughly to a concept, such as a thing or an event. This may be supplemented by finger spelling, in which different hand postures represent different letters of the alphabet. Kimura (1981) has reviewed cases of manual aphasia, or disorders in signing, in deaf patients who have suffered cerebral injury. Among nine right-handed patients, signing was impaired following damage to the left hemisphere, whereas in two left-handed aphasics, the damage was to the left hemisphere in one case and to the right in the other. Underwood and Paulson (1981) have since drawn attention to another left-handed patient with manual aphasia following left-cerebral injury. In some cases, at least, the deficit in signing could not be attributed to a more general apraxia. This pattern of results, although based on a small sample, closely resembles that observed in vocal aphasia: In right-handers, sign language is represented predominantly in the left cerebral hemispheres, whereas left-handers show a mixed pattern of cerebral lateralization. These results should dispel any notion that auditory input may be necessary for the left-cerebral dominance for language (e.g., Geschwind & Levitsky, 1968; Scholes & Fischler, 1979). It might also be noted that left-cerebral dominance applied as much to American Sign Language, which has a global, holistic quality, as to finger spelling, which is more analytic in character.

Kimura observed that most patients were impaired in their ability to comprehend as well as produce signs, suggesting that the left cerebral hemisphere is generally dominant for both reception and production of signs. Tachistoscopic studies of visual-hemifield differences in perception of signs in deaf subjects, by contrast, have often yielded a left-field advantage, implying right cerebral dominance (see Poizner, Battison, & Lane, 1979, for a review). Poizner *et al.* showed that this asymmetry disappeared when moving signs replaced static ones, suggesting that the contributions of left and right hemisphere may depend on the relative importance of dynamic and spatial aspects of the task. We saw in Chapter 3 that the direction of hemifield differences in perception of other verbal patterns may be similarly influenced by the relative importance of different components of the task even in normal subjects. Consequently, there is no firm evidence that the lateralization of the perception of signs by the deaf differs qualitatively from the lateralization of the perception of letters or words by the hearing.

There is evidence that the deaf differ from the hearing with respect to functional asymmetries in reading. All but one of the deaf aphasics described by Kimura showed severe impairment in writing, but reading remained apparently intact in the seven cases for which the relevent evidence was available. Tachistoscopic studies have generally revealed that the usual right-field advantage for words is either reduced, absent, or even reversed in the congenitally deaf (Poizner *et al.*, 1979). Kelly and Tomlinson-Keasey (1981) have also reported a reversal between deaf and hearing children in lateralization of a task requiring them to judge consecutive pairs of words or pictures as the same or different. The deaf were faster when the words or pictures were flashed in the left than in the right visual field, whereas the hearing children showed a right-field advantage. The deaf children were also faster overall. These various results need not imply a basic difference in cerebral lateralization for language between deaf and hearing, however. Kelly and Tomlinson-Keasey suggest that the deaf may adopt a right-hemispheric, visuospatial strategy for coding and comparing the stimuli, whereas the hearing children favor a verbal strategy. More generally, Kimura suggests that the deaf tend to read in a holistic rather than a syllabic fashion, which may explain why they are unimpaired by left-hemispheric lesions.

Finally, it has been claimed that North American Indians may show *right*-hemispheric dominance for language. In an unpublished manuscript, L. Rogers, TenHouten, Kaplan, and Gardiner (1976) described electroencephalographic evidence that this was so. Also, Scott, Hynd, Hunt, and Weed (1979) have reported a strong left-ear advantage among Navajo Indians in recognition of consonant–vowel syllables, whereas Americans of European stock displayed the usual right-ear advantage. McKeever (1981a), however, reported a right-visual-field advantage among Navajo Indians in latency to name tachistoscopically displayed objects, a task that reflects left-cerebral dominance in samples of European Americans, suggesting that the Navajo do not differ from other Americans with respect to cerebral lateralization. Given that there are no known left-handed cultures, it would be surprising indeed if any ethnic group were to show genuinely reversed cerebral lateralization for language.

An ambiguity that underlies all the research reviewed in this section is whether anomalies of lateralization are due to differences in the underlying neurological basis of lateralization itself or whether they reflect differences in the way subjects go about a particular task. Among the deaf, for instance, the usual right-field advantage in processing verbal material appears to be reduced or even reversed, but this may imply a spatial strategy rather than any reduction or reversal of underlying lateralization. A similar explanation may underlie the curious reversal of the asymmetry in dichotic listening among the Navajo Indians, reported by Scott *et al.* (1979). It has also been suggested that Genie's right-hemispheric mediation of speech reflects a holistic processing strategy rather than any fundamental anomaly in neurological organization (Fromkin *et al.*, 1974). I suspect that experience may play some role in the development of normal lateralization, despite the ambiguities in interpretation of the evidence. From the evidence reviewed, however, any variation due to environmental influences is minor when set against the biological forces that determine lateralization in the first place.

Sex Differences

I have already noted occasional instances where sex differences have emerged in the study of cerebral lateralization. It has in fact long been suggested that women may exhibit a lesser degree of cerebral lateralization, on average, than men do. McGlone (1980, p. 215) quotes the following comment by Crichton-Browne, published in 1880: "It would appear that the tendency to symmetry in the two halves of the cerebrum is stronger in women than in men." Crichton-Browne's conclusion was based on a study of differences in weight between the two sides of the brain. In a careful review of evidence from anatomical, clinical, and perceptual studies, McGlone herself concludes that there is indeed a good deal of evidence in support of the idea that cerebral lateralization is less pronounced in women than in men. It should be pointed out at once, however, that there is a great deal of overlap between men and women in the distribution of lateral asymmetries, and McGlone in fact notes that the most obvious overall conclusion is that "basic patterns of male and female brain asymmetry seem to be more similar than they are different [p. 226]." Any such differences are clearly too small to be classed as sexual dimorphism (Morgan, 1980).

The most convincing evidence is perhaps that collected by McGlone herself. In carefully matched samples of right-handed men and women with unilateral lesions, she found the incidence of aphasia following left-sided lesions to be at least three times as high among the men as among the women. When the aphasics were removed from the samples, men with left-sided lesions showed lower verbal intelligence and poorer verbal memory than did men with right-sided lesions, but there were no such differences between women with left- and right-sided lesions. Conversely, men with right-sided lesions performed more poorly on tests of mental rotation and memory for photographed faces than did men with left-sided lesions, but the side of the lesion did not influence women's performance on these tasks (McGlone, 1977, 1978). It might be noted that sex differences in degree of lateralization seem to apply more to the perception and comprehension of speech than to its production. There is little evidence that expressive speech is *ever* bilaterally represented in right-handed patients, whether male or female (Milner, 1975).

It may appear paradoxical that women should be less lateralized cerebrally when evidence reviewed in Chapter 2 suggested that they tend to show a higher incidence of manual asymmetry than men do. That is, the incidence of right-handedness appears to be slightly higher among women than among men. Part of the explanation for this seeming paradox is that McGlone confined her review to right-handers. This in turn, however, raises the possibility of an artifact in her data. If the sex difference in handedness is due to a response bias, as Bryden (1977) has suggested, then women may be more likely than men to declare themselves right-handed when they are truly left-handed or of mixed handedness. This may increase the relative number of non-right-handers among samples of putatively right-handed women, and so increase the percentage with bilateral representation of language.

Insofar as there is a genuine difference in degree of cerebral asymmetry between right-handed men and women, it seems likely that it reflects some developmental factor. In extensive reviews, both Witelson (1977b) and McGlone (1980) found little evidence for sex differences in degree of lateralization among children. Such differences, therefore, seem to be confined to adults. Indeed, D. P. Gordon (1980) found that the right-ear advantage in identification of syllables was clearly present in both male and female 9-year-olds, but was no longer present in girls by age 13, although it was still clearly evident in boys of that age. This suggests that the left-hemispheric specialization for the perception of speech may actually diminish in girls between childhood and puberty.

Just why this should happen is not clear. Conceivably, it is related to different life-styles increasingly adopted by boys and girls as they approach and pass through puberty, with girls indulging more in verbal pursuits and boys in exploration and spatial activities. Indeed, there is evidence that cognitive differences between girls and boys, with girls excelling in verbal skills and boys in some spatial skills, also become more evident with the approach of puberty; this pattern, moreover, is essentially the same in children from Scotland and from Ghana (Jahoda, 1979)! These differences may be due to experiential factors per se or to hormonal changes that bring about increasing physical differentiation between the sexes. An analogy is suggested by Nottebohm's (1972, 1977) discovery that singing in male chaffinches and canaries is controlled primarily by the left side of the brain. This asymmetry is not evident in female birds, who do not normally sing. Nottebohm (1980) reports, however, that when female canaries are treated with testosterone in adulthood they produce malelike song, and in four cases studied by Nottebohm, this song was also under left-cerebral control. One cannot, of course, draw strong inferences about human sex differences from the twittering of canaries, but these results surely at least raise the possibility that hormones may play a role in the development of human laterality.

Waber (1976, 1977) has suggested that the age of puberty, rather than sex per se may explain the observed results. She found that those who reached puberty earlier showed a less marked right-ear advantage on a verbal dichotic-listening task than did those who reached puberty later. Since girls generally mature earlier than boys do, this might explain why they typically show the lesser degree of cerebral asymmetry. Indeed, Waber (1977) found that when boys and girls were matched for sexual maturation rather than for chronological age, no sex differences in ear asymmetries were observed. However, Waber studied only adolescents between ages 13 and 16 years, and her account does not really explain why D. P. Gordon (1980) found a *decline* in cerebral asymmetry in girls between childhood and puberty.

Not all commentators have accepted that there truly is a sex difference in degree of cerebral asymmetry. Bryden (1980), for instance, suggested that the observed effects may be due to differences in strategy rather than to hemispheric asymmetry per se. Kimura (1980) suggested that language representation *within* the left cerebral hemisphere may be different in men and women, with more anterior representation in women and posterior representation in men. This might explain some of the observed findings, including McGlone's own results. Kinsbourne (1980) raised a number of methodological issues that, he claimed, render McGlone's results and those based on perceptual tasks suspect. He wondered if there might be extrascientific motives underlying reports of sex differences:

> Under pressure from the gathering momentum of feminism, and perhaps in backlash to it, many investigators seem determined to discover that men and women "really" are different. It seems that if sex differences (e.g., in lateralization) do not exist, then they have to be invented [p. 242].

Plasticity in Infancy

It is widely held that the infant brain exhibits considerable plasticity of function and in particular that the right cerebral hemisphere may take over the representation of language in the event of early injury to the left cerebral hemisphere. Hence, it is suggested that there is *equipotentiality* of the two halves of the brain for the representation of language. At first, the argument that each hemisphere has an equal potential for language representation was based simply on the apparent mirror-image relation between the two halves of the brain. Thus, Marie (1922) wrote:

> The inborn centers which we know (and they are not numerous) are always bilateral and very clearly symmetrical. The motor centers of the limbs, the centers of vision, have their locations in each of the two hemispheres in symmetrical regions. . . . How can we admit the existence of an inborn center for speech which would be neither bilateral nor symmetrical [p. 180; cited in translation by Dennis & Whitaker, 1977, p. 93]?

This argument, of course, is considerably undermined by the discovery of anatomical asymmetries in the brain, and especially in the language-mediating areas, that were documented earlier.

The argument for equipotentiality was placed on a somewhat firmer footing by Basser (1962) and McFie (1961), who reviewed evidence on the effects of infantile hemiplegia and hemidecortication. These authors claimed that in cases of severe brain injury during infancy, leading to hemidecortication, it did not matter which side of the brain was affected. According to Basser, damage to the left hemisphere prior to the onset of speech, at about 2 years of age, has no lasting effect on development of language, since the right hemisphere can take over the mediation of language functions normally subserved by the left. Between age 2 years and puberty, damage to the left hemisphere has increasingly disruptive effects, and damage after puberty produces essentially irreversible loss of language skills.

M. Dennis and Whitaker (1977) have argued that Basser's case for equipotentiality was exaggerated and based on only superficial assessment of language skills. Indeed, they note that other, earlier reviews of the effects of infantile hemiplegia show clearly that disorders of language are much more common in right hemiplegics than in left hemiplegics. These data raise serious doubts as to whether the right hemisphere can assume completely the linguistic functions of the left in the event of early left-hemispheric damage. M. Dennis and Kohn (1975) carried out a thorough analysis of the linguistic skills of nine infantile hemiplegics who subsequently underwent removal of the afflicted cerebral cortex, and observed that the left hemidecorticates were inferior to right hemidecorticates in certain syntactic skills, most particularly in comprehension of passive negative sentences.

Although the patients studied by Dennis and Kohn (1975) had been hemiplegic from early infancy, the ages at which they underwent hemidecortication ranged from 5 months to 20 years. It is commonly assumed that damage to the left hemisphere sufficient to produce right hemiplegia is also sufficient to induce right-hemispheric mediation of language, but as Dennis and Whitaker (1977) point out this need not be so. The damaged left hemisphere may continue to exert some influence over language functions, and any aphasic symptoms might therefore reflect left-cerebral damage per se rather than any reduced potential of the right hemisphere. For a surer test of infantile equipotentiality, therefore, it is important to study patients who have undergone hemidecortication in early infancy.

Such patients are unfortunately (or perhaps fortunately) rare. Dennis and Whitaker (1976) have described three critical cases, however—one right hemidecorticate and two left hemidecorticates, who underwent hemidecortication prior to the age 5 months. They were assessed at ages 9 and 10 years. All were making normal progress at school, had intelligence quotients within the normal range in both verbal and performance achievement, and were generally unimpaired in their phonemic and semantic abilities. Compared with the right hemidecorticate, however, the two left hemidecorticates were somewhat deficient in understanding spoken language, especially when meaning was conveyed by diversity of syntax. For instance, they were less able to understand passive or passive negative sentences and to judge whether complex sentences were grammatical or not. Dennis and Whitaker (1976) describe the defect as "an organizational, analytical, syntactic problem, rather than a difficulty with the conceptual or semantic aspects of language [p. 428]."

This evidence, although based on a very small sample, certainly suggests that equipotentiality might not be quite so complete as Basser (1962) suggested, although one might still be impressed by the high degree of verbal competence achieved by the left hemidecorticates. Given that lateralization for production of language is typically more pronounced than lateralization for language perception, one must also be impressed by the fact that speech was virtually unimpaired in these children; Dennis and Whitaker noted, in fact, that their expressive skills were in some respects better than their comprehension. These results in themselves, therefore, do not force a radical reassessment of the notion of infantile plasticity.

In Chapter 3 it was noted that left hemidecortication in adulthood does not impair language quite so much as one might expect from the effects of more circumscribed left-hemispheric lesions. Nevertheless, there is still a clear difference between adult and infantile cases. Summarizing the evidence, St. James-Roberts (1981) writes that

> although infant hemispherectomy cases have achieved apparently normal speech production, together with verbal IQs in the normal range, only one adult case has been reported to have normal speech comprehension; while speech production in adult left hemispherectomies has been limited to short phrases [p. 36].

St. James-Roberts nevertheless argues that the advantage of infantile over adult cases need not be attributed to infantile plasticity, as there are several systematic differences between infantile and adult cases other than the difference in age. For one thing, infantile cases have typically had a much longer period of recovery at the time of evaluation. Morbidity is also higher among the adult cases. Nearly half of the 31 adult cases reviewed by St. James-Roberts had died within 1 year of surgery, and all the cases of left hemidecortication in adulthood had died within 2 years of surgery. Older patients are also more likely to have suffered from injuries of endogenous origin, such as vascular accidents, and these are more likely to have irreversible effects than are lesions of exogenous origin (Kertesz & McCabe, 1977; Van Dongen & Loonen, 1977).

St. James-Roberts carried out several analyses of the effects of age, etiology, recovery-period, and experiential variables on Verbal and Performance IQ, which showed that age was of relatively minor importance. He concluded therefore that the notion of infantile plasticity was not supported. While this is a properly cautious conclusion based on the evidence, I suspect that it is premature to rule out the plasticity hypothesis entirely. It is not clear that St. James-Roberts's analyses are entirely successful in disentangling the independent variables or that the IQs are always comparably or appropriately measured. Moreover, he measured age with respect to the brain damage rather than with respect to hemidecortication, so that there is some doubt as to precisely when right-hemispheric compensation for left-hemispheric injury might be said to have begun.

The most critical evidence on infantile plasticity, in my view, remains that documented by Dennis and Whitaker (1976). Not only did their three cases undergo hemidecortication early in the first year of life, but subsequent development was also free of seizures and of other evidence of residual pathology.

Moreover, testing of their linguistic skills was comprehensive. The two left hemidecorticates probably gave a fairly accurate picture of the extent to which the isolated right hemisphere can mediate language. Although these two patients were somewhat deficient in syntactic skills, their sophistication in language was well beyond what one would expect of adult cases, even granted the extra considerations raised by St. James-Roberts. In short, there is evidence that the right cerebral hemisphere is capable of sophisticated production and comprehension of language and that it is more likely to achieve this potential if given the opportunity very early in life.

THEORETICAL OVERVIEW

Ideas about the development of lateralization have fluctuated considerably even within the course of the present century. It is worth briefly reviewing them, if only because it serves to remind us how transient are the doctrines of the moment. These doctrines, moreover, seem to depend as much on the prevailing zeitgeist as on the empirical evidence, and there is no good reason to suppose that our current ideas are any different in this respect.

Psychology in the twentieth century has been largely dominated by behaviorism. Within this framework, it is natural to regard handedness, at least, as a product of environmental contingencies. Thus, John B. Watson, founder of behaviorism, who carried out a series of studies on infants in the first year of life, wrote that "there is no fixed differentiation of response in either hand until social usage begins to establish handedness [1924, p. 101]." The idea that right-handedness might be of cultural origin is not restricted to behaviorist psychologists; as we have seen, it was also suggested by Collins (1970), a geneticist.

What, then, of cerebral lateralization? Weber (1904) argued that cerebral lateralization for language might arise as a direct result of the use of the preferred hand for writing, leading to a contralateral specialization for language skills generally. This idea has some superficial plausibility in that reading and writing are the only overtly asymmetrical acts associated with language. We have seen, however, that lateralization is apparent well before children learn to read or write, and is apparent even in illiterates. Gazzaniga (1970) suggested more generally that cerebral lateralization might be a consequence of handedness. He cited evidence that the corpus callosum is undeveloped in early life so that the infant is functionally "split-brained." Consequently, exploration of the environment with the preferred hand would stimulate only the contralateral hemisphere, which would in turn instigate further exploration. This hemisphere would thus be cumulatively enriched relative to the other hemisphere and so acquire the complexity required for the mediation of language.

The work of Ramsay, discussed earlier, suggests that there is indeed an association between the development of handedness and the onset of speech, and this might be taken as support for Gazzaniga's theory. However, the evidence reviewed earlier also suggests that cerebral asymmetries presumed to be related to the mediation of language can be detected very early in life, and even before birth.

The emphasis began to change in the 1960s, with the decline of behaviorism and the growth of neuropsychology, cognitive psychology, and psycholinguistics. Although Gesell and his colleagues (e.g., Gesell & Ames, 1947) had earlier emphasized maturational influences in the development of handedness, it was perhaps the work of Chomsky (e.g., 1957, 1965) on the nature of language that ultimately had the greatest impact, although the relevance of this work to lateralization was at first indirect. Chomsky argued that language was an innate, uniquely but universally human capacity that could not be reduced to the laws of operant conditioning. This point of view was nowhere better expressed than in Chomsky's (1959) famous, withering review of Skinner's (1957) book *Verbal Behavior,* which was (and still is) the most lengthy, sophisticated, and detailed exposition of the behaviorist approach to language.

Chomsky's ideas were placed in developmental and neuropsychological perspective by Lenneberg (1967) in his book *Biological Foundations of Language.* Lenneberg noted that language develops in children in an orderly, predictable way, suggesting that it is governed primarily by the biological process of growth. One aspect of this maturational process was the development of cerebral lateralization. Drawing primarily on the evidence reviewed by Basser (1962), Lenneburg argued that cerebral lateralization does not begin to develop until about the time the child begins to talk, and it is complete and irreversible around the time of puberty. According to this view, as we have seen, the two cerebral hemispheres exhibit equipotentiality for the mediation of language in the first 2 years of life, but language depends increasingly on the language-dominant hemisphere beyond age 2 years.

The evidence reviewed in this chapter confirms Lenneberg's conviction that lateralization is biologically rather than environmentally determined. Lenneberg was clearly in error, however, in supposing that lateralization is not manifest in the first 2 years of life. I have already recorded abundant evidence that lateralization can be detected at birth, and even before. Moreover there is very little evidence that lateralization per se shows any substantial development at all during childhood; on the contrary, several studies seem to suggest that the degree of lateralization remains essentially constant.

This new evidence immediately posed a problem: How could one reconcile infantile lateralization with infantile plasticity? That is, if the left cerebral hemisphere were already destined both functionally and anatomically for the representation of language even from before birth, by what mechanism could the right hemisphere assume the mediation of language if the left hemisphere were incapacitated very early in life? In the following sections, I contrast two possible answers to this question.

A Left–Right Maturational Gradient?

One possible answer is that the left cerebral hemisphere may develop earlier than the right, at least during the period of development when language is acquired and at least with respect to those areas of the brain that mediate language (Corballis & Beale, 1976; Corballis & Morgan, 1978; Moscovitch, 1977). According to this view, the left hemisphere would gain control over language functions, not because it is intrinsically specialized for them, but because it is the more advanced of the two hemispheres during the stages of development when language is learned. If the left hemisphere is incapacitated, however, the right hemisphere might then take over the representation of language, provided that this occurs early in development. If the right hemisphere has already developed beyond the so-called critical period for language, then no compensation would be possible. This account therefore explains how the two hemispheres can possess equal potential for the mediation of language and yet how it is normally the left hemisphere that is dominant for language.

It is also necessary to suppose that, in the course of normal development, the left hemisphere exerts an inhibitory influence over language representation in the right. If this were not so, one would expect the right hemisphere ultimately to develop the same degree of specialization for language as the left, albeit with a lag in development. Evidence on the lateralized representation of language in adults, reviewed in Chapter 3, shows clearly that this does not happen. It has been suggested that this inhibitory influence is exerted via the corpus callosum, which may therefore play a crucial role in the development of lateralization (e.g., Denenberg, 1981; Moscovitch, 1977; Trevarthen, 1974).

Evidence on this point comes from studies of lateralization in individuals with congenital absence of the corpus callosum. A useful review of 29 such cases is provided by Chiarello (1980). Among 10 cases given dichotic-listening tests of cerebral lateralization for language, 3 showed a right-ear advantage, 3 a left-ear advantage, and 4 a fluctuating asymmetry on different testing occasions or no ear advantage—an overall profile favoring neither cerebral hemisphere. In a more recent study, two further cases were shown to exhibit a left-ear advantage for both verbal and nonverbal material (Lassonde, Lortie, Ptito, & Geoffroy, 1981). Another patient was revealed to have bilateral representation of language by the sodium amytal test (Gott & Saul, 1978). It is also worth noting that 8 of the 29 cases reviewed by Chiarello, and 1 of the 2 described by Lassonde *et al.*, were left-handed or ambidextrous—nearly three times the proportion one would expect from the population at large. In spite of this evidence for bilaterality or reduced laterality in these cases of callosal agenesis, however, Chiarello notes that interpretation of this evidence is not straightforward. Some patients may have lateralized brain abnormalities in addition to agenesis of the corpus callosum, and they may also have developed a compensatory elaboration of ipsilateral sensory pathways, making the results of dichotic-listening tests difficult to interpret. Nevertheless, the results may be taken to be at least consistent with the idea that the corpus callosum is critical to the development of cerebral lateralization in normals.

As far as I know, there is no very direct evidence that one cerebral hemisphere develops earlier than the other, so the notion of a left–right gradient remains an hypothesis. Nevertheless, certain observations are at least consistent with it. It will be recalled, for instance, that Genie, a child who did not begin to learn language until nearly 13 years of age, appears to exhibit right-hemispheric specialization for language (Fromkin *et al.,* 1974). One might infer from this that the left hemisphere had developed beyond the critical period for the acquisition of language, which was thus committed to the lagging right hemisphere. We also saw that certain right-hemispheric skills, such as recognition of faces and other spatial skills, may not develop until late childhood, suggesting that the right hemisphere may undergo a period of growth at this stage.

A similar argument might be applied to the development of sex differences in lateralization. Suppose that the left hemisphere has the maturational advantage in early childhood, but the right hemisphere undergoes the more rapid growth late in childhood. It is during this later period that certain spatial skills, such as facial recognition and mental rotation (Kail, Pellegrino, & Carter, 1980), appear to develop, and these are represented primarily in the right hemisphere. However, if girls indulge more in verbal than in spatial activities in the years preceding and surrounding puberty, then verbal rather than spatial skills might well achieve some additional representation in the right hemisphere, perhaps at the expense of spatial abilities. This admittedly tenuous account implies that sex differences arise from the interaction between a maturational gradient common to boys and girls and the different environmental influences that they are subject to.

Morgan and I have suggested elsewhere that an early left-sided advantage in maturation might be quite general, not only in humans but in other species as well (M. J. Morgan, 1977; Corballis & Morgan, 1978). One example that suggests a remarkable parallel with the development of human cerebral lateralization comes from Nottebohm's (1971,1972, 1977) work on the lateralized control of singing in chaffinches and canaries. In normal birds, singing is controlled primarily by the left side of the brain, and section of the left hypoglossal nerve in the adult largely destroys the song pattern. If the left hypoglossal nerve is sectioned before the onset of spring song, however, subsequent acquisition of song is largely unaffected. The right side of the brain evidently takes over control, just as the right side of the human brain is thought to assume control of language functions if the left side is incapacitated early in life. Nottebohm (1972) has also reported evidence that normal acquisition of bird song may be influenced by a differential rate of growth on the two sides. Thus, the left hypoglossal nerve assumes control over the majority of song elements, but the right hypoglossal nerve assumes control over a few elements that emerge late in development. Nottebohm (1972) thus anticipates the theme of this section:

> Post-hatching neural lateralization could be determined by a bias as simple as different embryonic rates of growth of the left and right hypoglossus. One is led to wonder to what extent many phenomena of neural lateralization may not also develop out of a left–right differential rate of growth of the whole or part of the embryonic nervous system [p. 48].

A similar gradient might underlie development of the asymmetries of the heart and internal organs. In a classic study on the development of the heart in newts, Spemann and Falkenberg (1919) tied a human hair around the median plane of a newt embryo, producing two Siamese twin newts joined together on the medial surfaces. The twin on the left usually showed the normal asymmetry of the heart and other organs, but the one on the right quite often showed partial or complete reversal of these organs—a condition known as *situs inversus.* Spemann and Falkenberg inferred that the left–right asymmetry was governed by some factor inducing more rapid development on the left. However, constriction of the median plane could alter this gradient. In general, it could only enhance the gradient to the left of the median, but it might diminish or even reverse it to the right of the median, which explains why reversals were more frequent in the right twin. Subsequent evidence has generally confirmed that perturbations applied to the left are more likely to induce *situs inversus* in the developing embryo than are perturbations applied to the right, not only in newts, but in other vertebrates as well (see Oppenheimer, 1974, for a review). Von Kraft (1980) argues that the developmental gradient favoring the left is apparent only during a certain period in development of the internal organs, the so-called manifestation phase, and that it is only during this phase that *situs* can be affected. Again, there is a close analogy between these results and those concerned with equipotentiality in the development of human language.

I do not mean to imply that the same left–right gradient necessarily underlies *situs* of the internal organs as underlies cerebral lateralization or handedness, although in Chapter 7 I shall explore the possibility that this may be so. For the present, the main point is simply that there are biological precedents for supposing that left–right gradients may play the kind of role that is here hypothesized to underlie the development of cerebral lateralization.

Growth gradients do not always favor the left, in any case. In the amphibian brain, the habenular nucleus is larger on the left than on the right, but in some nonamphibian species, it is larger on the right (M. J. Morgan, 1977). In humans the right testicle is the larger and develops earlier than the left (Chan, Hsu, Chan, & Chan, 1960), although rather paradoxically the left testicle usually hangs lower—a phenomenon that male readers may be able to verify for themselves. Even in the human brain, the left-sided advantage in the temporal planum and posterior parietal region is offset by a right-sided advantage in other parts of the brain—indeed, LeMay (1980) claims that the right side of the brain is commonly wider than the left over no less than two-thirds of the brain's surface. Given the diversity of left- and right-sided advantages, Mittwoch (1980) suggests that lateral gradients may shift in the course of development. In the course of embryonic development, growth and differentiation occur first in the region of the head and then proceed tailward. Correspondingly, Mittwoch suggests that development first favors the left, then the right, then the left again. Thus, cerebral development is more advanced on the left, the right hand is developmentally dominant over the left, and the left leg is generally longer than the right.

Mittwoch's suggestions have to do with development during the first few months of embryonic growth. Nevertheless, fluctuations in the direction of growth gradients may well persist throughout development and may govern the allocation of specialized functions to the left or right sides of the brain or body. Hence, language may normally develop during a period of left-sided growth of the brain, but in the case of Genie, discussed earlier, language acquisition was delayed until a period in which growth was more pronounced on the right.

Ideas about the role of left–right gradients in the development of hemispheric specialization of course remain conjectural. That such gradients exist, however, is suggested by data on hemispheric differences in the onset of temporal-lobe epilepsy, reported by D. C. Taylor (1969). These data are summarized in Figure 5.1. If seizures begin in the first 2 years of life, they are more likely to be focused in the left than in the right hemisphere, whereas seizures of later onset are more likely to be focused in the right hemisphere. Taylor argues that the right hemisphere develops more rapidly than the left during the first 2 years, but that this state of affairs is subsequently reversed. This interpretation is based on the assumption that seizures are more likely to develop in the hemisphere that is *less* active at the time. Thus, Taylor suggests that the right hemisphere is the more active during the first 2 years, when the infant is primarily engaged in perceptuomotor activity. One could argue equally, however, that seizures are more likely to develop in the *more* active hemisphere and that left-cerebral dominance for language is established within the first 2 years of life.

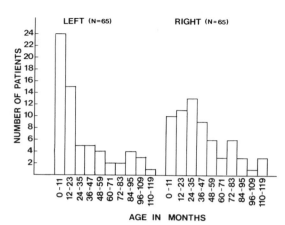

FIGURE 5.1. Distribution of age of onset of epileptic seizures among children with foci in left and right hemispheres. [Adapted from Taylor, 1969.]

According to this account, then, it is proposed that language is normally established early in development when the left cerebral hemisphere undergoes the more rapid growth, whereas certain spatial and nonverbal skills tend to emerge later in development when the right hemisphere undergoes a period of growth. This pattern of differentiation may be more extreme in boys than in girls, at least in those cultures in which boys tend to engage more than girls in spatial activities. If this view is correct, there is still a sense in which a priority attaches to left-hemispheric skills. In particular, so-called plasticity of function should be asymmetrical, with the right hemisphere better able to take over the specialized functions of the left hemisphere than is the left hemisphere to take over the specialized functions of the right. There is some evidence that this is so; summarizing evidence on spatial skills in hemidecorticates, Kohn and Dennis (1974) conclude:

> After early damage and hemidecortication of the left hemisphere, the processes regulating the analysis of spatial information appear to develop to a remarkably normal extent in the remaining right brain half. It seems, however, that the compensatory element which actually spares the performance of spatial (right-hemisphere) skills involves the reallocation of verbal processes to the right brain itself. In contrast, an atypical development of spatial rather than speech functions is more probable in instances of right-hemisphere disease and hemidecortication. The subjects' spatial abilities depend on a left-hemisphere (verbal) mediation of processes which are characteristic of right-hemisphere functions in the human brain [p. 45].

In other words, verbal skills may be reallocated to the right hemisphere if the left hemisphere is incapacitated early in life, whereas spatial skills are not reallocated to the left hemisphere if the right hemisphere is incapacitated. Rather, the intact left hemisphere deals with spatial problems in a linguistic or propositional manner that does not resemble the normal right-hemispheric mode of processing. Thus, the specialized praxic and linguistic functions normally associated with the left hemisphere preempt neural space in a way that spatial and nonverbal functions normally associated with the right hemisphere do not. In this sense, then, left-hemispheric skills can still be regarded as superimposed, in an evolutionary sense, upon a brain that is fundamentally bilaterally symmetrical, while right-hemispheric skills are lateralized by default.

In summary, the hypothesis of left–right gradients in growth patterns helps explain both the development of asymmetries and the plasticity of those asymmetries. In the event of injury to the dominant side or of severe evnironmental deprivation during a critical period of growth, the side that is normally nondominant can take over. This account stresses interactions between maturational and environmental influences in the development of neural representations.

Fixed Specialization of the Hemispheres?

The notion of a left–right maturational gradient underlying left-hemispheric specialization for language was developed to explain the apparent contradiction between early lateralization and the early equipotentiality of the two sides of the brain. An alternative possibility is simply that the two sides of the brain are not equipotential at all. Evidence reviewed earlier suggests, for instance, that left hemidecorticates remain inferior to right hemidecorticates in certain linguistic skills even when brain injury (M. Dennis & Kohn, 1975) or even hemidecortication (M. Dennis & Whitaker, 1976) is sustained very early in life. The analysis undertaken by St. James-Roberts (1981), moreover, suggests that the age at which unilateral damage is sustained is not a critical factor in determining the degree of compensation.

What is emerging, therefore, is a complete swing of the pendulum away from the environmentalist position that has, at least implicitly, dominated for much of the present century. The hemispheres are seen as specialized at least from birth, and the extent to which one hemisphere might take over the functions of the other is attributed simply to diaschisis (Von Monakow, 1914), or normal plasticity of function. Such plasticity is said to be independent of age per se (St. James-Roberts, 1981). This extreme nativist perspective is also consistent with the prevailing view that the two cerebral hemispheres differ in fundamental cognitive style rather than with respect to such specific functions as language or spatial skills. Thus, both hemispheres may be said to mediate language, but in different ways, with the left hemisphere specializing more in syntactic, phonemic aspects of language and the right hemisphere more in global, intuitive aspects.

I suspect that this rigidly nativist view is a manifestation of the overly dichotomized conception of cerebral lateralization that has emerged in recent years, a conception that stresses interhemispheric differences at the expense of the very considerable degree of functional overlap between the hemispheres. Such a conception does not square easily with the disturbing presence of left-handers, for instance, who do not display the same degree or consistency of lateralization as do right-handers. According to the alternative view that cerebral lateralization is governed by maturational left–right gradients, we may suppose that these gradients fluctuate in essentially random fashion among those lacking the so-called right-shift factor (Annett, 1972). Among left- and mixed-handers, therefore, cerebral asymmetries would not display the same consistent patterns as they do among the great majority of right-handers. More generally, the idea that asymmetries are governed by maturational gradients rather than by some fixed structural predisposition seems to me to offer a more realistic framework for understanding the interplay of organic and environmental influences in development.

Nevertheless, the truth may lie somewhere in between. At one extreme, we have the notion of two hemispheres as fundamentally the same and as interchangeable, but each programmed differentially by different rates of growth on the two sides. At the other extreme, we have the idea of the hemispheres as fundamentally different, each predestined to develop its own specialized functions. The one extreme emphasizes symmetry, continuity between humans and other species, and plasticity of function; the other stresses asymmetry, discontinuity, and rigid predetermination. Perhaps by keeping these extremes in mind, we shall be able in the future to arrive at a correct compromise. Or maybe we shall be forever doomed to swing with the pendulum.

6 Evolution of Laterality

Because of poor record-keeping in prehistoric times, conclusions about the evolution of laterality in human beings must be based very largely on speculation. It is nevertheless prudent to begin with a review of the available empirical evidence. I discuss first the evidence on handedness and cerebral asymmetry in prehistoric human beings. Although necessarily sketchy, this is the evidence that bears most directly on the evolution of human laterality. I then consider the evidence for laterality in our nearest relatives, the apes and monkeys. Finally, I briefly review evidence for laterality in other species. Here the search is for general principles that might govern the evolution of laterality, rather than for specific information about human laterality. Following the review of empirical evidence, I attempt to piece it together into an account of how and why we came to be so characteristically lopsided.

EMPIRICAL FINDINGS

Prehistoric Hominids

As we saw in Chapter 1, human beings of all races and cultures appear to have been predominantly right-handed since the earliest records were made (e.g., Coren & Porac, 1977). Precisely when right-handedness emerged in human evolution is a matter of some dispute, however. Some have argued that it evolved gradually during the Stone Age but was not clearly established until the Bronze Age, which dates from about 3000 to 100 B.C. (e.g., Blau, 1946; Wile, 1934). The idea that right-handedness was not clearly evident during the Stone Age is due primarily to de Mortillet (1890), who reported that stone scrapers from excavations in France and Switzerland, and dating from Neolithic times, were slightly more often shaped for the left hand than for the right. Earlier, however, de Mortillet (1882) had claimed a slight bias in favor of the right hand among Stone Age implements recovered from the Somme gravels, and Sarasin (1918) later observed evidence for a slight right-handed bias among implements discovered around Moustier in France. These observations nevertheless seem to stand in marked contrast to the strong right-handed bias observed in artifacts from the Bronze Age. The bronze sickle, for instance, seems to have been manufactured exclusively for right-handers (Blau, 1946).

More recent evidence seems to suggest, however, that the incidence of right-handedness during the Stone Age was considerably higher than claimed by de Mortillet and Sarasin. This evidence is based on a technique, pioneered by the Russian prehistorian S. A. Semenov, known as microwear analysis, in which the working edges and surfaces of tools are examined microscopically for polishing, striations, and other signs of wear. Semenov (1964) describes end-scrapers, evidently used for scraping hide, recovered from sites dating from the Upper Paleolithic, which covers the period from about 35,000 B.C. to about 8000 B.C. He claims that about 80% of these tools are worn on the right side, indicating that they were used in the right hand. This applies to end-scrapers recovered from widely dispersed sites in both eastern and western Europe and in North Africa. He cites several other instances of individual tools dating from the Upper Paleolithic having been used in the right hand, but no such instances of left-handed use.

Keeley (1977) also describes the results of microwear analysis of tools recovered from English sites dating from the Lower Paleolithic, about 500,000–100,000 years ago. Some of the tools recovered from Clacton were evidently used in a rotary action accompanied by downward pressure, as in boring. In each such tool examined (Keeley does not say exactly how many), the rotary movement was clockwise, suggesting that the users were right-handed. "The patterns suggest," writes Keeley, "that the Clacton woodworkers of perhaps 200,000 years ago were consistently right handed [p. 126]."

There is even evidence that right-handedness may go back to *Australopithecus africanus*, dating from the Pleistocene period some 2 million years ago. When the fossil remains of this creature were first discovered in 1925, it was widely hailed as the missing link between ape and human (Dart, 1959), although it has been suggested that it was not a direct ancestor of *Homo sapiens* (R. E. Leakey & Lewin, 1977). One characteristic that nevertheless seemed to reveal both its human-like quality and its handedness was its predilection for murder. It was able to hunt and kill baboons, despite its smaller size, because it was able to use a weapon—either a rock or the thighbone of an antelope—

that it could wield to crush the baboon's skull. Examination of these skulls revealed that most had been struck on the left side, evidently by right-handed attackers. One adolescent *Australopithecus* had also been hit just to the left of the point of the jaw, evidently murdered by a member of its own species (Dart, 1949).

Evidence for cerebral asymmetry among our prehistoric forebears is of course difficult to obtain. It has been claimed, however, that anatomical asymmetries, comparable to those in modern human brains, can be detected in prehistoric human skulls. For instance, the surface of the brain may leave an imprint on the inside of the skull, and this may reveal asymmetries. In Chapter 4, I noted that the Sylvian fissure in most human brains is angled more sharply upward on the right than on the left, and LeMay (1976) has claimed that this is also detectable in the imprint inside the skull of a Neanderthal man found at La Chappelle-aux-Saints in France. There is some dispute as to whether Neanderthal man, who lived over 40,000 years ago, is a true human ancestor, although LeMay argues that it was probably capable of language. She also suggests that the asymmetry of the Sylvian fissure is discernible in two other fossilized skulls, one from Peking man and the other from *Australopithecus africanus*.

The presence of these asymmetries is a matter of some dispute, however. In a personal communication dated 28 October 1980, Ralph L. Holloway of Columbia University writes that in his view the asymmetry of the Sylvian fissure cannot be reliably detected on the Neanderthal skull from La Chappelle-aux-Saints and has not been apparent in any of the 200 or so hominoid endocasts he has worked on. He does claim, however, that there is an enlargement on the left side of the so-called 1470 skull in the region corresponding to Broca's area (see also Leakey & Lewin, 1977). This skull is thought to be nearly 3 million years old and belongs to *Homo habilis*, who according to Leakey and Lewin is a direct ancestor of *Homo sapiens*. Holloway warns that the skull is somewhat distorted by damage, but he doubts that this is relevant to the asymmetry of Broca's area.

Holloway also notes that the counterclockwise torque mentioned in Chapter 4, with a backward protuberance of the left occipital lobe, is commonly found in hominid skulls and is present in the 1470 skull, although again there is the possibility of distortion through damage. It will be recalled from Chapter 4 that this asymmetry is more common among right-handers than among left-handers. LeMay (1976) observes that it is present in the first-found Neanderthal skull but not in that found at La Chappelle-aux-Saints.

Apes and Monkeys

Although right-handedness may go back as far as *Australopithecus africanus*, if not further, there is little evidence for it among present-day apes and monkeys. For instance, Jane Goodall (cited in Lancaster, 1973) observed chimpanzees in the wild using sticks or twigs to extract termites from their holes. This seems a clear example of the primitive use of a tool, even requiring some dexterity. Yet although individual animals showed consistent preferences for one or other hand, about as many were left-handed as were right-handed. As noted in Chapter 2, laboratory studies have confirmed the lack of any overall handedness, not only among chimpanzees (Finch, 1941), but also among baboons (Trevarthen, 1978) and monkeys (Cole, 1957; Lehman, 1978; Warren, 1977). About the only observation I know that suggests right-handedness of any form is that reported by Schaller (1963), who noted that of 72 male gorillas giving chest-beating displays 59 (82%) began with their right hands. However, he did not observe strong preferences in unilateral displays of leg kicking or throwing.

However, asymmetries of the skull resembing those observed in humans are to be observed in nonhuman primates, although Holloway (personal communication, 28 October 1980) claims that the particular combination of right-frontal and left-occipital protuberances is exclusive to hominids, including *Homo sapiens*. W. E. Le Gros Clark (1927) described the case of a gorilla known affectionately as John Daniels II, who exhibited the left-frontal protuberance as well as the asymmetry of the Sylvian fissure that is observed in most human skulls. John Daniels II was right-handed. Cain and Wada (1979) reported that in six of seven baboon brains, the frontal lobes protruded further on the right than on the left, but because of damage to the brains (of the baboons, it should be said), the authors were unable to measure occipital asymmetries. LeMay (1976) claims that the asymmetry of the Sylvian fissure described above in human brains is also prevalent in the brains of orangutans and chimpanzees, but not in gorillas, gibbons, siamangs, or various species of Old World and New World monkeys. Yeni-Komshian and Benson (1976) found the Sylvian fissure to be longer on the left than on the right in humans and in chimpanzees, but not in rhesus monkeys. Hence, if Holloway is correct in asserting that the pattern of anatomical asymmetries in human brains is unique to humans, it is clear that several elements of these asymmetries are present in the higher apes.

These anatomical asymmetries in nonhuman primates need not of course imply any *functional* cerebral lateralization resembling that in humans. There is one study, however, that does suggest a functional asymmetry in Japanese macaques that is somewhat analogous to the right-ear advantage in perception of speech in humans (M. R. Peterson, Beecher, Zoloth, Moody, & Stebbins, 1978). A group of five macaques displayed a right-ear advantage in discrimination of two "coo" sounds, presented monaurally, that were uttered by members of their own species and that signal meaningful events to them in the wild. Five Old World monkeys showed no such asymmetry, presumably because macaque coos conveyed no meaning to them. Curiously enough, there is little evidence for consistent anatomical asymmetries in macaque brains (LeMay, 1976.)

Evidence for functional cerebral lateralization in nonhuman primates comparable to that in humans is bound to be somewhat limited, however, simply because human cerebral lateralization is most pronounced with respect to language. Other primates do not possess language. Some advances have been made in teaching chimpanzees (R. A. Gardner & Gardner, 1969; Premack, 1970) and gorillas (F. Patterson, 1978) to communicate symbolically through nonvocal means, but it is fairly clear that the exploits of these linguistic apes bear only superficial resemblance to human language (Terrace, Petitto, Saunders, & Bever, 1979; Walker, 1978). Even so, it will of course be of interest to determine whether chimpanzees or gorillas taught to use a symbolic communication system from infancy will display consistent lateralization in the cerebral representation of that system.

Dewson (1978) has reported evidence for a functional asymmetry in Iris macaques in the discrimination of auditory signals. The task was to press a red panel if a pure tone was presented and a green one if a noise signal was presented; the colors green and red were switched randomly between the two available panels. Animals with lesions of the left superior temporal gyrus (chosen because it corresponds to Wernicke's area in humans) performed more poorly than those with lesions of the right superior temporal gyrus. However, this deficit occurred only when *variable* delays were introduced between the auditory signals and the lighting up of the panels for response; it did not occur with no delay or when the delay was constant over trials. This result must be considered somewhat preliminary, since there were only four animals in the left-temporal group and two in the right-temporal group. It is a difficult result to interpret, but it may imply some specialized role of the left hemisphere in temporal processing.

One might also enquire whether nonhuman primates exhibit any asymmetry comparable to human right-hemispheric specialization for spatial and other nonverbal skills. Some investigators have reported hemispheric dominance in monkeys in the learning of visual discriminations (Gazzaniga, 1963; Hamilton & Lund, 1970; Hamilton, Tieman, & Farrell, 1974), but the results are conflicting and are in any case based on small samples. Hamilton (1977) followed up these earlier studies with a systematic series of experiments but failed to find any convincing evidence of cerebral lateralization for either the learning or the retention of visual discriminations.

In summary, the evidence reviewed so far, while sketchy and incomplete, suggests that human right-handedness may extend back at least as far as *Australopithecus africanus* some 2 million years ago, and cerebral lateralization at least as far back as *Homo habilis* about 3 million years ago. This suggests that human laterality has evolved over millions rather than thousands of years, and offers little support for Jaynes's (1976) contention that cerebral lateralization evolved since the time of Homer! In marked contrast, however, there is little evidence of any consistent bias in handedness among nonhuman primates of

the present day. The higher apes, though, appear to show rudimentary anatomical asymmetries of the brain that resemble human asymmetries known to
correlate with handedness and cerebral lateralization. Such asymmetries are not
so conspicuous in monkeys, although there is some evidence that macaque
monkeys show a functional left-cerebral specialization for the perception of
meaningful species-specific vocalizations. The fact that these cerebral asymmetries have proven more conspicuous than handedness suggests that cerebral
lateralization may have been prior to handedness per se in the evolution of
laterality.

Other Species

Although the particular combination of right-handedness and left-cerebral
dominance for language and for sequencing appears to be uniquely human,
there are a great many examples of lateral asymmetries in other species. These
include such obvious cases as the leftward displacement of the heart in all vertebrates, the asymmetrical coiling of snail shells or climbing plants, the asymmetrical pincers of crabs and lobsters, and the curious asymmetry of flatfish,
in which the two eyes are on the same side of the body—the reader is referred
to Neville (1976) for an extensive review. Many of these asymmetries are not
of immediate concern here, except insofar as they serve to remind us that asymmetry per se is not an unusual or a mystical phenomenon; it occurs frequently
in nature as an adaptation to particular environmental contingencies. In the
following review, I shall be concerned only with those asymmetries that bear
at least some resemblance to handedness and cerebral lateralization in human
beings or that offer some clues as to the evolutionary contingencies that might
have brought about this characteristically human pattern of laterality.

There are remarkably few parallels to human right-handedness in any other
species. We have seen that nonhuman primates may show consistent preferences within individuals, but there is no convincing evidence for a consistent
bias over a species as a whole—save possibly for the right-handed bias in the
chest-beating displays of mountain gorillas! The same is true of rats and mice,
as we saw in Chapter 2. Although Cole (1955) observed a slight left-paw bias
in cats, data reported by Webster (1981) suggest a slight bias toward the right
paw.

Curiously enough, the most striking analogy to human right-handedness
comes, not from primates or even mammals, but from parrots. Friedman and
Davis (1938) observed that South American parrots showed a strong overall
tendency to use the left foot in picking up bits of food or in manipulating
objects. In a reanalysis of these data, Rogers (1980) discovered that six species
were left-footed, one was right-footed, while eight showed no obvious bias or
else the sample size was too small to yield acceptable evidence. Rogers also

investigated footedness in nine species of Australian parrots and cockatoos. The data are reproduced in Table 6.1; notice that all but one species exhibit a degree of left-footedness at least comparable to that of right-handedness in humans. The exception, *Platycercus elegans,* is right-footed.

Since the left-footed parrot must balance on its right foot in order to pick up or manipulate an object, there might be some question as to which foot is truly dominant. In my view, there is little reason to diagnose right-footedness in this case, for it is truly the left foot that is the more manipulative, as it is the right hand in most humans that is the manipulative one. Most human beings are of course also right-footed, and I suspect that most would prefer to balance on the left foot and use the right foot if asked to perform some manipulation with the foot or toes. Even in kicking a ball, which most people do with the right foot, it is the left foot that might be said to provide the balance.

Footedness in parrots nevertheless resembles human handedness in that the asymmetry is functional rather than structural. That is, there is no obvious indication in the structure of the feet themselves as to which is the preferred one. In other species, there is clear specialization evident in the structure of the limbs themselves. In the coconut crab (*Birgus latro*), the left claw is larger and stronger than the right. It is specialized for dragging heavy food, for breaking hard materials such as coconut shells, and for combat. The right claw performs more delicate operations, such as scraping the meat from a coconut shell or scooping out soft portions of fruit (T. A. Davis, 1978). In some crabs, such as the family *Paguridae*, the asymmetry is round the other way, as it is typically the right claw that is the larger (Vermeij, 1978). In yet others, such as *Alpheus heterochelis*, the direction of the asymmetry is apparently random, with the larger claw equally often on the left as on the right (E. B. Wilson, 1903).

TABLE 6.1

Observations of the Foot Used to Manipulate Food or Objects by Some Australian Cockatoos and Parrots[a]

Species	Number using left foot	Number using right foot	Percentage of left-footedness
Cacatua roseicapilla	58	10	89
Cacatua galerita	98	15	87
Cacatua sanguinea	14	1	93
Cacatua tenuirostris	17	2	89
Cacatua leadbeateri	24	0	100
Calptorhynchus funereus	7	0	100
Platycercus elegans	17	73	23
Platycercus f. flaveolus	6	0	100

[a] From L. J. Rogers (1980).

It is perhaps appropriate to mention a further example from our feathered friends and to introduce the reader to the New Zealand wry-billed plover. This engaging bird has its beak bent to the right, an adaptation that helps it turn over stones in the search for food (Neville, 1976). While scarcely to be classed with handedness, this example illustrates again how readily asymmetries may evolve in the context of manipulation.

Turning now to cerebral lateralization, it is again the birds rather than the primates who provide the clearest examples. As mentioned in the previous chapter, singing in chaffinches and canaries is controlled predominantly by the left side of the brain (Nottebohm, 1977). The same is true of sparrows (Lemon, 1973; Nottebohm & Nottebohm, 1976). It is not true of all birds, however, and is not obviously related to the complexity of the vocal repertoire. For instance, Nottebohm (1977) cites evidence that vocalization is under bilateral control in the talkative parrot, *Amazona amazonica*, even though this was one of the left-footed species in Friedman and Davis's (1938) sample (L. J. Rogers, 1980). On the other hand, there is an asymmetry in vocal control in the vocally unsophisticated domestic chick, since the left hypoglossal nerve innervates both sides of the syrinx, whereas the right one innervates only the right side (Youngren, Peek, & Phillips, 1974).

Domestic chickens nevertheless do exhibit cerebral lateralization with respect to other functions. Rogers and Anson (1979) tested the ability of 2-day-old chicks to discriminate food crumbs from pebbles scattered on a plexiglass floor. When cycloheximide was injected into the chicks' left forebrains, their ability to learn this discrimination was markedly worse than when this substance was injected into their right forebrains or than when saline was injected into either forebrain. Cycloheximide is an antibiotic that inhibits ribosomal protein synthesis and may be supposed to retard the formation of memory traces. Rogers and Anson's result therefore suggests that the mediation of visual discrimination is normally restricted largely, if not exclusively, to the left cerebral hemisphere in young chickens.

Injections of cycloheximide into the left forebrains of chickens has also been shown to retard habituation to a repeated sound (L. J. Rogers & Anson, 1979) and to reduce their ability to switch attention from one visual stimulus to another (Rogers, 1980). However, left-sided injection *increased* attack and copulation in 11-day-old chicks, whereas injection into the right side or into both forebrains did not affect these activities. Howard, Rogers, and Boura (1980) have observed the same pattern of results with injections of monosodium L-glutamate rather than of cycloheximide. Thus, visual and auditory discriminations seem to be mediated primarily by the left cerebral hemisphere. Attack and copulation appear to be mediated by the right hemisphere, but are inhibited by the left.

These asymmetries can be demonstrated simply by occluding one or the other eye, since each eye projects solely to the contralateral hemisphere. R. J. Andrews, Mench, and Rainey (1980) found that chicks could learn to discriminate crumbs from pebbles more rapidly when viewing with the right eye than when viewing with the left eye. With the left eye open, however, they emitted "peep" calls, indicating fear, but they did not do this with the right eye open. The right forebrain therefore seems to mediate emotional reaction, whereas the left hemisphere mediates visual learning.

Rogers and Anson (1979) have suggested that lateralization of visual and auditory learning could result from asymmetrical sensory input in embryonic development. Inside the egg, the embryo is positioned so that the left eye and the left ear are shielded either by the yolk sac or by the left side of the body. Only the right eye would be exposed to light filtering through the eggshell, and the right ear would similarly receive more auditory stimulation than the left. This asymmetrical input might bestow an early advantage on the contralateral left hemisphere, either in growth itself or in the early establishment of engrams. Rogers (1981) also cites unpublished work of her own showing that attack and copulation are not uniformly lateralized in the right hemisphere in chicks hatched from eggs incubated in darkness; under these conditions, lateralization of function does eventuate, but its direction appears to be random. This finding suggests that right-hemispheric specialization for attack and copulation is secondary to left-hemispheric specialization for visual and auditory learning, which in turn depends on asymmetrical stimulation of the embryo.

Webster (1972) has reported functional asymmetries between the cerebral hemispheres of the cat. Cats were first taught various visual discriminations. They then underwent section of the optic chiasm and forebrain commissures, and each disconnected hemisphere was retrained on each discrimination. Relearning was more rapid, on the whole, in the hemisphere ipsilateral to the preferred paw. Although this effect was not observed on all discriminations, Webster suggested that it reflects a specialization of the hemisphere for spatial representation. Since cats are not uniformly left- or right-pawed, this asymmetry does not represent a consistent asymmetry, and in any event it seems to be rather weak. Nevertheless, it suggests that the hemisphere opposite the hemisphere controlling the preferred paw may be the more specialized for spatial tasks—a specialization possibly achieved by default. This may well be analogous to the right-hemispheric specialization for spatial processing in humans.

Webster has also studied anatomical asymmetries in the patterns of fissures in the cat's brain. Such asymmetries, which often take the form of a complete fissure on one side but a mere dimple on the other, are more frequent in the posterior than in the anterior cortex and might be thought to relate to the asymmetry of spatial representation (Webster & Webster, 1975). However,

Webster (1981) could find no relation between anatomical asymmetries and paw preference in cats. If nothing else, this evidence warns against a too ready association of functional asymmetries with gross morphological asymmetries.

Denenberg (1981) has summarized evidence for cerebral asymmetries in rats. These asymmetries are somewhat complex and indirect, and in some cases rather weak, so it may be premature to attach too much weight to them. Nevertheless, a brief review of Denenberg's main conclusions is in order. Rats appear to show a slight preference overall for the right arm of a Y-maze or the right-hand lever in a two-lever operant task. These asymmetries appear to be independent of paw preferences, and according to Denenberg imply a dominance of the left cerebral hemisphere. Denenberg also cites evidence for a specialized right-hemispheric involvement in spatial representation and in emotional reactivity (e.g., as expressed in muricide, or mouse killing). This right-hemispheric involvement may be manifest only in rats that have been handled from infancy. Denenberg concludes that the effect of handling is to remove an inhibitory influence of the left over the right hemisphere and so permit expression of the right hemisphere's specialized capacities.

Denenberg suggests that a common pattern may underlie cerebral asymmetries in different species, including birds, rodents, primates, and humans: The left hemisphere tends to be specialized for communication and for "when an auditory or a visual input carries information [p. 16]," whereas the right hemisphere tends to be specialized for spatial and emotional representation. There are difficulties, however. For instance, the visual and auditory discriminations that appear to be lateralized toward the left hemisphere in chickens may be simply a result of asymmetrical stimulation of the embryo, as proposed by Rogers and Anson (1979). In any event, one would not expect these functions to be mediated by the left hemisphere in human beings; if anything, one would anticipate a right-hemispheric bias. More generally, Bureš, Burešová, and Křivánek (1981) accuse Denenberg of distorting the evidence; they write:

> Denenberg makes this case from a dozen studies showing lateralization of several specific functions, but he does not mention the hundreds of papers that demonstrate the symmetry of the brain for the majority of behavioral, electrophysiological, metabolic, and morphological indices [p. 22].

Despite this necessary corrective, some of the evidence, especially that from birds, does seem convincing, and it is surely a worthwhile enterprise to seek common principles underlying cerebral asymmetries in different species.

In summary, some of the functional asymmetries reviewed in this section bear at least some resemblance to human cerebral asymmetry and, in one instance, to human handedness. However, in my view, it is premature to argue that higher animals are lateralized in the same basic way, as Denenberg (1981) has suggested, although there are of course some tantalizing parallels. These include the left-hemispheric control of singing in passerine birds and the left-hemispheric control of speech in humans, the right-hemispheric specialization (or bias) for emotional expression in birds and in human beings, and spatial representation in the hemisphere contralateral to the preferred hand or paw in human beings and in cats. On the other hand, left-cerebral dominance for visual and auditory discriminations in chickens has no obvious counterpart in human beings, and parrots are predominantly left-footed, whereas human beings are predominantly right-footed. Moreover, evidence from animals overwhelmingly suggests symmetrical cerebral organization and lack of any consistent bias in handedness or pawedness; the asymmetries remain very much the exception and are in most cases weaker in degree than those in human beings.

I suspect, therefore, that these asymmetries have evolved in relatively isolated and independent contexts, and do not represent some common evolutionary thread. Common principles may nevertheless underlie different asymmetrical adaptations. To give an analogy, different species have independently evolved the same basic locomotory mechanisms; for instance, birds, reptiles, insects, mammals, and even a species of fish have all evolved wings for flying. These mechanisms bear a good deal of resemblance to one another; all, for instance, are characterized by bilateral symmetry. Similarly, the various manifestations of cerebral and manual asymmetry may be similar but independent adaptations to common environmental contingencies.

THEORETICAL REVIEW

Evolution of Symmetry

In attempting to arrive at an overview of the evolution of handedness and cerebral lateralization, the first point that must be stressed is that bilateral symmetry is itself an evolutionary adaptation, constructed from building blocks that are fundamentally asymmetrical. The biologist Jacques Monod, for instance, suggests that bilateral symmetry is actually merely a surface phenomenon and that asymmetry represents the true order of living things:

> The truth of course is that these morphological, macroscopic symmetries are superficial, and do not reflect the fundamental order *within* living things. I am not even now referring to the fact that we possess only one heart, on one side, and a single liver, on the other, although this is enough to show that our outwardly "bilateral" appearance is something of a fake. I am referring now to the microscopic structures which are re-

sponsible. . . . for all the properties of living things, namely proteins and nucleic acids [1969, pp. 16–17].

Clearly, then, for bilateral symmetry to have emerged in so precise and comprehensive a fashion, there must have been adaptive advantages associated with symmetry sufficiently strong to overcome a natural organic predisposition to asymmetry. Bilateral symmetry applies particularly to ectodermic tissue, including the skeleton and skeletal muscles, but does not apply to endodermic structures, such as the heart, gut, liver, and pancreas. Presumably, bilateral symmetry of the ectodermic and mesodermic structures has to do with interactions between the organism and an environment that is without systematic left–right bias. Thus, for instance, locomotion nearly always involves a bilaterally symmetrical motor apparatus, whether legs for walking, fins or flippers for swimming, or wings for flying. Hermann Weyl explains it this way:

> Factors in the phylogenetic evolution that tend to introduce inheritable differences between left and right are likely to be held in check by the advantage an animal derives from the bilateral formation of its organs of motion, cilia or muscles and limbs: in the case of their asymmetric development a screw-wise instead of a straight-motion would naturally result. This may help to explain why our limbs obey the laws of symmetry more strictly than our inner organs [1952, p. 27].

To a freely moving animal, the advantages of bilateral symmetry are not confined to motor systems but apply equally to the sensory apparatus, especially since there are in general no systematic biases in the stimuli impinging on one or the other side. "The slightest loss of symmetry, such as the loss of a right eye," writes M. Gardner (1967, p. 70), "would have immediate negative value for the survival of any animal. An enemy could sneak up unobserved on the right!" The motor and sensory systems of animals, and thus their external bodily structures, are therefore constrained in large part to be bilaterally symmetrical because of the fundamental equivalence of left and right in the natural environment. This bilateral symmetry in turn must dictate the bilateral symmetry of the brain and nervous system, especially those parts of it that are concerned with locomotion, spatial perception, and reactions to environmental events.

It was against this prior evolution of bilateral symmetry that human laterality emerged. Human right-handedness and cerebral asymmetry involve those very structures that are characterized by bilateral symmetry in most other species and that must also have been symmetrical for most of our own evolutionary history. What was it, then, in human evolution that led to a reversal of evolutionary pressures, so that a lateralized system was preferred, at least in some limited aspects of cerebral and manual functioning, to a bilaterally symmetrical one?

Evolution of Upright Walking

The decisive influence was very likely the evolution of upright walking, or bipedalism. The evidence suggests that this occurred in the genus *Ramapithecus*, the common ancestor to *Homo habilis* and the australopithecines and the first true hominid, and was brought about by the transition from a woodland habitat to the open savanna of East Africa some 12 million years ago. R. E. Leakey and Lewin (1977) suggest three factors associated with this transition that might have favored a standing posture. One was an increased need in the open savanna for protection against predators, achieved by brandishing large branches or by hurling projectiles. Another was surveillance: Amid the long grass of the savanna, the ability to stand up and achieve a wider view of the surroundings was a clear advantage. The third was the ability to carry things, undoubtedly a great asset to a species that gathered food and brought it to some meeting point for the meal. Precisely when bipedalism emerged in *Ramapithecus* is not clear, however, since according to Leakey and Lewin there is virtually no trace of the early hominids during the period lasting from about 10 million to about 5 million years ago.

Bipedalism would have freed the hands from any direct involvement with locomotion, removing one of the pressures for bilateral symmetry. The hands could then evolve new specializations, such as feeding, food gathering, manipulation, and the use of tools and weapons. This in turn would have freed the mouth from some of these activities and so allowed it to specialize somewhat for communication. The upright stance would have contributed to this in other ways: It allowed individuals to confront one another more directly, and it meant that the face was further from the ground, so that it was easier to reach for things with the hand than with the mouth. It was, no doubt, a hand-to-mouth existence. Life on the open savanna also required cooperation and group cohesiveness for survival, which further favored the evolution of communication. These various influences do not of course constitute a linear causal chain, but make up a complex system of mutual reinforcement and feedback. The hominids thus evolved into socially cohesive, communicative, manipulative creatures, distinctly different from the other primates.

Emergence of Laterality

Which of these newly evolved characteristics favored the emergence of laterality? According to one point of view, laterality evolved first in the context of manipulation. Unlike locomotory or reflexive actions, most manipulative acts put no special premium on bilateral symmetry and are in some respects better served by an asymmetrical system. Manipulation is an operation upon the environment rather than a reaction to it; it is planned and directed from within, rather than elicited from without. Bruner (1968) has pointed out that many manipulative acts require the hands to adopt complementary roles, favoring the evolution of different specialized functions in each. In most people, then, the right hand is specialized for operating, whereas the left is specialized for holding: The left hand holds the banana, while the right peels it; the left holds the nail, while the right swings the hammer; the left steadies the paper, while the right moves the pen across it.

Bruner also suggests that the distinction between holding and operating may have extended to the cerebral hemispheres and apply to cognition as well as to manual skills. Hence, the right hemisphere may "hold" a context, while the left hemisphere "operates" upon it to produce speech. This theory, however, seems too metaphorical, too dependent on analogy, to be entirely convincing. Besides, if it were true, one might expect commissurotomized patients to be very deficient in ordinary spoken discourse, since the hemisphere controlling speech would be deprived of context, supposedly held in the other hemisphere. There seems no good evidence that commissurotomized patients are in fact deficient in this way.

Hewes (1973) has argued for a more direct link between handedness and cerebral lateralization for language, suggesting that the earliest human language was gestural, carried on with signs of the hands and arms:

> The peculiarly human association of right-handedness and left-hemispheric dominance for both language skills and precise manual manipulations could well be the outcome of a long selective pressure for the clear separation of the precision grip from the power grip, combined with manual-gesture language exhibiting a similar (and related) asymmetry. If tool-making and tool-wielding already had a pronounced dextral bias, one would expect gestures derived from weapon-making and wielding to present the same preference for the right hand. . . . I believe that the phenomenon of cerebral lateralization can best be envisaged as the joint selective product of more precise tool and weapon manipulation, pressures for a much greater terrain cognizance, involving right–left cognizance with respect to responses to visible landmarks, and the growth of a manual-gesture language; in other words, I think lateralization precedes the development of speech [p. 9].

Lieberman (1975) has argued that human speech is dependent on a vocal tract of a particular shape, containing among other characteristics a sharp right-angled turn. This gives humans the capacity, unique among primates, to produce three different, distinctive vowel sounds to which most other elementary speech sounds are pegged. A cast of *Australopithecus*'s vocal tract does not display this sharp right angle, and indeed it resembles that of the modern chimpanzee (Lieberman, 1975, p. 173), suggesting that *Australopithecus* could produce only a limited range of sounds. We have seen, however, that *Australopithecus* probably wielded weapons made of bone or stone and may even have been right-handed (Dart, 1949). His contemporary *Homo habilis* probably also used stone implements, and did so unimanually (M. D. Leakey, 1971). This suggests that these creatures possessed the precision of control over the movement of the upper limbs sufficient to be able to gesture, but they probably had only a very limited vocal range. This line of reasoning is at least consistent with the view that gestures preceded vocal speech in evolution. In fact, it is not until *Homo erectus,* perhaps a half million years ago, that we find evidence for the right-angled vocal tract (Lieberman, 1975).

It is also noteworthy that chimpanzees apparently cannot be taught vocal speech but can be taught a form of sign language (B. T. Gardner & Gardner, 1971; R. A. Gardner & Gardner, 1969)—although this does not have the sophistication and flexibility of human language, as we saw earlier (Terrace *et al.,* 1979). Right-handed human beings commonly gesture with their right hands as they talk, suggesting a close association between right-handedness, gesture, and language (Kimura, 1973a). Evidence reviewed in the previous chapter indicates that sign language, like vocal language, is mediated primarily by the left cerebral hemisphere in deaf subjects. These observations lend further support to Hewes's theory.

Yet there must be doubt as to whether left-cerebral dominance for language was secondary to handedness. For one thing, as we saw in Chapter 4, the percentage of the population with left-cerebral dominance for language is higher than the percentage of right-handers, suggesting that it may be the more entrenched manifestation of lateralization. Moreover, the evidence reviewed earlier in this chapter suggests that some degree of cerebral lateralization can be discerned in some nonhuman primates, but there is virtually no evidence of consistent handedness, even in the manipulative chimpanzee. Finally, if the primary manifestation of lateralization lay in differential specialization of the two hands, then one might have expected *structural* differences between the hands, as in lobsters and crayfish. Since the hands retain a very high degree of structural symmetry, it seems clear that the asymmetry resides, not in the hands themselves, but in the brain structures that control them.

Some writers have urged that handedness was secondary in evolution to the lateralization of language. For instance, Brain (1945) argued that, because animals appear to be divided about equally in their preferences for one or the other hand (or paw), it must have been the appearance of a "motor speech centre" in the left cerebral hemisphere of humans that brought about the predominance of right-handedness. W. W. Roberts (1949) gave the argument a more ontogenetic emphasis, but with an evolutionary undertone:

It is not improbable that the infant passes through an earlier, fleeting, simian phase [in which] rudimentary handedness may be detected. But true human handedness occurs only after the beginnings of speech, by which it is directed and to which it is linked. Its essential quality is its determination by speech [p. 567].

Certainly, there are precedents for the emergence of cerebral lateralization in the absence of any overt manual asymmetry or indeed of any obvious specialization for manipulation. The clearest example is the lateralized control of singing in passerine birds. Hence, it is not altogether unreasonable to suppose that human laterality evolved primarily in the context of communication and that left-cerebral control of expressive language led secondarily to right-handedness.

The truth, however, may be more complicated. Language and manipulation have elements in common, and it is conceivable that lateralization evolved in both contexts, with some positive feedback between the two. Both might be described as praxic, in the sense that they are sequential, internally planned and generated operations upon the world rather than reactions to it. The manipulation of tools and weapons, in particular, implies communication; implements were presumably shared, as were the various tasks involving them, such as scraping hides, cutting up meat, and killing animals. Perhaps the earliest forms of communication were indeed gestural, ranging from the brandishing of weapons to demonstrations of how to use simple implements. However, it may have been the common praxic quality of communicative and manipulative acts, rather than any specific property of either, that favored the evolution of lateralization.

What is it about praxic functions that favored lateralized representation in the brain? Frost (1980) suggests that the evolution of skill with tools created a large and relatively sudden demand for "neural space." Since using tools implies the skilled use of only one of the hands at any one time, the neural organization devoted to this skill need be localized in only one hemisphere. Moreover, in the competition for neural space, localization of praxic organization primarily in one cerebral hemisphere minimizes any compensatory loss in nonpraxic organization, which would remain essentially intact in the other hemisphere. Lateralization is thus the outcome of an evolutionary cost–benefit analysis. This account implies that the left-cerebral specialization of praxic functions was superimposed on a brain that was hitherto bilaterally symmetrical, a theme already developed in Chapter 3.

Although I am sympathetic with Frost's account, I suspect that lateralization of praxic functions may have had as much to do with the resolution of interhemispheric conflict as with the competition for limited neural resources. As already noted, the praxic skills that emerged predominantly after the appearance of the bipedal stance differed qualitatively from the more stimulus-bound behaviors that predominated earlier: They were internally generated, involved sequential planning, and were operations on the environment rather than reactions to it. Bilateral symmetry is no longer so important and indeed may prove a disadvantage, since there would be potential conflict if both sides of the brain were equally disposed to initiate sequential actions. In this context, it is worth recalling from Chapter 3 that lateralization is more pronounced with respect to production than with respect to perception.

A similar argument may apply to the lateralization of song in chaffinches and canaries. Bird song is not to be compared to human speech in all respects, of course, but it shares with speech the properties that it is sequential, internally generated, and independent of spatial constraints. Again, one suspects that bilateral control might create interhemispheric conflict. L. J. Rogers (1981) notes also that the avian brain does not possess a corpus callosum, although there are several other lesser commissures. This might make "on-line" resolution of interhemispheric conflict difficult. Similarly, in the human brain, the elaboration of cortical function *within* hemispheres might be said to have exceeded the elaboration of interhemispheric connections, and if both hemispheres were equally disposed to initiate complex sequences of action, there might well be a danger that interhemispheric communication is too meager to permit a resolution of potential conflicts. "Lateralization," suggests Rogers (1981, p. 36), "would prevent hemispheric competition and eliminate redundancy of neural capacity."

Right-Hemispheric Specialization

The account developed so far is consistent with that of Chapter 3, in that it suggests that left-hemispheric specialization was effectively superimposed on a system that was hitherto bilaterally symmetrical. As a consequence, however, nonpraxic functions, including spatial representation, would tend to be lateralized toward the right cerebral hemisphere, at least among that majority of individuals (RS+, in Annett's, 1972 terminology) who exhibit consistent lateralization.

Some authors have argued that *right*-hemispheric specialization was primary in the evolution of laterality. For instance, Denenberg (1981) cites a personal communication from Geschwind suggesting that attention had to be the first process that was lateralized, since attending was necessary before action could occur. In Geschwind's view, attention is primarily a right-hemispheric specialization and must have preceded left-hemispheric specialization for praxic functions (cf. Geschwind, 1981). It is to me dubious whether attention must be lateralized prior to the lateralization of action, but in any event, it is questionable whether attention is truly lateralized in the right cerebral hemisphere. As we saw in Chapter 3, one can make a case for supposing that certain aspects of attention are *left*-hemispheric rather than right-hemispheric, and I suspect that it depends very much on the nature of the processes to which attention is directed. Geschwind's argument for the right-hemispheric control of attention is based primarily on the phenomenon of spatial hemineglect, which occurs more often following right-hemispheric lesions than following left-hemispheric lesions. However, this is of course a spatial context; one would expect *verbal* attention to be primarily under the control of the left cerebral hemisphere, and there is evidence that this is so (Kinsbourne, 1975).

A more impressive argument for the primacy of right-hemispheric specialization has been advanced by Webster (1977). He suggested that right-hemispheric specialization for spatial representation evolved in the context of territoriality. Life on the savanna would no doubt have created new pressures for our hominid ancestors to analyze and remember spatial locations. Webster draws on an argument, familiar to me (Corballis & Beale, 1970, 1976), that a bilaterally symmetrical organism would be unable to tell left from right. He suggests that a bilaterally symmetrical brain would therefore create difficulties for an animal that needed to record accurate spatial representations of the environment. Consequently, spatial representation tended to become localized in the right cerebral hemisphere, thus obviating any difficulties with directionality. Denenberg (1981) makes the further suggestion that this would tend to polarize emotional representation toward the same hemisphere, "since fright, fight, and flight are behaviors associated with defence of territory [p. 20]." (I know of some who are rendered emotional by words, however, and trust that the reader is not one of them.)

I think it is questionable, however, whether lateralization evolved primarily in the context of territoriality or spatial representation. Indeed, I have already suggested that the fact that the spatial environment exhibits no consistent left–right bias would have favored the evolution of bilateral *symmetry*, not of asymmetry. One might therefore expect those parts of the brain concerned with reactions to spatial events to be symmetrical rather than asymmetrical. It is nevertheless true that a symmetrical brain could not tell left from right, and so could not discriminate left–right mirror images from one another, and there is corresponding evidence that most animals have difficulty with such tasks (see Corballis & Beale, 1976, for a review). So, for that matter, do human adults, although only in a residual fashion (e.g., Farrell, 1979). Confusion of left–right mirror images might actually be regarded as left–right *equivalence*, a tendency to treat left–right mirror images as the same rather than different. This presumably has adaptive significance in the natural world, where the same pattern may appear in mirror-image orientations. For instance, faces or bodies of other creatures may appear in left or right profile. Hence, the inability to tell left from right might be regarded as adaptive rather than maladaptive in the natural environment, and it is favored by symmetrical rather than asymmetrical representation in the brain. Animals other than humans are seldom if ever required to discriminate left–right mirror images, but there are many situations in which it is adaptive to treat them as equivalent.

To be sure, humans are the exception. We need to be able to tell left from right in order to read and write, at least in the case of scripts that are written laterally in a consistent direction. Left–right discrimination is also involved in remembering which side of the road to drive on and giving verbal directional instructions. Thus, the left–right axis forms the basis of several codes that we use. It seems unlikely, however, that these requirements constituted an evolutionary pressure for the emergence of lateralization—reading, writing, and transportation are too recent to have been decisive evolutionary influences. Rather, I suspect that prior lateralization of the brain enabled us readily to attach different meaning to left and right, and to exploit them in our culture. In short, discrimination of left and right was a spin-off from lateralization, rather than a cause of it.

One might still argue that left–right discrimination is important in navigation or in the internal representation of terrain. Certainly, we often make use of the labels ''left'' and ''right'' in navigating or in giving directional instructions, although this may be because the labels are available and convenient rather than because they are necessary. In navigating over familiar terrain, it is generally, perhaps always, possible to find one's way with respect to landmarks independently of the concepts of left and right. For instance, if you try to give instructions on how to go to a certain location in your own neighborhood without using the labels ''left'' and ''right,'' you should find it possible to do so, albeit rather inconvenient.

Some sense of left and right does appear to be necessary in migrating over unfamiliar territory, where specific landmarks may be unknown. For instance, certain warblers migrate every year from central Canada to the southeast coast of the United States, where they pause to accumulate subcutaneous fat before continuing on the long overwater flight to the Lesser Antilles on the northern coast of South America. According to DeSante (1973), these birds calculate the direction of flight relative to the north–south line and thus fly *left* of this line in a southeasterly direction. Presumably this calculation requires an internal sense of which is left and which is right, implying some structural (perhaps cerebral) asymmetry. Some birds, however, make a left–right confusion and fly south*west* instead of southeast. These so-called vagrant warblers can be observed, according to DeSante, in the area around San Francisco before they set out on a futile overwater flight, only to perish in the Pacific.

DeSante experimentally studied the preferred directional orientations of the vagrant warblers by holding them in cages under clear, moonless night skies. They showed clear but equal preferences for two axes: one running northwest to southeast, representing the correct line of migration; the other running northeast to southwest, the vagrant direction. DeSante concluded that these birds were unable to tell left from right. He argued that the vagrant warblers choose the direction of migration according to the direction of the prevailing wind. This is usually from the west, but an occasional easterly wind across the Canadian prairies brings a fresh crop of vagrants to California. The majority of birds are not affected by the wind and choose the correct direction anyway.

Now, warblers belong to the order of passerine birds, as do chaffinches and canaries. It will be recalled that singing in chaffinches and canaries is controlled primarily by the left side of the brain. I do not know whether warbling in warblers is also under left-hemispheric control, but it is conceivable that the asymmetry governing the direction of migration is related to an asymmetry in vocal control. Which would have come first? DeSante observes that the migration of warblers is probably a fairly recent phenomenon, occurring within the last 20,000 years. If these birds do indeed display an asymmetry in vocal control, it seems very likely that this would have preceded the evolution of migration. This lends further credence to the idea that the motor asymmetry is prior but permits a complementary asymmetry governing migration. It is analogous to the argument that cerebral asymmetry in humans evolved first in the context of praxic skills but permitted an asymmetry of spatial representation that has allowed us to exploit a sense of the left–right distinction.

I have dwelt on the migration of warblers, not because I think we are descended from them (a delightful but improbable thought), but because they illustrate the sorts of pressures toward lateralization that might have existed. Nevertheless, the account I have given is highly conjectural. If it could be shown that warblers do indeed exhibit an asymmetry of vocal control, then it would be of great interest to determine whether the same asymmetry was present in vagrant warblers. DeSante's suggestion that the vagrant warblers represent a subgroup lacking a directional sense is reminiscent of Annett's (1972) theory that certain people, including most left-handers, belong to a subgroup lacking consistent cerebral lateralization. To carry the avian analogy to its logical conclusion, therefore, one might expect vagrant warblers *not* to display consistent lateralization in the control of song.

To return to the point at issue, I suspect that lateralization evolved first in the context of praxic function—whether in human beings or in birds. Complementary specialization for spatial skills was achieved by default. Nevertheless, it is conceivable that the distinction between primary and secondary lateralization is blurred. In the case of the early hominids, for instance, life on the savanna would have led to the emergence of tools and communication, creating pressures toward a lateralized brain. At the same time, lateralization of spatial representation might have proven an advantage, in removing uncertainties over left–right orientation and so sharpening the representation of particular locales. This suggestion, it may be recalled, was implicit in the extract from Hewes (1973), quoted earlier.

On the Direction of Lateralization

One issue not so far discussed has to do with the direction of lateralization. In the review of empirical evidence earlier in this chapter, it was clear that the direction of lateralization is sometimes constant within a species and sometimes random. For instance, the asymmetry between the claws of lobsters and crabs might be quite marked, but it may vary in direction in random fashion from individual to individual. There seems no compelling reason why asymmetry is random in some cases but follows a directional rule in other.

If Annett's (1972) theory is correct, human laterality is characterized both ways; in the majority of cases (RS+), the direction of lateralization is uniform, whereas in some minority (RS−), it fluctuates in apparently random fashion. One of the advantages of consistency is that asymmetrical tools need be manufactured in only one of two mirror-image forms. Indeed, throughout the ages, such implements as the sickle, scissors, and golf clubs have been manufactured almost exclusively for right-handers. Only recently, with the emergence of left-handed-shops, have left-handers been catered to. It is conceivable but perhaps unlikely that the convenience of having to manufacture tools in just one left–right orientation was a decisive factor in the evolution of directional asymmetry.

Any speculation as to why lateralization follows a uniform directional principle in the majority of humans leads inevitably to the question of why a minority does not exhibit uniformity. I suggested in Chapter 3 that certain advantages may derive from fluctuating asymmetries, including perhaps an element of serendipity. That is, the brain that is *not* subject to a uniform lateralizing influence might include unusual combinations of specific asymmetries. Individuals in this category might suffer a slightly greater risk of minor disorders of language or sequencing, but they might also exhibit superior creative ability. Further, it might be advantageous to the species as a whole to ensure that such individuals are in the minority. To be a left-hander in tennis, for instance, may prove an advantage precisely because it represents a departure from the norm. The same argument may apply, perhaps, to departures from the usual pattern of cerebral lateralization.

A final question is: What explains the particular direction of asymmetry exhibited by the majority of humans? One classic theory, attributed to Carlyle (Froude, 1884), is that right-handedness evolved as a consequence of its survival value in early warfare. The warrior who held his sword or stick in his right hand and his shield in the left hand was less likely to be wounded in the heart, since the heart is displaced slightly to the left. This theory is generally not considered convincing, since the displacement is too small to have been decisive and since the incidence of right-handedness is slightly lower among men than among women, who did not fight. In any event, Carlyle's theory does not square with the main argument of this chapter, which is that lateralization evolved in the context of cerebral control rather than of handedness itself.

It is possible that a uniform lateralizing principle was necessary to achieve a sufficient degree of lateralization. We have seen that other mammals, including rats, mice, cats, monkeys, and chimpanzees, exhibit clear paw or hand preferences, but these fluctuate randomly between individuals and are not as distinctive as human handedness. We have also seen that many humans assumed to fall into Annett's RS– category do not show clear manual asymmetry. In Chapter 8, I shall review evidence that weak or inconsistent cerebral lateralization in some individuals may create difficulties in reading or in speech. Yet the examples of fluctuating asymmetries *can* be both random and of marked degree.

My own view is that the direction of human laterality does not need any special explanation, any more than does the leftward displacement of the heart or the left-cerebral control of bird song in chaffinches and canaries. I suspect that there are intrinsic biological asymmetries, possibly of cytoplasmic origin, that may govern the direction of consistent asymmetries when they do emerge in evolution. Further speculation on the molecular and genetic origins of laterality will be pursued in the following chapter.

SUMMARY

It seems likely that lateralization evolved somewhere in that dark region between perhaps 12 and 5 million years ago, as the first hominids adjusted to life on the savanna. Although the evidence is of course far from definitive, lateralization had probably emerged by the time *Homo habilis* and the australopithecines appeared. I have suggested, following Hewes (1973), Kimura (1979), Frost (1980), and others, that it emerged first in the context of sequential manipulations, including gestural language, and that sophisticated vocal speech appeared later. Written language is of course much more recent, but it too is represented asymmetrically in the brain. The initial lateralization for manipulation, however, was presumably not so much a specialization of the hands themselves as a specialization of the neural structures controlling them. To some extent, this accounts for the mystery of handedness, that it is apparent in function but not in structure. Right-hemispheric specialization appeared at first as a secondary consequence of superimposing left-hemispheric functions on a brain that was hitherto for the most part bilaterally symmetrical. With the march of time, however, it is conceivable that right-hemispheric specialization may have achieved an evolutionary autonomy of its own, as pressures for complementarity superseded those for bilateral symmetry.

7 Inheritance of Laterality

There is little doubt handedness is at least partly inherited. That is, a person is more likely to be left-handed if one or the other parent is left-handed than if both parents are right-handed, and more likely still if both parents are left-handed. But as with the inheritance of money, transmission from one generation to the next is far from perfect. Even if both parents are left-handed, the chances that an offspring will be left-handed are no better than even.

The vast majority of families are of course predominantly right-handed, so any evidence for a left-handed lineage must command special interest. As we have already seen, there is no convincing evidence that any race or culture has ever been predominantly left-handed, and I have never heard of any family in which the majority, over a sufficiently large sample, may be said to be left-handed. There is however an age-old tradition that those with the surname of Kerr, or its anglicized form Carr, tend to be left-handed. Indeed the name is derived from the Gaelic *caerr*, meaning awkward, and the terms *car-handed*, *ker-handed*, and *carry-handed* are still used in some places to refer to the left-handed. An article in *The Times* of London on 4 January 1972 quotes the following anonymous poem:

> But the Kerrs were aye the deadliest foes
> That e'er to Englishmen were known,
> For they were all bred left-handed men,
> And 'fence against them there was none.

However, *The Times* conducted a quick survey of Carrs and Kerrs listed in *Who's Who?* and discovered that "rather more than half" were right-handed.

To say that handedness includes an inherited component is not to say that it is *genetically* inherited. Left-handed parents may tend to teach their children to be left-handed, or else children may tend to imitate their parents. I have already argued at length that *right*-handedness is not simply a product of imitation, learning, or culture, but that it is biologically preprogrammed. It is still conceivable, however, that *left*-handedness is determined by environmental or even pathological influences. In this chapter, I shall argue that variations in human laterality are in fact partly determined by genetic variation. I shall focus mainly on handedness, simply because there is a good deal more evidence on the inheritance of handedness than on the inheritance of cerebral asymmetry as such. Because of the close relation between the two (see Chapter 4), however, there are reasonable grounds for drawing some general inferences about the inheritance of laterality.

There has been remarkably little agreement about the inheritance even of handedness despite centuries, even millenia, of observation and speculation. Even in recent times, left-handedness has been attributed to such diverse causes as cerebral anoxia at birth (Bakan, 1971; Bakan, Dibb, & Reed, 1973) or "emotional negativism" (Blau, 1946). Collins (1970) argued against a genetic mechanism for the inheritance of handedness, suggesting that the correlations between generations "result from cultural inheritance or from an unknown extrachromosomal biologic predisposition to asymmetry [p. 135]." The consensus of opinion may well lie with genetic theories, but even these vary widely in the precise form they take (e.g., Annett, 1967, 1972; Levy & Nagylaki, 1972; Rife, 1950; Trankell, 1955).

One reason for this diversity of opinion is that attempts to explain variations in handedness have been exercises in the fitting of mathematical models rather than in biology. Genetic models, for instance, depend on rather arbitrary assumptions, with little or no backing in molecular biology. Needless to say, there have been no published experiments on selective breeding for handedness in humans, and nothing is known of the genetic code for handedness or cerebral lateralization at the molecular level. It is therefore prudent to begin with a discussion of the general problem of how asymmetries might be coded and of what role the genes might play. This will provide some biological backing for the assessment of genetic models reviewed later in the chapter.

BIOLOGICAL BACKGROUND

Positional Information

The coding of lateral asymmetries is part of the general problem of morphological differentiation. All the cells of the body are thought to contain identical genetic information, and yet they develop into different structures, such as skin, bone, muscle, and neural tissue. That is, the genes the cells contain are unequally expressed, depending on the particular environment each cell finds itself in. As Wolpert (1969) put it, cells that differentiate according to their position in the embryo must have access to some "positional information" that tells them where they are. There seems no way in which this information could itself be coded genetically, although it must of course interact with genetic information in morphogenesis.

In particular, if an organism is to develop some consistent left–right asymmetry—be it a leftward displacement of the heart or a predisposition to language in the left cerebral hemisphere—there must be some source of information that allows cells to "know" whether they are on the left or right side of the body. There seems no logical way in which this information could be coded in the genes themselves. The genetic code is highly abstract. Although the DNA molecule, which contains the genetic information, is a double clockwise-coiling helix, this directional aspect does not itself constitute part of the genetic code, which is represented in the sequence of bases along the spiraling strands. As M. J. Morgan (1977) has put it, the genetic code is essentially "left-right agnosic."

Bateson (1980) makes a similar point. Discussing the development of bilateral symmetry and asymmetry in the frog, he notes that there must first be some definition of the median plane to distinguish the left and right sides. The unfertilized egg is characterized by two poles, which can specify no more than radial symmetry. At fertilization, the spermatozoon enters the egg, typically at a point somewhat below its equator, and the two poles and the entry point then define the median plane that determines the frog's bilateral symmetry. The side of the egg on which the spermatozoon enters becomes the ventral side of the frog. The question then is: What distinguishes the left from the right side? There must be some systematic distinction, for although the frog remains strikingly symmetrical in ectodermic structures (skin, brain, eyes) and in mesodermic tissue (skeleton and skeletal muscles), it is grossly asymmetrical in its endodermic structures (gut, liver, pancreas, etc.). What is the nature of the information that distinguishes left from right? Bateson (1980) answers as follows:

> So far as we know, there is no moment after fertilization at which this information could be delivered. The order of events is first extrusion from the mother, then fertilization; after that, the egg is protected in a mass of jelly throughout the period of segmentation and early embryonic development. In other words, the egg must surely already contain the information necessary to determine asymmetry *before* fertilization. In what form must this information exist? . . .
>
>   I believe that there can be, in principle, only one sort of solution (and I hope that somebody with a scanning electron microscope will look for the evidence). It must be so that the answer is in the egg before fertilization and therefore is in some form that

will still determine the same asymmetry *regardless of which meridian is marked by the entering spermatozoon.* It follows that every meridian regardless of where it is drawn, must be asymmetrical and that all must be asymmetrical in the same sense.

This requirement is satisfied most simply by some sort of *spiral of nonquantitative or vector relations.* Such a spiral will cut every meridian obliquely to make in every meridian the same difference between east and west [p. 179; Bateson's italics].

Bateson's suggestion was earlier given explicit form by Lepori (1969), who carried out experiments in which he sectioned duck blastoderm, the disc-like sheet of cells at one pole of the egg yolk, to produce twin embryos. Nearly all the embryos showed the normal asymmetry of the heart and inner organs regardless of the orientation of the cut; that is, left and right were distinguished in identical fashion whichever way the blastoderm was spliced. Lepori, like Bateson, postulated a spiral structure, illustrated in Figure 7.1. This figure shows the two poles and different possible locations of the median plane. According to Lepori, the cytoplasmic structure of the egg somehow constrains the cells to slide against one another in a counterclockwise spiraling direction, illustrated by dotted lines in the figure. The arrows represent the direction of movement of cells during the period of development known as gastrulation. This movement is coincident with the direction of the spiraling constraint on the left side, but antagonistic to it on the right side, regardless of how the median plane is defined.

Lepori's model implies more rapid development on the left than on the right. This growth differential explains a good many of the facts about the

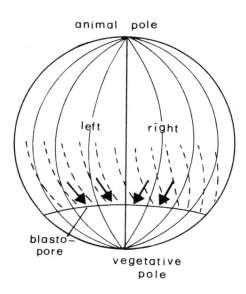

FIGURE 7.1. Schematic representation of amphibian gastrula at an early stage of development. During gastrulation, the cells move toward the blastopore, as indicated by the arrows. The dotted lines show the counterclockwise spiraling tendency, indicated by some presumed cytoplasmic property. This tendency is aligned with the spiraling tendency on the left of the embryo but antagonistic to it on the right. This is so regardless of possible locations of the meridian plane, indicated by the solid longitudinal lines. [Reprinted by permission from N. G. Lepori, Asymmetric blastomere movement during gastrulation, *Behavioral & Brain Sciences*, 1978, *2*, 304–305.]

development of endodermic asymmetries, including the induction of *situs in-versus* by interventions that tend to slow development on the left and so reverse the direction of the left–right differential (Lepori, 1969, 1978; M. J. Morgan, 1977; Spemann & Falkenberg, 1919; von Woellwarth, 1950; Wehrmaker, 1978). In Chapter 5, however, I noted that not all the evidence on the development of lateral asymmetries favors the hypothesis of a left-sided advantage, and one must suppose that right-sided advantages also occur, depending perhaps on the stage of development and on the structures involved.

The important point is that the actual spatial information that specifies structural asymmetries probably does not reside in the genetic code as such, but is extrachromosomal. (For further speculation on the nature of this code, the interested reader is referred to Collins, 1978, and Wolpert, 1978.) It should not be concluded that the genes are unimportant, however. Clearly, the genetic information must interact with the directional information to determine the precise form that structural asymmetries will take. As an analogy, imagine a swimmer who cannot tell left from right, who plunges into a river. She may decide to swim upstream or downstream, but she cannot explicitly decide to swim left or right. Her movement, moreover, is more likely to be downstream than upstream, although she may plausibly compensate for the stream and swim straight ahead. Similarly, it is suggested that the genes cannot explicitly instruct leftward or rightward growth, but they can yield to asymmetries in the embryonic environment.

Genetic Influences

One consequence of the foregoing discussion is that the genetic code is more likely to have an influence over the presence or absence of an asymmetry than over the direction of an asymmetry (Collins, 1977, 1978; Dahlberg, 1943; M. J. Morgan, 1977; M. J. Morgan & Corballis, 1978). Hence, directional information is very largely ignored (or overridden) in ectodermic and mesodermic structures, which are largely bilaterally symmetrical, but it is strongly expressed in endodermic structures. Although *situs inversus* of the heart and internal organs is occasionally observed in humans and can be induced experimentally in animals, there is no evidence that it ever results from a genetically instructed reversal; rather, as noted earlier, the probable cause of *situs inversus* in experimental studies has to do with some mechanical or chemical interference with relative growth on the two sides of the embryo.

In contrast, there is evidence that genetic instructions can cancel the directional asymmetry of the internal organs, but not explicitly reverse it. Hummel and Chapman (1959) have described a mutant strain of mice, assigned the gene symbol *iv*, in which 50% of homozygous (*iv–iv*) animals displayed *situs inversus* of the viscera. Layton (1976) has since reported that even after many years of inbreeding the incidence of *situs inversus* in this strain has remained at 50% and has proven resistant to selection for *situs*. The simplest explanation is that the normal allele of the *iv* gene locus specifies normal *situs*, but that the recessive allele in these particular mice cancels the asymmetrical instruction, so that the direction of *situs* is assigned randomly. That is, the gene locus does not specify the *direction* of *situs*, but determines in Mendelian fashion whether or not some underlying asymmetry will be expressed. Layton speculates that many cases of *situs inversus*, both in humans and in animals, and even when experimentally induced, may be the outcome of a random process rather than of a systematic reversal.

It is perhaps not entirely true to say that the direction of an asymmetry is *never* under genetic control. One example is provided by the snail *Limnaea peragra*, which has a coiled shell. The direction of coiling is apparently under the control of a single diallelic locus, with dextral (or clockwise) coiling controlled by the dominant allele and sinistral coiling controlled by the recessive allele (Levy, 1977; Sturtevant, 1923). However, it is the allele carried by the mother, not the allele carried by the individual itself, that determines the direction; that is, if the mother carries the dominant gene, all her offspring are dextral, regardless of their own genotypes. Moreover, the sinistral phenotypes do not always breed true. If sinistral phenotypes are allowed to self-fertilize, they should produce all sinistral offspring, but the incidence of dextral phenotypes may be quite high, and in one exceptional case reached 80% (Diver & Andersson-Kottö, 1938). By contrast, self-fertilization of dextral phenotypes very rarely results in sinistral offspring. As M. J. Morgan (1978) puts it:

> It thus appears that there is something inherently asymmetrical about the inheritance of asymmetry in *Limnaea*. One "gene," the dextral, has no difficulty in producing its appropriate phenotype; the other "gene," the sinistral, has greater difficulty. Therefore we ask why there should be this asymmetry if the respective genes code in themselves the direction of laterality [p. 330].

Another example of apparent genetic control over the direction of an asymmetry has been documented by Policansky (1982). It has to do with flatfish, which inhabit the seabed and sensibly have both eyes on the same side of the head, presumably in order to keep watchful eyes upward. Some species are sinistral—that is, both eyes are on the left—whereas others are dextral, and a few are divided between sinistral and dextral. Among one species, the starry flounder, those found in the waters off the coast of Japan are nearly 100% sinistral, whereas those found around the United States are about evenly divided between sinistral and dextral. Policansky obtained a number of these fish from both Japanese and American waters and produced crossbreeds. Preliminary results are shown in Table 7.1. There is clearly a strong tendency for sinistral parents to produce sinistral offspring. This is not a case of maternal inheritance, as it was with snails, since the fathers as well as the mothers influenced the direction of the asymmetry—this can be seen by examining the columns of Table 7.1. Another point of interest about the results is that there was evidently an environmental component as well as a genetic one. The fish were bred in the New England Aquarium, and it is noteworthy that the offspring of sinistral Japanese parents were about 13% dextral, compared with less than 1% in Japanese waters. What it is about the United States that turns their eyes to the right I cannot guess.

It is not necessary to conclude from this rare example that directionality is directly coded in the genes themselves. Given the abstract nature of the genetic code, it still seems most likely that the directional information is supplied by some extrachromosomal source, to which the genetic code makes reference; I do not see how the genes could simply issue the commands "eyes left" or "eyes right." Further research might help clarify the kind of mechanism involved. For instance, it is worth noting that the flatfishes are initially externally

TABLE 7.1
Ratios of Sinistral (L) to Dextral Offspring of Crosses Between Sinistral and Dextral Starry Flounders[a]

Males	Females			
	60L[b]	82L	91R	97L
59L[b]	79L:12R 86.8%L	121L:47R 72.0%L	264L:248R 48.4%L	—
61L[b]	—	—	27L:29R 48.2%L	—
62L[b]	49L:10R [c]	—	—	501L:83R 86.9%L
85L	—	4L:3R [c]	47L:150R 23.9%L	—
87R	—	7L:11R [c]	42L:88R 32.3%L	204L:67R 75.3%L
89R	—	36L:27R 57.1%L	134L:230R 36.8%L	—
95R	—	115L:160R 41.8%L	14L:66R 17.5%L	—
96L	—	—	63L:61R 50.8%L	—
98L	545L:149R 78.5%L	106L:102R 51.0%L	78L:110R 41.5%L	189L:38R 83.3%L

[a] From Policansky (1982).

[b] Japanese fish. The others are American.

[c] Percentages not calculated when total progeny less than 50.

symmetrical and undergo a metamorphosis later on in which one eye migrates from one side to the other. Policansky states that the age at which this metamorphosis takes place varies widely, from a few weeks to several months. One wonders if the age of metamorphosis might be related in some systematic fashion to sinistrality or dextrality. If so, then the coding for sinistrality or dextrality might arise indirectly from some genetic code for the regulation of growth. The directional information might thus be provided by the embryonic conditions prevailing at different stages of growth rather than by the genes themselves.

The examples of asymmetries considered so far bear little resemblance to handedness or cerebral lateralization in humans. So far as I know, nothing is known about the inheritance of cerebral asymmetry in passerine birds, or footedness in parrots, or any of the anatomical cerebral asymmetries to be observed in nonhuman primates. There is evidence, however, that the direction of pawedness in rats and mice is not under genetic control. As we saw in Chapter 2, individual rats and mice typically do show consistent pawedness, but as many are left-pawed as are right-pawed. Collins (1969) found that the proportions of left- and right-pawed mice remained equal after three generations of selective breeding for left-pawedness, and G. M. Peterson (1934) reported that left- and right-pawed rats persisted in equal numbers even after eight generations of selective breeding. It was partly on the basis of such evidence that Collins (1970) was led to question whether human handedness was under genetic control.

The main purpose behind this detour into developmental biology has been to gain some a priori notion of what a genetic theory of human laterality might entail. On the basis of evidence on other asymmetries, it seems unlikely that different alleles of a gene would directly code different directions of handedness or of cerebral asymmetry, and genetic models that postulate this begin with one strike against them. It is more likely, on both empirical and logical grounds, that there might be genetic control over whether or not some underlying asymmetry is expressed.

GENETIC MODELS OF LATERALITY

Fitting the Data on Inheritance

As noted at the outset of this chapter, there is a correlation in handedness between parents and their offspring. Table 7.2 shows the proportions of right-handed children born to right-handed parents, parents of opposite handedness, and left-handed parents, according to a survey of 2178 offspring of 687 couples undertaken by Rife (1940). The data are based on a somewhat arbitrary and conservative definition of right-handedness—Rife designated as right-handed only those who professed to use the right hand for each of 10 familiar operations (throwing, bowling, playing marbles, sewing, writing, and using a knife, spoon, hammer, saw, and scissors), while all others were designated as left-handed. Nevertheless, the data do illustrate the declining proportion of right-handers as the parents depart from right-handedness.

These data rule out any simple model in which direction of handedness depends on a single gene locus. For instance, Ramaley (1913) suggested that right-handedness might be attributed to a dominant allele and left-handedness to a recessive allele carried by about one-sixth of the population. If such a model were true, however, then left-handed couples should always produce left-handed children. This is contrary to fact, as Table 7.2 shows (see also Annett, 1974). To explain such departures from a strict Mendelian segregation law, several modifications have been proposed.

Some authors have invoked partial penetrance. Trankell (1955), for instance, argued that only some of the individuals homozygous for left-handedness will actually be phenotypically left-handed. Rife (1950) suggested that partial penetrance applied to heterozygotes rather than to recessive homozygotes; that is, some heterozygotes are left-handed or ambidextrous rather than right-handed. This idea was pursued by Annett (1964), who proposed that the gene controlling handedness also controlled cerebral lateralization for language. According to this theory, individuals homozygous for one allele are all right-handed and left-cerebrally dominant for language, whereas those homozygous for the other show the reverse pattern. Heterozygotes are variable; most will be right-handed and left-cerebrally dominant for language, but in some, the recessive allele will produce a tendency toward left-handedness or ambilaterality, and toward right-hemispheric dominance for language. If it is supposed that about 25% of the population of heterozygotes show the reversed pattern and that the proportions of dominant and recessive alleles are about .8 and .2, respectively, then the model provides a reasonable fit to the data of Table 7.2. However, this model does not readily explain why the majority

TABLE 7.2
Number and Proportion of Right-Handed Offspring as a Function of Parental Handedness[a]

	Parental matings		
	R–R (N = 620)	R–L (N = 62)	L–L (N = 5)
Total offspring	1993	174	11
Number right-handed	1842	140	5
Proportion right-handed	924	805	455

[a] From Rife (1940).

of left-handers have language represented primarily in the *left* cerebral hemisphere (see Chatper 4).

Levy and Nagylaki (1972) suggested a model in which different patterns of laterality depend on two genetic loci. One determines which hemisphere is dominant for language and for control of the preferred hand, with left-hemispheric dominance represented by the dominant allele. The other locus determines whether hemispheric control of the hands is contralateral or ipsilateral. Hence, ipsilateral control is thought to be a recessive condition, perhaps associated with lack of decussation of the pyramidal tract, and it is this condition that gives rise to left-handers with left-cerebral representation of language and to right-handers with right-cerebral representation of language. With suitable choice of parameters, this model provides a reasonable fit to the data of Table 7.2 and also to the data relating handedness to cerebral lateralization for language.

This model had not won general acceptance. Hudson (1975) presents a detailed critique, noting for instance that the model does not provide adequate fits to other data, including those of Chamberlain (1928) and Annett (1973), on the inheritance of handedness. Perhaps the most controversial aspect of the model is the suggestion that somewhat over half of the population of left-handers should lack decussation of the pyramidal tract or should otherwise show ipsilateral cerebral control over the hand. Levy and Nagylaki had also proposed that these particular individuals are distinguished by the "hook" or inverted style of writing, but as we saw in Chapter 4, this particular proposition has not been supported by the subsequent evidence (Weber & Bradshaw, 1981).

The models described so far assume genetic control over the *direction* of laterality. Levy and Nagylaki's model is unusual in that it postulates direct genetic control over the direction of cerebral lateralization, but only indirect control over the direction of handedness. It follows, according to this model, that cerebral lateralization should follow Mendelian segregation laws. Preliminary evidence based on dichotic listening suggests that the heritability of cerebral lateralization is too low for this to be likely (Bryden, 1975), although this conclusion should be tempered by the fact that dichotic listening provides a rather unreliable index of lateralization (e.g., Blumstein *et al.,* 1975). But in any event, I observed earlier in the chapter that it is difficult to find precedents in biology for genetic control over the direction of asymmetries, and it is more likely on both logical and empirical grounds that the genes would influence the *degree* of asymmetry, or the *presence or absence* of asymmetry, rather than its direction. In the case of handedness, moreover, there is nothing in the data themselves to suggest that the direction of handedness is under genetic control.

By contrast, the data conform quite well to a model that asserts that the presence or absence of asymmetry is controlled in Mendelian fashion by a single gene locus. This model is the one proposed by Annett (1972)—it should not be confused with Annett's (1964) earlier model—and has been discussed already in Chapters 2 and 4. To recapitulate, the essence of the model is that the majority of people inherit a right-shift (RS +) factor that results in right-handedness and left-cerebral dominance for language, while a recessive minority (RS −) lack this factor and exhibit no consistent bias in handedness or in cerebral asymmetry. Annett (1972) initially attributed control to the presence or absence of a right-shift gene. Corballis and Beale (1976) suggested that control might be better attributed to a diallelic gene locus, with the RS − allele recessive, and Annett (1981) seems to have adopted this position, but the point is academic. In either case, the presence or absence of the right shift is controlled in Mendelian fashion. Those inheriting the right shift include dizygotes as well as those homozygous for the RS + allele, whereas those lacking the right shift are made up of those homozygous for the RS − allele. For simplicity, however, I shall continue to refer to the former as the RS + group and the latter as the RS − group.

Annett's model does not rigidly specify the phenotype but allows for a random component in the distribution of handedness. Those inheriting the right shift are therefore assumed to make up a distribution that is shifted to the right of the point of equality between the hands, but some small proportion will be left-handed, perhaps because of extreme environmental or pathological influences. Those lacking the right shift make up a distribution centered theoretically on the point of equality, although environmental pressures or bias in the measure of handedness may be modeled by allowing this distibution to be centered away from precise equality between the hands. The reader is referred to Figure 2.3 (in Chapter 2) for illustrations of these hypothetical distributions.

Elsewhere, I have fitted Annett's model to the data shown in Table 7.2 (Corballis, 1980a). The probability of occurrence of the RS + allele was estimated to be .6244. The proportion of individuals belonging genotypically to the right-shifted population is therefore estimated to be $.6244^2 + (2 \times .6244 \times .3756) = .8589$. This leaves a proportion of .1411 recessive individuals who lack the right shift. The proportion of left-handers in the RS + population was estimated to be .0136, and the proportion of left-handers in the RS − population was estimated to be .6457. One may wonder why this last estimate is higher than .5. Recall, however, that Rife used a biased criterion to classify handedness, since he designated individuals "left-handed" if they performed but 1 of 10 activities with the left hand. A more neutral criterion would presumably have shifted the proportions of left-handers in the sample and resulted in an estimate closer to .5. This fit to the data was exact since the equations upon which it was based were fully determined—that is, there were three equations for three unknowns—and the fit is therefore not truly a test of the model.

Nevertheless, the estimates do make reasonable sense in terms of what one would expect.

In Chapter 4, we saw that Annett's model also accounts reasonably well for the data on the joint distribution of handedness and cerebral lateralization for language. In fact, Annett (1979) has shown that a parameter estimated from data on cerebral lateralization can then be used to fit the data on the inheritance of handedness. In an earlier study, Annett (1975) had reported that 9.27% of patients with speech disorders following unilateral lesions had right-sided lesions. Doubling this percentage yields a value of .1854 as an estimate of the proportion of RS− individuals, and by simple Medelian logic, the square root of this—namely, .43—is the estimated incidence of the RS− allele. Subtracting from unity yields an estimate of .57 for the incidence of the RS+ allele—a value not grossly different from the value of .6244 I estimated from Rife's data. Annett then used these estimates to provide further estimates of the proportion of left- handers born to right-handed, mixed-, and left-handed couples, and these estimates did not differ significantly from data that she herself collected.

By assuming that the right shift is expressed more strongly in women than in men, Annett was able to model two slight but persistent trends that occur in most surveys, including her own. One is that the incidence of left-hand-edness is lower among girls than among boys, and the other is that children are slightly more likely to be left-handed if their mothers are left-handed than if their fathers are left-handed. However, Annett's assumption that the right shift is expressed more strongly in women seems to conflict with the evidence that women show the lesser degree of cerebral lateralization (McGlone, 1978; and see Chapter 4), since the right shift and the left-cerebral dominance for language are assumed to depend on the same fundamental lateralizing influence. The conflict can be resolved, however, if it is supposed that handedness is more susceptible to environmental or pathological influences than is cerebral lateralization for language (Satz, 1972) and that boys are more prone to these influences than are girls, especially in early infancy. Biologically, the lateralizing influence might well be expressed more strongly in boys than in girls, perhaps because boys tend to mature later (Waber, 1977). With respect to handedness, however, boys may be more susceptible to environmental effects, which negate their biological predisposition toward greater lateralization.

There is one respect in which even quite large surveys on the inheritance of handedness do not provide a very exacting test of Annett's model: There are typically very few families in which both parents are left-handed. In Rife's (1940) survey, for instance, there were only five such families, and in Annett's (1979) survey only four. Yet such families are of particular interest in relation to Annett's model, because in the absence of pathological left-handedness, they may be supposed to represent the recessive RS− subpopulation. Consequently, one would expect the children of left-handed parents to lack any over-all handedness (or cerebral lateralization, for that mattter). In a separate study, Annett (1974) has found this to be so. She located 24 left-handed couples who were apparently free of any history of perinatal difficulty or other pathology that might have influenced their handedness. Of the 45 children of these couples, 23 were faster with the right hand and 22 were faster with the left hand on the peg-moving test (described in Chapter 2), and the mean difference between the hands over the group as a whole was essentially zero. This result provides striking support for Annett's model.

Annett rejected from her initial sample of 29 left-handed couples 5 who had shown evidence of early pathology, and the children of these couples were predominantly right-handed on the peg-moving task. Again, then, we have evidence for two categories of left-handers: those whose genotype is RS + but who are left-handed because of extreme environmental or pathological influences, and those whose genotype is RS − and who owe their left-handedness essentially to chance—or the "asymmetry lottery." In Chapter 4, I estimated the relative proportions of these two categories to be about even, based on a comparison of left- and right-handed aphasics. Annett's (1974) sample of left-handed couples suggests that the majority of left-handers are in the RS − category. According to my own parameter estimates based on Rife's data (Corballis, 1980a), some 89% of left-handers are estimated to belong to the RS − category, with only about 11% owing their left-handedness to pathology or to extreme environmental influences. Annett's (1979) analysis yields relative estimates of the same order. The higher estimated frequency of RS + left-handers among aphasics may reflect a higher degree of early pathology in those with speech disorders, or it may reflect a higher proportion of men, who appear to be more susceptible than women to early cerebral pathology.

If left-handers in the RS + category owe their left-handedness primarily to some early pathology, such as cerebral anoxia at birth (e.g., Bakan *et al.*, 1973), and if such pathology influences handedness rather than cerebral lateralization for language (Satz, 1972), then one might expect RS + and RS − left-handers to show different patterns of cerebral asymmetry. That is, one might expect RS + left-handers to show the usual pattern of left-cerebral dominance for language, whereas RS − left-handers should show mixed dominance, with neither hemisphere dominant over the group as a whole. There is in fact some support for these expectations.

Hécaen and Sauguet (1971) examined the effects of unilateral lesions on language functions in two groups of left-handers, those with and those without left-handers in their immediate families. Thus, the *familial* group had one or more left-handed sibling, parent, or child, whereas the *nonfamilial* group had no such left-handed relatives. Roughly speaking, then the familial group may be considered largely RS − , whereas the nonfamilial group may be considered to include the larger proportion of RS + individuals. Hécaen and Sauguet found that those in the nonfamilial group were essentially indistinguishable from right-handers in that language disorders resulted only from left-sided lesions. Familial left-handers, by contrast, showed evidence of a higher incidence of bilateral representation of language, with more diffuse representation both within and between hemispheres.

Other investigators have similarly found that the lack of consistent cerebral lateralization so often observed in left-handers applies particularly to familial left-handers, and not to nonfamilial ones (e.g., R. J. Andrews, 1977; Satz, Fennel, & Jones, 1969; Zurif & Bryden, 1969). The evidence is not entirely unequivocal, however, since some have not found familiarity to be important (e.g., Bryden, 1975; McKeever & Van Deventer, 1977; Newcombe & Ratcliff, 1973), and Warrington and Pratt (1973) reported the reverse result—namely, that familial left-handers were *less* likely than nonfamilial ones to reveal right-cerebral representation of speech. In a review of this evidence, Hécaen, De Agostini, and Monzon-Montes (1981) note that earlier studies may have been contaminated by the effects of age, sex, and variations in the degree of handedness. In a carefully controlled study, they selected 141 cases of left-handers with unilateral lesions and were able to confirm essentially the earlier conclusions of Hécaen and Sauguet. That is, familial left-handers showed a higher incidence of ambilateral representation of language, whereas nonfamilial left-handers resembled right-handers in that language was represented predominantly in the left cerebral hemisphere. The same was true of a sample of 130 *right*-handers; that is, those with familial left-handedness revealed a more diffuse representation of language than those without.

Hécaen *et al.* did not observe the same effect with respect to right-hemispheric specialization for spatial functions; in fact, the familial left-handers appeared more likely to show right-hemispheric specialization than did the nonfamilial ones, which is contrary to what one would expect from Annett's model. The authors point to a possible artifact in their results, however, and other authors have obtained results on the lateralization of tasks normally thought to be right-hemispheric that are more consistent with expectations; that is, lateralized representation in nonfamilial but not in familial left-handers (M. L. Albert & Obler, 1978; Gilbert, 1977; Varney & Benton, 1975). Taken overall, the results show rather good support for Annett's model, the more so when one realizes that the distinction between familial and nonfamilial left-handedness can be only a crude approximation to the distinction between RS − and RS + genotypes.

In summary, of the genetic models so far suggested, Annett's (1972) model seems clearly the most parsimonious and the most biologically apt. It accounts for the principal facts concerning the inheritance of handedness and the relations between handedness and cerebral lateralization. It allows for environmental as well as genetic variation, and so permits one to accept that some left-handers may owe their left-handedness to early cerebral pathology rather than to any genetic predisposition. Above all, the model implies genetic control over whether or not an asymmetry is expressed rather than control over the direction of asymmetry, which accords with the idea that the genes are fundamentally "left–right agnosic" (M. J. Morgan, 1977). There is, however, one impediment to Annett's model, and indeed to *any* genetic model of laterality, and it is to this that we now turn.

Distribution of Laterality in Twins and Siblings

If handedness is indeed subject to a genetic influence, one would expect some degree of concordance between siblings. This should be highest among monozygotic twins, who possess identical genes. Indeed, according to a model such as Levy and Nagylaki's in which handedness is fully determined by two gene loci, the concordance should be perfect; that is, in the absence of pathological left-handedness, monozygotic twins should always display the same handedness. The facts, however, are quite to the contrary.

Table 7.3 summarizes data on the distributions of right-handed, mixed-, and left-handed pairs among monozygotic twins, dizygotic (fraternal) twins, and pairs of nontwin siblings. Notice that the concordance is far from perfect, in that about one-third even of monozygotic twins are discordant for handedness. Concordance is most succinctly expressed by the ϕ coefficient, defined as follows:

$$\phi = \frac{p_{RR} - p_R^2}{p_R (1 - p_R)}$$

where p_{RR} is the proportion of pairs who are both right-handed, and p_R is the overall proportion of right-handers. A deterministic genetic theory implies that ϕ should be unity for monozygotic twins and greater than zero for dizygotic twins and for nontwin siblings. A value of zero, by contrast, implies a binomial distribution. The most parsimonious explanation is simply that handedness is determined independently in each twin or sibling, so that discordances arise purely by chance. In fact, ϕ lies very close to zero in all three sets of data in Table 7.3. It was this observation that led Collins (1970) to reject genetic models of handedness.

One genetic model that can be fitted to the data on twins is that proposed by Rife (1950). In this model, handedness is determined by an allelic gene pair

TABLE 7.3

Incidence of Concordant and Discordant Handedness in Monozygotic Twins, Dizygotic Twins, and Pairs of Nontwin Siblings

Source	R–R	R–L	L–L	ϕ
Monozygotic twins[a]				
Frequencies	261	71	6	
Proportions	.761	.222	.017	.009
Dizygotic twins[a]				
Frequencies	164	45	2	
Proportions	.777	.213	.009	−.039
Nontwin siblings[b]				
Frequencies	3067	467	41	
Proportions	.856	.133	.011	.075

[a] From Rife (1950).

[b] From Rife (1940).

in which there is partial penetrance of left-handedness among heterozygotes. Although Rife assumes that most singly born heterozygotes are right-handed, he assumes that heterozygotic twins are always of opposite handedness, whereas homozygotic twins are always concordant for handedness. This model predicts a binomial distribution of handedness among monozygotic twins and a near-binomial distribution among dizygotic twins, and indeed the predictions lie very close to the distributions reported by Rife himself. Collins (1970) has re-marked, however, that the assumption of opposite handedness among heter-ozygotic twins "requires a special type of environmental determination of handedness in twin pairs which should not be accepted in the absence of con-clusive evidence [p. 27]." Rife's model therefore has a post hoc quality that detracts from its plausibility.

Can the data be reconciled with Annett's (1972) model? This model does of course include a random element, and even in the case of monozygotic twins, one would expect binomial distributions *within* each of the RS+ and RS− subpopulations. However, the sum of two binomial distributions is not in general binomial, and one must in fact predict a value of ϕ greater than zero. Using the parameters from the fit of Annett's model to Rife's (1940) data on the inheritance of handedness (see earlier), I computed an expected value of .525 for monozygotic twins and .203 for dizygotic twins and for nontwin siblings (Corballis, 1980a). These values are significantly above the values com-puted from an augmented sample of twins described by Rife (1950). The em-pirical values are shown in Table 7.3. Even when I corrected for the higher incidence of left-handedness in twins than in the singly born in Rife's surveys, the predicted value of ϕ for monozygotic twins was .393, still well above the empirical estimates and significantly different from them (see Corballis, 1980a, for details). I also attempted to correct the estimate of ϕ for paired nontwin siblings for a bias evident in Rife's data—namely, that right-handed parents had more children than parents of mixed-handedness, who were in turn more prolific than left-handed parents. Even the corrected estimate of .156 failed to match the empirical value of .075.

However, one should probably not take such mathematical exercises too seriously. It is possible, for instance, that the particular assumptions I made in fitting Annett's model to the data on the inheritance of handedness distorted the fit to the data on twins. Annett (1978) has also fitted her model to Rife's (1940) data on the inheritance of handedness, as well as to other such data, and then shown that the model provides an excellent fit to data on the distribution of handedness in monozygotic twins and dizygotic twins reported by Zazzo (1960)! Her reasoning was similar to my own, but it differed sufficiently in its initial premises to yield rather different parameter estimates, and these in turn allowed much closer fits to the data on twins than my own estimates did.

Annett began by estimating the probability of the RS+ allele to be .57; as explained earlier, this estimate was based on her earlier (Annett, 1975) data on the incidence of aphasia in left-handers suffering unilateral lesions. She also allowed the proportion of left-handers in the RS+ and RS− subpopulations to vary between generations, and in fact estimated these proportions in Rife's (1940) survey to be .0050 and .2611, respectively, for the parents and .0149 and .4071, respectively, for the children. These estimates allowed an acceptable, though not perfect, fit to the data. Notice that these estimates imply a bias toward *right*-handedness in Rife's survey, whereas my own solutions indicate a bias toward *left*-handedness. Hence, Annett's solution implies that the RS− and RS+ distributions are closer to one another than my own solution implies. In order to fit the model to the distribution of handedness among twins, Annett assumed further that the right shift is expressed more weakly than in the singly born—an assumption equivalent to assuming a higher proportion of "pathological" left-handedness in twins. Her model then predicted ϕs of .098 for monozygotic twins and .037 for dizygotic twins. These did not differ significantly from empirical values of .099 and .022, respectively, computed from Zazzo's (1960) data. The point that emerges from these analyses, I think, is not that one solution is more "correct" than another but that the fitting of models can be heavily influenced by seemingly minor changes in assumptions.

Should Twins Be Allowed?

In any event, there has been considerable debate as to whether evidence on twins is admissible in the testing of genetic models. Nagylaki and Levy (1973) have argued that it is not. For one thing, they claim, twins are especially susceptible to pathological influences, and this raises the incidence of left-handedness due to pathology. McManus (1980), however, has reviewed 19 studies of handedness in twins and concluded that there is no good evidence for a higher incidence of left-handedness in twins than in the singly born. His conclusion is guarded, however, since there are few studies in which the handedness of twins and singletons has been assessed by the same methods. McManus notes one exception, the study by Zazzo (1960), who is quoted as having observed no difference in handedness between twins and singletons. He might also have observed, however, that in the survey by Rife (1940) the incidence of left-handedness was considerably higher among both monozygotic twins (11.38%) and dizygotic twins (15.41%) than in the sample as a whole (4.49%), even though the same criterion of handedness was presumably applied. Ironically, Springer and Searleman (1980) have independently reviewed the evidence, including most of the same studies reviewed by McManus, and concluded that the incidence of left-handedness in twins may be as much as double that in singletons.

The possibility that twins may be more prone to pathological left-handedness is not especially critical to Annett's model, in any case, since pathological left-handedness is readily incorporated in the model, as we have seen. A more critical possibility raised by Nagylaki and Levy is that monozygotic twins may be subject to a special mirror-imaging effect that artificially increases the proportion of twins who are discordant for handedness relative to those who are concordant for handedness. This mirror-imaging process is believed to apply particularly to ectodermally derived tissue and to include handprints and hair whorls, as well as possibly, handedness and eye dominance (e.g., Newman, 1940).

Although mirror imaging rarely applies to the viscera, some suggestions as to how it might operate have come from studies of *situs inversus* of the viscera. We saw in Chapter 5 how conjoined (Siamese twin) newts may be produced by tying a hair around the median plane of the embryo and that the twin on the right often shows complete or partial reversal in the *situs* of the internal organs (Spemann & Falkenberg, 1919). Similarly, in cases of conjoined human twins, it is commonly observed that one twin exhibits *situs inversus* of the viscera, and according to Schlumberger and Gotwals (1945) this reversal occurs in the twin on the right in 90% of cases. However, *situs inversus* is rare in twins born separately, perhaps as rare as in the general population (Torgerson, 1950). It has been suggested that the extent of mirror imaging increases as the age at which twinning occurs increases (e.g., Carter-Saltzman, 1979; Newman, 1940). If the embryo divides to form twins very early on, before the basic bilateral symmetry of the body is defined, then each half is likely to develop the normal asymmetry. If division occurs after the two sides of the embryo have been defined, then reversals are likely to occur, especially in the right-hand twin. Such reversals, however, are likely to affect only the ectodermal tissue, unless division is very late or does not occur completely at all, as in conjoined twins.

This account is highly speculative, and there is little direct evidence that mirror imaging depends on the age at which the embryo splits to form twins, although Hay and Howie (1980) have furnished indirect evidence. They observed that monozygotic twins were more likely to be of different handedness if the difference in their weights at birth was relatively large than if they were nearly equal in weight. Differences in birth weight are in turn thought to be larger if the embryo splits late than if it splits early. Hay and Howie also noted that the non-right-handed twin was not necessarily the lighter one, suggesting that the departure from right-handedness was not due simply to birth stress.

As Springer (1978) points out, it is conceivable that some percentage of left-handers are simply the survivors of a twinning event in which the right-handed co-twin perished at an early stage of prenatal development. Indeed, it is conceivable that *all* left-handers are formed in this way; thus, Boklage (1980) writes that ''there is very little to keep us from imagining that every left hander in the world is a survivor of just such an embryonic disturbance [p. 125].'' For every Leonardo, there is a mirror twin who failed to materialize.

Yet there remains very little evidence for any special mirror-imaging mechanism related to the twinning process, at least with respect to handedness and cerebral lateralization. The incidence of left-handedness is essentially the same in dizygotic as in monozygotic twins (McManus, 1980; Springer & Searleman, 1980), suggesting that it may be a consequence of prenatal environmental conditions rather than of the twinning process. Moreover, the fact that the distributions of concordant and discordant handedness are approximately binomial in the case of both monozygotic and dizygotic twins suggests that reversals are due to chance rather than to any systematic mirror imaging. Springer and Searleman (1980) have described weak evidence that there may be a mirror-imaging effect in cerebral lateralization, however, They measured cerebral lateralization for language using a dichotic-listening test and found that the intraclass correlation between twin pairs was $-.34$ for monozygotic twins discordant for handedness but $.09$ for dizygotic twins discordant for handedness. Although the difference between these correlations was not statistically significant, this is one of the very few results that suggests *any* systematic difference between monozygotic and dizygotic twins in the distribution of laterality. In spite of this, however, I suspect that the popular notion of mirror twins is little more than a superstition, based on the chance occurrences of mirrored features and sustained by the human quest for symmetry. Even if the right-sided twin of Leonardo never existed, he would have to have been invented sooner or later. I hereby offer him, Odranoel!

If the apparently increased incidence of left-handedness in twins (pace McManus, 1980) has nothing to do with the embryology of twinning, it may well be due to conditions prevailing in the womb (e.g., Rife, 1940; P. T. Wilson & Jones, 1932). This would of course explain why the incidence is about equal in dizygotic and monozygotic twins. However, Springer and Searleman (1980) assert that there is little evidence that bears directly on whether the positioning of twins in utero would indeed tend to increase the incidence of left-handedness. They also recall a suggestion by Danforth (1919) that the positions taken up by twins *after* birth may be influential. According to Danforth, twin babies generally face one another in their cribs, exposing opposite sides of the head and opposite hands. Again, however, any such influence would tend to produce a mirroring effect, and the near-binomial distributions of handedness in twins suggests that chance, not mirror imaging, is the major determinant of reversals in twins.

On balance, then, it seems unlikely that special mirror-imaging effects play a significant role in increasing the number of twins discordant for handedness, but it does seem reasonable to conclude that the proportion of "pathological" left-handers is higher among twins than among the singly born. If this is so, then Annett's model should fit the data, since this model allows for both genetic and environmental variation, but not for special mirror-imaging effects. The question of whether Annett's model does fit the data depends perhaps on whether one accepts my own analysis (Corballis, 1980a) or Annett's analysis. Given the other evidence in favor of the model, it would seem churlish not to give it the benefit of the doubt.

A Nongenetic Model

But although the data on twins can be reconciled with Annett's model, albeit with some post hoc adjustment and choice of assumptions, the disturbing fact remains that binomial distributions suggest a much more parsimonious explanation. This is simply that handedness is distributed between twins, and between paired siblings, on a random basis. One is reminded again of Collins's (1975) "asymmetry lottery"—left-handedness befalls about 1 in 10, but the selected few are picked out merely by chance. It is cold comfort to the genetic modeler that the distributions appear to deviate slightly from the binomial, so that the ϕ coefficients are typically a little above zero, since this can be predicted from nongenetic considerations.

Now it is clear from Table 7.2 that the probability of being left-handed does depend on the handedness of one's parents, but let us suppose that this is simply a matter of learning or imitation. Suppose too that this parental influence operates independently on different siblings within a family. If this is so, then we must expect binomial distributions within families of right-, mixed-, and left-handed couples, but a systematic departure from binomiality when the distributions are pooled across family types. This may be illustrated from

Rife's (1940) data, summarized in Table 7.2 (Corballis, 1980a). Among the offspring of right-handed couples, the probability of a child being left-handed is .0758, so that the expected binomial probabilities of right-handed, mixed-handed, and left-handed *pairs* are .8541 ($= .9242^2$), .1401 ($= 2 \times .9242 \times .0758$), and .0057 ($= .0758^2$), respectively, and among offspring of left-handed couples .2066, .4959, and .2976, respectively. If we weight these distributions according to the number of families within each category and compute the weighted average across categories, we obtain the values .834, .156, and .010, yielding a ϕ of .027. In short, this approach yields a value of ϕ slightly above zero and quite close to the values shown in Table 7.3 for twins and for paired siblings. In other words, the data are reasonably consistent with the assumption of systematic variability *between* families, but random or binomial variability *within* families.

In order to extend this nongenetic approach to account for the relations between handedness and cerebral lateralization, one need simply suppose that the parental influence on handedness is stronger than that on cerebral lateralization. This would not be surprising, given that handedness is the more overt and thus the more susceptible to learning or to imitation. Indeed, one must suppose that the influence on cerebral lateralization occurs indirectly through the influence on handedness; thus, somewhat less than half of those who are left-handed are influenced to the extent of exhibiting right-cerebral dominance for language. Milner (1975) notes that there appears to be little if any correlation between the degree of left-handedness and the degree of right-cerebral specialization for language. Nevertheless, this is not decisive evidence, and one might well argue that some, if not all, cases of right-hemispheric dominance for language are due to early cerebral pathology.

According to this model, the parental influence is nongenetic. As counterevidence, Hicks and Kinsbourne (1976) have reported that parental handedness is predictive of a child's handedness only if the parent is biologically related to the child. The handedness of adopted children was not related to that of their stepparents. According to Hicks and Kinsbourne, this finding suggests a genetic component in parent–child correlations. The evidence is scarcely conclusive, however, since the children surveyed, whose average age was just over 20 years, had been living with their stepparents for an average of only 7.24 years. There seems little doubt that the handedness of the great majority of the stepchildren had been established well before they began living with their new parents.

In a more convincing study, Carter-Saltzman (1980) found evidence for both genetic and sociocultural effects on handedness. She examined the influence of parental handedness on the handedness of 400 children who were the biological offspring of their parents, and of 408 children who had been adopted in infancy. The data are summarized in Table 7.4. Notice that the

TABLE 7.4
Percentage of Left- and Right-Handers among Biological and Adoptive Children
as a Function of Parental Handedness[a,b]

Parents' handedness (Father x Mother)	Handedness of children					
	Biological			Adoptive		
	N	right	Left	N	right	Left
RxR	340	89	11	355	86	14
RxL	38	76	24	16	75	25
LxR	22	73	27	37	95	5

[a] From Carter-Saltzman (1980).

[b] Right-handers were defined as those with positive scores and left-handers those with negative scores on the Edinburgh Handedness Inventory (Oldfield, 1971). There were only five children whose parents were both left-handed, so data for the LxL group could not be meaningfully tabulated. Twins were also excluded.

proportion of left-handers among those with a left-handed mother and a right-handed father was essentially the same in the two groups (25% and 24%, respectively). Among those with a right-handed mother and a left-handed father, however, the proportion of left-handers was much less in the adopted group (5%) than in the biologically related group (27%). These results suggest that the paternal influence is largely genetic, while the maternal influence may be at least partly sociocultural. The data cannot be considered definitive, however, since the critical group of adopted children with left-handed stepmothers contained only 16 children.

Although there may well be a nongenetic component underlying variations in handedness, then, Carter-Saltzman's data suggest that there is a genetic component as well. Again, this is broadly consistent with Annett's model, which allows for both genetic and nongenetic sources of variaton.

Indirect Evidence for Genetic Control

So far, the argument for genetic control of variations in laterality has been based primarily on the distribution of handedness itself. An alternative approach is to try to discover some trait known to be genetically heritable that is correlated with laterality (e.g., Levy, 1976; Rife, 1943, 1955). In particular, it has been argued that handedness is correlated with asymmetries in hair whorls and in hand- or fingerprints, and that these traits are in turn under genetic control. By association, then, one can argue for a genetic component underlying handedness.

Most people have a single hair crown that whorls either clockwise or counterclockwise, although a few individuals have two crowns. The direction of whorling does not appear to be correlated with handedness (Lauterbach & Knight, 1927; Newman, 1934), and in any event, there is considerable dispute over whether variations in the direction of whorling are under genetic control. Reviewing the evidence, Bhalla and Kaul (1968) conclude that studies of the inheritance of hair whorls

> make it fairly clear that the direction of hair whorls is rather inconsistent and its mode of transmission indefinite . . . Its erratic behavior could only be explained in the words of Scheinfeld (1956) who remarked that the clockwise or counterclockwise expression of this trait may be influenced by chance factors in prenatal development [p. 102].

There is clearly little support for a genetic model of laterality here (see also M. J. Morgan, 1977).

As further evidence against a simple Mendelian model, it is noteworthy that hair whorls are often opposite in direction in monozygotic twins, and indeed the frequencies of concordant and discordant hair whorls fall very close to binomial expectancies (Lauterbach, 1925; Newman, 1923; Rife, 1933). Although Rife's (1950) genetic model predicts a binomial distribution, it does so in somewhat post hoc fashion, as explained earlier in relation to handedness. In any event, a binomial distribution suggests random allocation much more obviously than it suggests genetic determination.

Hair whorls may also be located to the left or right of the midline. This is somewhat independent of the direction of coiling, although clockwise coiling is more commonly associated with whorls to the right than to the left (Wunderlich & Heerema, 1975). According to Friedman, Golomb, and Mora (1952), there *is* a correlation between handedness and the position of the hair whorl. They used a rather extensive battery of items to determine handedness and obtained the results shown in Table 7.5. Notice that 98% of both men and women with a left-sided hair whorl were right-handed, whereas those with a right-sided hair whorl were much more evenly split, with a small majority again being right-handed. These data again conform rather well to Annett's (1972)

TABLE 7.5
Percentage of Left- and Right-Handed Men and Women in Each Hair Whorl Category[a]

Location of hair whorl	N	Men Percentage right-handed	Men Percentage left-handed	N	Women Percentage right-handed	Women Percentage left-handed
Left side	175	98	2	191	98	2
Right side	53	58	42	34	56	44
Midline	15	93	7	23	100	0
Double	7	100	0	2	100	0

[a] From Friedman, Golomb, and Mora (1952).

model, in that they imply a division between those who are consistently lateralized (right-handed, left-sided hair whorl) and those who are inconsistently lateralized. Wunderlich and Heerema (1975) remark, however, that neither the position nor the direction of hair whorls follow the Hardy-Weinburg distribution for a population that breeds randomly, so Friedman *et al.*'s data cannot therefore be considered strong evidence for a genetic model of handedness.

Friedman *et al.* suggest that the side of the hair whorl may indicate cerebral dominance rather than handedness per se, and indeed if one substitutes cerebral dominance for language for side of hair whorl in Table 7.4, one obtains figures that correspond quite well to those presented in Chapter 4. It is somewhat disturbing, however, that whereas Friedman *et al.* report that the majority of people have the whorl on the left side, Wunderlich and Heerema (1975) report a preponderance of right-sided over left-sided whorls and suggest that "the hair whorl tends to lie over the nondominant hemisphere [p. 1049]."

Dermatoglyphic patterns, otherwise known as handprints and fingerprints, may offer a more promising avenue for the documentation of a genetic component in laterality. Rife (1955) summarizes the results of five independent investigations involving handprints of a total of 3095 right-handers and 1642 left-handers, in which asymmetry between the hands was found to be slightly but significantly less among left-handers than among right-handers. Notice again that this conforms to Annett's (1972) model. Rife notes that handprints are established at about midterm in fetal development and do not change thereafter except in size. He also states that they are highly heritable. This association between handedness and handprints therefore suggests a genetic basis for variations in handedness.

Estimates of the heritability of handprints are actually somewhat variable. In particular, measures taken from the palm appear to have somewhat lower heritability than do those taken from the fingers, and yet the association with handedness seems to be stronger for palmar than for digital measures (Jantz, Fohl, & Zahler, 1979). For instance, Loesch (1974) reported heritability estimates of around 50% for most measures taken for the palm, whereas estimates of the heritability of digital measures range from about 70% (Froehlich, 1976; Loesch, 1971) to 95% for the total number of dermal ridges on the fingers (Holt, 1968). However, L. Y. Morgan, Juberg, and Faust (1977; cited in Jantz *et al.*, 1979) failed to find any correlation between measures of fingerprints and lateral preference.

According to Holt's (1968) heritability estimate of 95%, the number of dermal ridges on the fingers must be among the most heritable of all human traits. Consequently, any clear correlation with handedness would provide reasonably secure evidence for a genetic basis for variations in handedness. However, in a detailed comparison of finger ridge counts between left- and right-handers, Jantz *et al.* (1979) found only slight and rather unsystematic differences, although there was a general trend for left-handers to have fewer ridges. Both left- and right-handers had more ridges, on average, on the fingers of the right hand than on the fingers of the left, but contrary to Rife's (1955) evidence, this asymmetry was if anything greater among the left-handers.

One interesting difference between left- and right-handers had to do with the correlations between different measures. Jantz *et al.* took a count from the radial and ulnar sides of each finger to yield a total of 20 measures for each person. They then intercorrelated these measures separately for men and women within each handedness category. The majority of correlations were higher for the right-handers than for the left-handers. Jantz *et al.* argue that this implies a difference between left- and right-handers in the control of development, and may or may not reflect genetic variation. That is, left-handers appear to be more susceptible to extraneous environmental influences early in prenatal life. Jantz *et al.* also note that this is consistent with Annett's model, in that left-handers represent a group in which consistent lateralization is lacking so that handedness is determined by chance.

In summary, evidence on the association between handedness and other asymmetries believed to be heritable does not provide clear-cut evidence for a genetic basis underlying variations in handedness. The association with dermatoglyphic patterns need not imply that the asymmetry of those patterns is highly heritable; rather, asymmetries of dermatoglyphic patterns may reflect development mechanisms or gradients that are independent of the genes themselves. Even so, this approach is one that holds some promise.

CONCLUSIONS

It should be stressed again that the predominant pattern of human laterality, in which the great majority are right-handed and left-cerebrally dominant for language and praxic functions, is almost certainly biologically preprogrammed. It would be surprising if this pattern did not depend in some way on the genetic makeup of human beings. The source of the asymmetrical influence may not be genetic, however; following M. J. Morgan (1977), I have argued that the genes themselves are "left–right agnosic." Morgan suggests, in fact, that the asymmetry may depend ultimately on some molecular asymmetry in the ooctye. This asymmetry may also govern other systematic bodily asymmetries, such as those of the viscera. However, whether the asymmetry is expressed, and how it is expressed, no doubt depends on genetic factors.

This chapter has been concerned with the question of why some human beings depart from this predominant pattern of laterality; that is, with why some people are left-handed or ambidextrous, or have language represented bilaterally or predominantly in the right cerebral hemisphere. Specifically, the question is whether at least some of the within-species variation in laterality is of genetic origin. The evidence reviewed in this chapter does not permit a conclusive answer to this question, although most of this evidence is at least consistent with the proposition that there is a genetic component.

In particular, the evidence continues to offer support for Annett's (1972) theory that a minority of people simply lack the consistent lateralizing influence that governs the direction of handedness and cerebral lateralization in the majority. Whether this lack can be attributed to a recessive allele at the locus that controls the expression of the lateralizing influence remains unproven, but the model based on this premise can provide reasonably good fits to the data on the inheritance of handedness, on the interrelations between handedness, cerebral lateralization, and other indices of lateralization, and (perhaps less satisfactorily) on the distribution of handedness among twins. It is worth recalling that Layton (1976) has similarly argued that the presence or absence of a consistent lateralizing influence underlying *situs* of the viscera in mice—and by implication in other species as well, including humans—is also governed by a gene pair. The locus of the gene governing *situs* would of course be different from that of the gene governing the direction of handedness and cerebral lateralization, but the underlying asymmetry and the nature of the genetic control over its expression may well be the same.

It is of course still possible, and in some respects valuable, to play devil's advocate and maintain that variations in laterality are due entirely to environmental influences. Thus, Bakan (1978) is still able to argue that deviations from right-handedness are due to prenatal or perinatal events leading to brain hypoxia, which in turn has a damaging effect on cells of the pyramidal system in the left motor cortex. He cites independent evidence that the left hemisphere is the more vulnerable to hypoxia or asphyxiation, not only in humans (Bruens, Gastaut, & Giove, 1960), but even in monkeys (Braun & Myers, 1975). It is difficult to disprove such a theory, however, especially since Bakan argues that recovery from such pathological events is "remarkable in degree and rapidity [p. 280]." Even so, there seems a reasonable consensus that pathological factors cannot plausibly explain all deviations from right-handedness (see, e.g., Leiber & Axelrod, 1981).

A variation on Bakan's theme has been proposed by Geschwind and Behan (1982), who also note a higher incidence of pathology in the left-handed. In particular, they found that the strongly left-handed were more likely than the strongly right-handed to suffer from developmental learning disorders, migraine, and immune disorders (such as ulcerative colitis, celiac disease, and Hashimoto's thyroiditis). Since the relatives of left-handers also showed an elevated frequency of these disorders, however, Geschwind and Behan suggest that the cause is genetic rather than pathological. They speculate that the critical ingredient is testosterone, which slows development of the left cerebral hemisphere and also plays a major role in the development of the immune system. Since the fetal testes secrete testosterone, this might explain the higher incidence of both left-handedness and developmental learning disorders in males than in females. It is perhaps too early to tell whether this theory can be reconciled plausibly with Annett's.

One of the advantages of Annett's model is that it readily incorporates both a genetic and an environmental component. Rather than argue that variations in laterality are due entirely to one or the other, the more constructive approach is surely to ask how much of the variation is genetic and how much environmental, and Annett's model provides a vehicle for doing this. At the same time, the model possesses a degree of simplicity, or parsimony, that prevents it from simply stretching to accommodate the data. At the present time, this model seems to me to provide the most appropriate framework within which to evaluate and structure the bewildering range of evidence on variations in laterality.

8 Congenital Disorders of Speech and Language

Some people are afflicted with disorders of speech or language, and yet they display no other signs of neurological deficit or indeed of any other obvious perceptual, motor, or intellectual impairment. Perhaps the most obvious and incapacitating disorder of speech is stuttering. One well-known victim was Lewis Carroll, and the Dodo in *Alice in Wonderland* was named after the way Carroll was apt to pronounce his own real name: "Do-Do-Dodgson." Another celebrated stutterer was the English writer W. Somerset Maugham. Carroll and Maugham illustrate the common observation that stuttering may afflict even those who are otherwise unusually gifted, verbally as well as intellectually.

Another highly specific disorder is reading disability, also known as developmental dyslexia. Paradoxically, this disorder may also afflict those who are in other respects gifted. In 1896, the English physician Pringle Morgan described the case of a 14-year-old boy suffering from what Morgan called "congenital word blindness." Despite his inability to read properly, the boy was talented in other academic areas, including mathematics. Critchley (1964) observed that the reading problems exhibited by the dyslexic "are unlike those met with in the case of a dullard, or a poorly educated person [p. 11]." Thompson (1971) has examined case histories of several prominent men who appear to have been dyslexic, including the inventor Thomas A. Edison, the brain surgeon Harvey Cushing, the sculptor Auguste Rodin, and President Woodrow Wilson. Critchley (1970) notes that Hans Christian Andersen may be classified as dyslexic. Clearly, reading disability is also no respecter of intellect.

In recent years, the somewhat more general term *developmental dysphasia* has been used to describe deficits of language that somewhat resemble the aphasias caused by brain injury but that occur in individuals who are apparently neurologically sound (Wyke, 1978). The nineteenth-century physician William Wilde (1853) may well have had this category in mind when he wrote of children who were "dumb but not deaf," and "neither paralytic nor idiotic."

These disorders are not well understood, despite a good deal of investigation and debate. Although their chief characteristic is precisely that there are no accompanying signs of neurological disorder, it remains a possibility that they are due to undetected cerebral injury. For instance, Pringle Morgan was prompted to describe the case of the boy with congenital word blindness because of evidence presented a few years earlier that damage to the angular gyrus of the left hemisphere also produces a specific deficit in reading (Dejerine, 1891, 1892), and he suggested that congenital word blindness might be due to a lag in development of this area of the brain. Some investigators have continued to draw attention to the similarities between developmental dyslexia, where there is no evidence of brain injury, and so-called acquired dyslexia (also known as alexia), where brain damage is clearly implicated (e.g., Aaron, Baxter, & Lucenti, 1980; Benton, 1978; Jorm, 1979).

The evidence on this point is equivocal, however. In particular, a good deal of attention has been directed toward so-called deep dyslexia, a form of acquired dyslexia in which the patient does not appear to have access to the phonological rules for pronouncing words (Coltheart, Patterson, & Marshall 1980). For instance, such patients are unable to read orthographically regular nonwords, such as *brone* or *dake* (K. E. Patterson & Marcel, 1977). Jorm (1979) suggested that developmental dyslexics suffer the same incapacity and therefore try to read in a holistic, nonphonological way, as one might read Chinese ideograms. We saw in Chapter 3 that this holistic strategy also seems to characterize the way in which commissurotomized patients read words projected to their right hemispheres (Zaidel & Peters, 1981), and indeed it has been suggested that the right hemisphere is responsible for reading in the deep dyslexic (Coltheart, 1980; Saffran, Bogyo, Schwartz, & Marin, 1980). Similarly, it has been suggested that developmental dyslexics also adopt inappropriate "right-hemispheric" strategies for reading (e.g., Kershner, 1977; Witelson, 1977a). However, Baddeley, Ellis, Miles, and Lewis (1982) have shown that developmental dyslexics, unlike deep dyslexics, can read orthographically regular nonwords, so the parallels between the two forms of dyslexia should not be pushed too far.

Even if developmental disorders are not due to cerebral injury, there is a broader question of whether they are best understood in neurological terms or whether they can be linked to environmental influences. The neurological approach was especially prominent in the 1920s and 1930s, mainly because of the pioneering influence of Samuel Torrey Orton, an American psychiatrist and pediatrician. Orton argued that disorders of language, including reading disability and stuttering, were due to poorly established cerebral dominance. This argument is the focus of this chapter.

The so-called dominance theory of language disorders gradually lost favor in the years following World War II. With respect to reading disability, part of the reason for this was that Orton's rationale for proposing a link with poorly established dominance seemed suspect. In 1960, Zangwill wrote of Orton that

> he linked his observations with a decidedly speculative theory of brain function which few have had the temerity to accept. For these and other reasons, Orton's work has fallen into disrepute, especially among educational psychologists. None the less, Orton deserves great credit for being the first to discuss these problems in a systematic way and to envisage them within the framework of genetic neurology [p. 14].

I shall describe Orton's theory and explain what was wrong with it later on in the chapter.

The dominance theory of stuttering, although initially suggested by Orton (e.g., 1928), was taken up by Orton's colleague Lee Edward Travis, who made it a cornerstone of his influential book *Speech Pathology,* published in 1931. But it, too, lost favor. According to Wendell Johnson, who succeeded Travis as director of the Speech Clinic at Iowa, it lapsed for want of evidence. Describing the outcome of many years of research at Iowa, Johnson (1955) wrote that "the more skilled and meticulous the investigators became, the more they found stutterers to be, from a neurophysiological point of view, like other people [p. 9]." Johnson himself favored the view that stuttering could in most cases be linked to a vicious cycle in communication between the child and his or her parents: The parents admonish the child for what are at first minor inadequacies in speech, and the child then perceives his or her speech as faulty, which then increases the impediment, leading to further admonitions, and so on.

I suspect, however, that objections to Orton's theories were not entirely based on rational or empirical argument. After World War II, it became generally more acceptable, perhaps fashionable, to attribute maladaptive behaviors to emotional or psychological causes rather than to neurological or constitutional ones. This trend may have had to do with observations of the traumatic effects of war. It might also be attributed to the confluence of two streams that were in other respects often in opposition to one another. One was the gradual acceptance of "depth" psychology, and especially of Freudian theory. The other was the coming of age of learning theory and of its application to practical problems. The change in emphasis with respect to theories of stuttering illustrates the trend, although to my knowledge attempts to link stuttering to the vicious cycle proposed by Johnson (1955) have not proven especially convincing or useful.

As for reading disability, evidence on its relation to lateralization has proven variable and at times inconsistent (e.g., Satz, 1976), and is in any event susceptible to methodological problems (e.g., Naylor, 1980), and this has tended to undermine Orton's theory. Besides, anomalies of lateralization could themselves be attributed to psychological or emotional factors. In his classic monograph *The Master Hand*, for instance, Blau (1946) argued that left-handedness was not inherited, but was due to "emotional negativism." As the preceding chapter made clear, I think that this conclusion is certainly wrong, but it does illustrate the nature of the zeitgeist that prevailed after the war.

In spite of this change of emphasis, a number of influential authors, such as Critchley (1970), Benton (1978), and Zangwill (1978a), have continued to maintain a neurological perspective, and this has been reinforced over the past two decades by the emergence of neuropsychology as a discipline. Indeed, it is probably fair to say that the emphasis has swung back in favor of a neuropsychological approach. And although Orton's own particular neurological ideas about reading disability and stuttering have not fared so well, there remain good reasons for supposing that developmental disorders of language can be related to anomalies of lateralization.

One reason is simply that research continues to emphasize that the representation of linguistic skills is strongly lateralized toward the left cerebral hemisphere in most human brains. This in itself provides good grounds for supposing that weak or inconsistent lateralization might lead to disorders of speech and language. A deeper reason, however, is the growing realization, documented in earlier chapters, that lateralization evolved primarily in the context of praxic skills—skills involving sequential planning and organization. As we shall see, developmental dyslexia, stuttering, and developmental dysphasia may all be interpreted, albeit in different ways, as deficits of sequencing.

Another reason stems from the evidence reviewed in the previous chapter that some minority of the population inherit the lack of consistent lateralization. This minority is the RS— subpopulation of Annett's (1972) theory. Both reading disability and stuttering, in particular, have been linked to weak or reversed lateralization, and both appear to exhibit a significant degree of heritability. It seems reasonable to postulate, therefore, that the risk of language disorders is higher among the RS— minority than among the RS+ majority.

This is not a strong claim. That is, I do not propose that all RS— individuals display disorders of language, nor that developmental language problems are linked exclusively to the RS— genotype. For instance, estimates of the incidence of developmental dyslexia vary considerably, depending on the criteria used and to some extent on geography and language, but Bannatyne's (1971) estimate of a 2% incidence for Western countries is probably a representative if slightly conservative figure. At most, then, the odds of an RS— individual being classed as developmentally dyslexic cannot be more than about one in six. Moreover, the RS— genotype per se does not specify the form of language disorder. Some individuals in this category may be prone to stuttering, others to problems of reading and writing, still others to problems of speech, while the majority probably have no difficulties at all. Hence, the dominance theory of language disorders, at least as I have adapted it from the earlier writings of Orton and Travis, is not so much a theory as a unifying framework for discussing a range of disorders.

There is a final disclaimer I wish to make before considering specific disorders in more detail. It is not my intention to provide an exhaustive or even an unbiased review; the literature is simply too vast for that to be possible here. The evidence is also notoriously inconsistent. To some extent, this may be due to variations in how different disorders are defined or in the criteria used to select cases for different groups. Additional problems arise in attempts to relate lateralization to specific disorders. For instance, there is little agreement as to how to measure laterality, especially when it is important to compare individuals or groups (e.g., Richardson, 1976), and the difficulties of both measurement and interpretation are compounded in the comparison of groups of different ability (e.g., Naylor, 1980; A. W. Young & Ellis, 1981). Besides this, noninvasive indices of lateralization, such as those based on dichotic listening or tachistoscopic presentation, typically have rather low reliability, as we saw in Chapter 3, and yet the majority of studies have relied on indices of this sort. The following review is simply an attempt to capture the evidence on developmental dyslexia, stuttering, and to a limited extent developmental dysphasia within the framework of Orton's (1937) dominance theory, suitably updated to take into account recent developments in theory and technology. The reader interested in general treatments of these disorders, or in other approaches to them, should consult other sources.

DEVELOPMENTAL DYSLEXIA

Orton (1925, 1937) argued that lack of cerebral lateralization makes an individual especially prone to left–right confusions and reversals. The victim would thus have special difficulty discriminating left–right mirror images, such as b and d; would tend to confuse reversed sequences of letters, such as was and saw; and would generally have difficulty with scripts that depend on a consistent left–right directionality. According to Orton, the reason for these difficulties with left and right is simply that a bilaterally symmetrical brain, by virtue of its symmetry, must record engrams with opposite left–right orientation in the two cerebral hemispheres. Hence, if an engram corresponding to the letter sequence **ABC** is registered in one hemisphere, then the reversed engram is necessarily registered in the other hemisphere, and corresponds to the sequence **ƆꓭA**. Orton's (1925) diagram illustrating this state of affairs is reproduced in Figure 8.1.

As Zangwill (1960) apparently recognized, this theory does not make sense (Corballis, 1974; Corballis & Beale, 1976). To suppose that one-half of the brain records patterns correctly, while the other half records them incorrectly is scarcely a symmetrical state of affairs. Orton appears to have assumed that it is the right hemisphere that has the misfortune to record patterns as though they were reversed, but why should it be the *right* hemisphere that is thus singled out? Clearly, it has been the victim of an asymmetrical decision. In fact, there is no more reason to expect the two sides of a symmetrical brain to record patterns with opposite orientation than there is to expect a symmetrical camera to register pictures with opposite orientation on each side of exposed film.

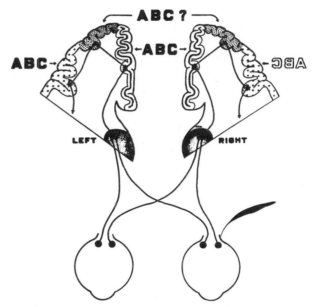

Figure 8.1. Schematic representation of Orton's theory of how the stimulus **ABC** is represented in the brain. The normally dominant image is in boldface and the normally elided one in outline. In those lacking cerebral dominance, the reversed image in the right hemisphere is hypothesized to compete with the correctly oriented one in the left, creating left–right confusion. [Reprinted by permission from S. T. Orton, "Word-blindness" in school children, *Archives of Neurology & Psychiatry*, 1925, *14*, 581–615. Copyright 1925, American Medical Association.]

There is nevertheless a germ of truth in Orton's theory. It is true that a bilaterally symmetrical brain could not tell left from right, in the sense that is required for discriminating left–right mirror images (such as b and d) or for consistently responding with a consistent left–right directionality, as in reading or writing those scripts that are arranged laterally (Corballis & Beale, 1970, 1976; Mach, 1897). A symmetrical person with a symmetrical brain would write backward as often as forward and would have no way of telling whether **YAW** spells *yaw* or *way*. To understand that this is so, let us suppose we have a symmetrical device that does shriek "yaw!" when the stimulus **YAW** appears and "way!" when **WAY** appears. Now imagine everything to be mirror reversed, as in a looking glass. Mirror reflection does not alter the device at all, since it is symmetrical, but it does change **YAW** to **WAY** and vice versa. Hence, we now witness the very same device bellowing "yaw!" to **WAY** and "way!" to **YAW**. Its original behavior must therefore have been impossible, for it is now contradicted by the mirror reflection.

Notice that this account says nothing about how the stimulus is encoded, or even about which "hemisphere" it is registered in. That a symmetrical device could not tell left from right is a truth that applies to any such device, however it encodes, whether or not it has hemispheres. This truth has not always been grasped by those who have encountered it.

Another point that is often misunderstood is that this theory does not imply any perceptual confusion. It is commonly asserted that the dyslexic has a tendency to "see things backward," but this is extremely unlikely to be true. There is no reason why our symmetrical device could not see which side of the stimulus the **Y** or the **W** is on, and point to that side accordingly. What it cannot know is which side to begin on when reading the word. Even Orton (1931) was clear on this point: "I believe that children with these problems *see as others do* but fail to elide completely one of the two antitropic engrams registered as a pattern for later comparison which forms the basis of recognition [p. 166; emphasis added]."

One might argue that the very acts of learning to read and write would create asymmetrical engrams and so instill the necessary structural asymmetry to enable the individual to tell left from right. This might be offset, however, by a built-in tendency for the brain to preserve its structural symmetry despite the recording of asymmetrical experiences. Such a tendency would have adaptive significance in a world in which left and right are essentially equivalent; it would enable an animal to later recognize another animal that had originally appeared in opposite profile or, if attacked from one side, to later cope with attacks from either side. All children, for instance, and not just those classified as dyslexic, have initial difficulty with left–right discriminations and seem naturally to treat mirror-image letters as the same (see Corballis & Beale, 1976, for a review); even adults retain a strong tendency to treat mirror-image shapes as equivalent (Rock, 1973). This symmetrizing tendency may well be accomplished by a process of left–right reversal in the transfer of engrams from one cerebral hemisphere to the other (Corballis & Beale, 1970), and there is evidence that this may involve the anterior commissure, at least in monkeys (Achim & Corballis, 1977).

It follows at least logically from this adaptation of Orton's theory that an individual lacking the usual human predisposition to lateralization might well have special difficulty in learning to read and write scripts that depend on a consistent left–right directionality. Whether this is in fact the explanation for dyslexia, or for any specific category of dyslexia, is another matter. Let us consider first the evidence relating dyslexia to lateralization.

Laterality and Dyslexia

The earlier studies on the relation between laterality and reading disability focused on handedness and eyedness rather than on cerebral lateralization per se, since no simple ways of measuring cerebral lateralization in intact subjects were available. Orton (1937) noted that many of his dyslexic patients were ambidextrous or showed such mixed patterns of laterality as opposite handedness and eye dominance, or came from families with a high incidence of mixed- or left-handedness. Many other studies also revealed a high incidence among developmental dyslexics of mixed laterality (e.g., Eames, 1934; A. J. Harris, 1956; Monroe, 1932; Schonell, 1940, 1941) or of left-handedness (e.g., Dearborn, 1933; Wall, 1945, 1946). Nevertheless, some authors failed to observe any association between reading disability and lateral preferences (e.g., Gates & Bond, 1936; J. Jackson, 1944; L. C. Smith, 1950; L. S. Wolfe, 1941). Vernon (1960) and later Benton (1975), reviewing the evidence, concluded that there was in fact little convincing evidence for any such association.

More recently, investigators have tried to measure cerebral lateralization in dyslexic and normal readers more directly, using the tachistoscopic, dichotic, and dichaptic techniques described in Chapter 3. Naylor (1980) has reviewed this evidence, and the results are summarized in Table 8.1. The results are clearly somewhat inconsistent, which is perhaps not altogether surprising given the rather poor reliability of the measures and the diversity of criteria used to define reading disability. Naylor notes, however, that most if not all the studies are beset by methodological difficulties. For instance, the disabled readers typically performed more poorly than the normal readers, and this makes comparison of laterality scores difficult. In some of the visual studies, the stimuli were exposed for longer intervals for the disabled readers in order to compensate for their poorer performance, but this adds a further contaminating factor. A. W. Young and Ellis (1981) note further methodological difficulties, such as the failure to control fixation in the visual studies, failure to consider the

TABLE 8.1

Summary of Cerebral Lateralization Studies with Reading-Disabled and Control Children[a]

Population studied and authors	Asymmetry (R < L) in relation to control group[b]			
	Greater	Equal	Less	None
Visual half-field studies				
School-younger (8–9 years)				
T. Marcel, Katz, and Smith (1974),				
J. Marcel and Rajan (1975), Olson (1973)			4	
School-older (10 years and older)				
Bouma and Legein (1977), Kershner (1977), Naylor, Lambert, Sassone, and Hardyck (1980), McKeever and Huling (1970), Olson (1973), Yeni-Komshian, Isenberg, and Goldberg (1975)	1	7	1	1
Clinic-older				
McKeever and Van Deventer (1975)		2	1	
Dichotic-listening studies				
School-younger				
Bakker (1973),[c] Bakker, Smink, and Reitsma (1973),[c] Bryden (1970), Darby (cited in Satz, 1976), Leong (1976), Satz, Rardin, and Ross (1971), Sparrow and Satz (1970)	2	3	2	
School-older				
Bakker (1973),[c] Bakker et al. (1973),[c] Bryden (1970), Darby (cited in Satz, 1976), Satz et al. (1971), Sparrow and Satz (1970), Yeni-Komshian et al. (1975), Zurif and Carson (1970)		4	3	1
Clinic-younger				
Witelson (1976)		1		
Clinic-older				
McKeever and Van Deventer (1975), M. E. Thomson (1976), Witelson (1976), Witelson and Rabinovitch (1972)		2	2	
Dichaptic tactile study				
Clinic-younger				
Witelson (1976)		2		
Clinic-older				
Witelson (1976)			2	

[a] From Naylor (1980).

[b] R = right hemisphere; L = left hemisphere.

[c] Monaural testing.

possibility that poor readers might use different strategies, and failure to compare normal and poor readers matched for reading ability rather than for age. Naylor concludes that the studies she reviewed ''do not support the hypothesis that reading disability is related to incomplete or inconsistent cerebral asymmetry [p. 537].'' Notwithstanding the methodological problems, and the fact that a good many of the studies fail to show any difference in lateralization between normal and poor readers, it is still worth noting that studies showing the poor readers to be less lateralized than the normal readers outnumber those showing the reverse result by a ratio of five to one.

Several investigators, seeking anatomical evidence for anomalies of lateralization, have examined computerized brain tomograms in dyslexic patients. Although the relation between anatomical and functional asymmetries may not be entirely straightforward, these studies at least escape the methodological criticisms leveled at studies of perceptual asymmetries. In one investigation, Hier, LeMay, Rosenberger, and Perlo (1978) examined computerized tomograms from 24 dyslexic patients and noted that 10 of them revealed a greater width in the right than in the left parieto-occipital region. This asymmetry is the reverse of that observed in most people (see Chapter 4). Indeed, among normals only 9% of right-handers and 27% of left-handers show the reversed asymmetry (LeMay, 1977—although these values are based on skull measurement, not computerized tomograms), and on the basis of these figures, one would have expected only 3 of the dyslexics to show it. Six of the dyslexics were left-handed. It is also worth noting that, as a group, the dyslexics showed essentially no asymmetry—10 showed the reversed asymmetry, 8 the usual asymmetry, and in the remaining 6, the two sides of the parieto-occipital region were of equal width.

In another study, Rosenberger and Hier (1981) found that 22 of 53 children and young adults with learning disabilities showed the reversed asymmetry of the parieto-occipital region. This corresponds to 42%, and contrasts with the figure of 25% obtained from 100 patients undergoing computerized tomography for other reasons. All the learning-disabled patients had shown deficits in reading of at least two grade equivalents at some point in their school careers, although many had also shown deficits or delays in spoken language. The subjects were selected partly on the basis that their Verbal IQs were substantially below their Performance IQs on the Wechsler scale, and there was a reliable correlation (Pearson's $r = .38$) between the degree of reversed asymmetry and the extent of this discrepancy between Verbal and Performance IQ.

A study by Haslam, Dalby, Johns, and Rademaker (1981), however, fails to confirm the high incidence of reversed parieto-occipital asymmetry; only 3 out of 26 dyslexic boys showed it. In this study, the main difference between the dyslexics and normal readers was that 11 of the dyslexics showed no asymmetry, compared with only 1 of the 8 control subjects—a result that at least conforms to Orton's theory. It is also perhaps worth noting that 13 of the dyslexics revealed so-called soft neurological signs (Touwen & Sporrel, 1979), and 12 had records indicating abnormal pregnancy or delivery, suggesting that their reading difficulties may have been of pathological origin.

Taken overall, the evidence does suggest a higher incidence of reversed asymmetries, or of lack of the usual asymmetries, among dyslexics as compared to normal readers. The evidence is not overwhelming, but it is at least persistent. It does not seem unreasonable to conclude, therefore, that some nontrivial proportion of dyslexics owe their condition to a congenital lack of any predisposition to asymmetry, as postulated by Annett (1972, 1978). It is perhaps also fair to conclude, however, that there is a complementary proportion who are dyslexic for pathological reasons, just as it was concluded earlier that left-handedness is sometimes of pathological origin. That is, although a distinction can be drawn in theory between developmental and acquired dyslexia, it may not always be possible to distinguish them in practice.

Types of Dyslexia

Besides the distinction between developmental and acquired dyslexia, there may be different types within these categories. Some of the conflicting evidence may therefore be due to different criteria used to define dyslexia in different studies, so that there are both qualitative and quantitative differences between groups of dyslexics.

One influential classification scheme has been devised by Boder (1971, 1973), who divides dyslexics into three types. Those she terms *dyseidetic* have difficulties that are primarily spatial. They have difficulty in perceiving words as wholes or in knowing what words look like, but they appear to understand phonological rules and their spelling mistakes are phonetically acceptable. Another type is termed *dysphonetic*. Subjects in this category appear not to have access to phonological rules. Like the deep dyslexics described earlier, they have difficulty knowing how new or unfamiliar words should be pronounced, and they make bizarre, nonphonetic spelling mistakes. Boder also identifies a *mixed* category who appears to exhibit both kinds of difficulty.

In their study of computerized tomograms in dyslexic patients, described in the preceding section, Haslam *et al.* (1981) did attempt to classify the patients as dyseidetic, dysphonetic, or ''nonspecific'' (apparently implying neither dyseidetic nor dysphonetic), but these groups did not appear to differ with respect to cerebral asymmetry. The groups were small, however, and at least half of the subjects in each group showed some evidence of early cerebral pathology. Obrzut (1979) classified dyslexics according to Boder's system and found that the three groups did not differ significantly with respect to the right-ear advantage on a verbal dichotic-listening task. However, normal readers and the dyseidetic group performed significantly more accurately than the dysphonetic and mixed groups, not only on dichotic listening, but also on a test of immediate memory for simultaneous sequences of visual and auditory items.

Despite these negative findings, Pirozzolo (1979) has claimed that cerebral asymmetry may depend on the type of dyslexia. He divided his dyslexic subjects into those he termed *auditory-linguistic,* corresponding roughly to Boder's dysphonetic category, and those he termed *visuospatial,* corresponding to the dyseidetic category; unlike Boder, he had no mixed category. Pirozzolo found that the auditory-linguistic group showed no overall asymmetry in identification of tachistoscopically presented words, whereas normal readers and the visuospatial group showed the usual right-hemifield (left-hemispheric) advantage.

Spatial Problems in Dyslexia

It is the dyseidetic (or visuospatial) dyslexic who most resembles the classic Ortonian dyslexic, given to spatial confusions and reversals. It may therefore seem surprising that this group should appear to show the usual left-hemispheric specialization for language, according to both tachistoscopic and dichotic-listening tests, in seeming contradiction to Orton's theory. Yet there is also a sense in which it is not unexpected, if we define the dyslexic to be one whose deficit is restricted to the processing of script but whose linguistic skills are otherwise normal. Orton's theory of left–right confusions does not appeal specifically to cerebral dominance for language, and it is possible that the asymmetry required to overcome left–right confusions is of a different sort. Indeed, the anomaly that gives rise to the so-called dyseidetic pattern may have to do with directional scanning and eye movements, since these are directly linked to the directional component of script.

Along with this line of reasoning, there is evidence that at least some dyslexics are indeed deficient in making eye movements. While reading, their eye movements are erratic compared to those of normal readers and include frequent regressive movements in the wrong direction (Lesèvre, 1968; Zangwill & Blakemore, 1972). Zangwill and Blakemore suggest that dyslexics are not aware of the direction of their eye movements and simply process the symbols as they are encountered, which accounts for the frequent reversals and poor spelling. They found that their dyslexic patient had normal saccadic eye movements to flashing lights, but Pavlidis (1981) has reported that a group of dyslexics were markedly worse than a control group in tracking a sequence of five lights that lit up in turn from left to right or from right to left. The deficit seems to be one of programmed sequencing rather than one of reacting to visual signals; that is, it is a praxic dysfunction.

J. Stein and Fowler (1981) have proposed that disordered movements may result from unstable ocular dominance. To test this, they measured ocular dominance in dyslexic and normal readers, using a test devised by P. Dunlop (1972). The subject views different slides with each eye. The slides depict scenes that are the same except for a particular feature unique to each eye and are fused in binocular vision. The slides are then moved apart laterally, so that in order to maintain fusion the subject's eyes diverge. This creates a conflict between oculomotor and retinal information, since each retinal image remains stable while the eyes move relative to one another. The result is typically an illusion of movement in which the feature presented uniquely to one eye seems to move while the feature presented to the other eye remains motionless. The eye that registers no movement, and is thus the "reference eye" with respect to the perception of location, is defined as the dominant eye.

Stein and Fowler defined a child as having stable ocular dominance if the same eye was found to be dominant 8 or more times out of 10 trials. By this criterion, 50 out of 80 dyslexic children showed unstable dominance, compared with only 1 out of 80 control children matched for age and intelligence. Moreover, all 50 of the dyslexics belonged to a subgroup of 52 who had been classified as "visual" dyslexics—details are not provided, but it seems reasonable to suppose that this category is comparable to the visuospatial category identified by Pirozzolo (1979) or to Boder's (1971, 1973) dyseidetic category.

It is not altogether clear why unstable ocular dominance would lead to poor control of eye movements. Stein and Fowler suggest that a subject with unstable dominance might be unable to resolve the conflicting oculomotor and retinal information in a consistent fashion during converging eye movements when the subject fixates an object. This would lead to some degree of imprecision in determining where the object is located, and this in turn would affect the precision of saccadic eye movements. This does not seem to me to have much bearing on reading disability, however, since the degree of binocular convergence presumably remains more or less constant while a subject is reading. An alternative explanation for Stein and Fowler's results is simply that unstable ocular dominance might reflect an instability of cerebral control over eye movements; that is, neither hemisphere assumes unique executive control over internally programmed eye movements. Such an account emphasizes again the praxic quality of eye movements involved in reading, and it is precisely this quality that suffers if cerebral dominance is not clearly established.

Dunlop, Dunlop, and Fenelon (1973) used the same technique that Stein and Fowler used to measure ocular dominance, and they also used a more standard test of monocular sighting dominance (i.e., the eye the subject used to view a distant object through a cardboard cylinder). Among 15 dyslexic children, 10 showed crossed dominance according to the Dunlop test, and 8 showed crossed dominance between the writing hand and the eye used for sighting. The comparable figures for 15 normal readers were 1 and 3, respectively. The majority of dyslexics also showed deficits of binocular convergence and stereopsis.

Curiously enough, Stein and Fowler did not observe any relation between crossed dominance and dyslexia in their study, but other authors have. For instance, Orton (1937) claimed that 69 out of 102 cases of dyslexia in his files showed opposite handedness and eye dominance. Denckla (1979), although self-confessedly unsympathetic to Orton's theorizing, records one fact that she has "tried in vain to escape": Nearly two-thirds of her dyslexic patients have been right-handed, right-footed, but *left*-eye dominant. G. M. Stein, Gibbons, and Meldman (1980) classified children as "left movers" or "right movers" depending on which direction they first looked when asked a reflective question, and discovered that the great majority of children classified as disabled learners were right-handed but left movers. Normal children, by contrast, although predominantly right-handed, showed no overall bias in their directional looking.

Crossed control may well underlie some of the directional confusions and scanning difficulties that many dyslexics show. There is evidence that skills learned with one hand tend to be left–right reversed in transfer to the other hand (Milisen & Van Riper, 1939), which may be taken as an instance of a more general principle, referred to earlier, of left–right reversal in the transfer of engrams from one cerebral hemisphere to the other (Corballis & Beale, 1970). Assuming that there is also some transfer of directional habits between hand and eye, this implies that skills learned with one hand might be reversed in transfer to the eye controlled by the opposite hemisphere, and vice versa. In some cases, for instance, dyslexics seem actually better at visually scanning from right to left than from left to right (Orton, 1937; Pavlidis, 1981; Zangwill & Blakemore, 1972), despite the persistent attempts of educators to instill the left-to-right scan. Some dyslexics also show a surprising talent for mirror writing, even though most of their painful experience has been with normally oriented script.

An example of mirror writing, taken from a dyslexic girl, is shown in Figure 8.2. Both her normal writing and her mirror writing are accomplished with the right hand, but she is left-eye dominant according to a monocular sighting test. Notice that her spelling errors tend to be phonologically correct—*sorce* for *source, bodys* for *bodies, ecenchal* for *essential, enormus* for *enormous, sholders* for *shoulders.* Characteristically dyseidetic, she knows what words sound like and she knows phonological rules, but she does not know what words *look* like. These errors are also characteristic of "surface dyslexia," which is one of the categories of acquired dyslexia (K. E. Patterson, 1981).

Not all investigators have found dyslexics to be especially prone to left–right confusions. Although some authors have claimed support for Orton's

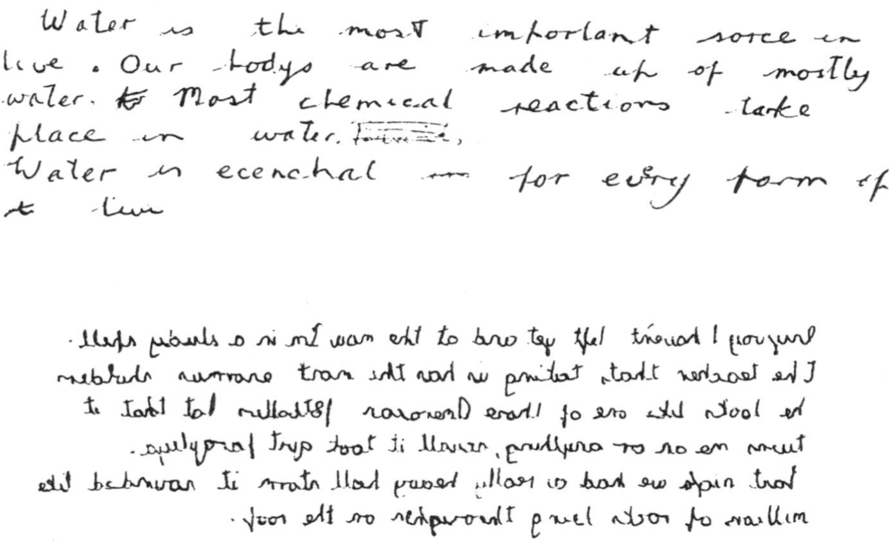

Water is the most important sorce in live. Our bodys are made up of mostly water. Most chemical reactions take place in water. Water is ecenchal ... for every form of live

[mirror writing]

FIGURE 8.2. Examples of normal and mirror writing from an adolescent dyslexic girl.

(1937) observations (e.g., Irwin & Newland, 1977; Sidman & Kirk, 1974; Zangwill, 1960), others have found left–right confusions to play only a minor role (e.g., Belmont & Birch, 1965; Benton & Kemble, 1960; Coleman & Deutsch, 1964; Ginsberg & Hartwick, 1971). It is sometimes suggested that left–right confusions are prominent only among genuine dyslexics referred for remedial treatment, and not among poor readers in the classroom (e.g., Corballis & Beale, 1976; Liberman, Shankweiler, Orlando, Harris, & Berti, 1971), but a study by Fischer, Liberman, and Shankweiler (1978) offers only limited support for this.

These authors studied reversals of letters and letter sequences among two groups of poor readers—one consisting of children diagnosed as dyslexic according to medical and psychoeducational criteria, and the other consisting of children in the lower third of an elementary school class on a standard test of reading. The children were aged between 8 and 10 years. The groups did not differ significantly in the incidence of reversal errors, and such errors were infrequent compared with other sorts of errors in both groups. However, in a special analysis of confusions among the letters *b, d, p,* and *g* (*sic*), the dyslexic group made relatively more left–right confusions—that is, confusions of *b* with *d* and *p* with *g*—whereas the school group confused these letters more indiscriminately. Moreover, among the dyslexic group, there was a correlation between reversals of sequence (e.g., reading *pal* for *lap*) and letter reversals, whereas there was no such correlation among the children from the classroom. Fischer *et al.* conclude that the dyslexics may have failed to establish stable left-to-right habits of scan.

The majority of errors made by both groups, however, were what Fischer *et al.* describe as linguistic errors, reflecting difficulties in phonemic segmentation, phonetic recoding, and mastery of the orthography. This suggests that the majority of the children may have belonged to Boder's dysphonetic and mixed categories, rather than to the dyseidetic category.

Difficulties in establishing an appropriate directional scanning habit should have little influence on perceptual skills other than those involved in reading. Script is more or less unique in that it has a consistent directional aspect. If the world is viewed through a looking glass, printed words are conspicuous by their unfamiliarity, while all else looks more or less ordinary. Slides and photographs are often mirror reversed in error, and it is often difficult or impossible to tell whether this has occurred *unless* there are words or letters represented in the scene. The perception of words, therefore, has a strong directional aspect and is strikingly disrupted if the directionality is reversed. Hence, if dyslexia is indeed a consequence of failure to establish the appropriate directional habit, this would explain the specificity of the deficit; other perceptual and motor skills that are not dependent on consistent directionality would not be affected.

In a sense, then, we might suppose that the normal reader's perception of reversed script somewhat resembles the dyslexic's perception of normal script. I do not of course mean that the dyslexic sees script backward, but simply that the verbally opaque, somewhat hieroglyphic quality of script viewed in a looking glass might give some measure of what the dyslexic has to cope with.

Learning to read and write involves close cooperation between hand and eye. What I am suggesting is that left–right confusions may be especially likely to occur when eye movements are controlled predominantly by one cerebral hemisphere and hand movements by the other. The source of these confusions may be a left reversal in the transfer of directional engrams between hemispheres, and not, as Orton proposed, a reversal in the way the engrams are laid down in the first place. Crossed dominance of hand and eye may well be a manifestation of the RS− genotype discussed in the previous chapter. This is not to say that all RS− individuals will display crossed dominance. Rather, some proportion of individuals lacking a consistent biological predisposition to asymmetry will show it, simply as a consequence of random enviromental influences, or of the "asymmetry lottery."

Sequencing Problems in Dyslexia

Some authors have stressed temporal rather than spatial deficits in developmental dyslexia (e.g., Bakker, 972; Corkin, 1974; Denckla, 1979). This is in some ways a curious emphasis, since script is by its very nature spatial rather than temporal. Many children with reading difficulties seem quite normal with respect to the perception and production of oral speech, which is by contrast sequential and time bound. Hence, if dyslexia is at root a problem of temporal sequencing, one might expect the problems with oral language to exceed those with written language.

This conclusion is somewhat simplistic, however, for although script is spatial, reading is not. Indeed, in some respects, reading places demands on the specialized sequential skills of the left cerebral hemisphere in ways that the perception of speech does not. Reading requires sequential, internally generated eye movements, which have precisely the praxic quality that distinguishes the specialized functioning of the left cerebral hemisphere. In the perceptual analysis of spoken speech, by contrast, the temporal structure is provided by the speaker, not the listener, whose role is relatively passive. It is therefore possible that deficits in left-hemispheric specialization are more readily apparent in reading than in perception of speech.

Notwithstanding this argument, it seems likely that some dyslexics display sequencing deficits unrelated to eye movements. Tallal (1980), for instance, found that reading-impaired children were deficient in the perception of rapid sequences of tones. In this respect, they resembled children classified as developmentally dysphasic (e.g., Tallal & Piercy, 1973, 1974) except that their deficit was less severe. Shankweiler, Liberman, Mark, Fowler, and Fischer (1979) also found poor readers to be deficient in the processing of verbal acoustic information. Again, Denckla, Rudel, and Broman (1981) compared learning-disabled boys with and without reading difficulties and found that the reading-impaired ones were the more prone to what they termed *dysphasic errors*—a slowness in naming and an excess of circumlocutions and paraphrasic errors. The distinction between the dyslexic and the more generally dysphasic may be a fine one, especially in the case of the dysphonetic or auditory-linguistic dyslexic. Indeed, it is conceivable that tests of reading provide a more sensitive index of general language difficulties than do tests of oral comprehension.

Errors are in general much more noticeable in written than in spoken language. We can tolerate mispronunciations, sequential reversals, misplaced phonemes, and so on, more readily than we can tolerate comparable spelling mistakes. I know a woman who always says "aksed" instead of "asked," but her grown-up daughter has never noticed it. Spoonerisms make more immediate sense when spoken than when read; try "hopgrasser," for example. There are several reasons why speech is the more flexible medium. It has evolved over millions of years to become part of our biological heritage, whereas script has developed over only a few thousand years, is still primarily arbitrary and cultural, and must be painstakingly taught. Speech is ephemeral; a mispronounced word is tied to the moment of its utterance, whereas a misspelled word stares back at us for as long as we care to look at it. Finally, speech is acoustic, whereas script has both a visual and a phonetic aspect; a misspelled word both looks wrong and (usually) sounds wrong.

This last point would apply in particular to those scripts—such as those of most Indo-European languages, including English—where symbols are mapped onto sound at the phonemic level, since it is at this level that the temporal acoustic demands are greatest. Chinese logographs, by contrast, represent units of meaning (morphemes) rather than of sounds, although they also incorporate clues as to their pronunciation. In Japan, *Kanji* script consists of Chinese logographs, whereas *Kana* is a sound-based system in which the symbols map onto syllables, not phonemes (Hung & Tzeng, 1981). One would therefore expect the reader prone to dysphonetic dyslexia to have much less difficulty with these scripts than with Western scripts, and there is evidence that this may be so. Makita (1968) has reported that reading disability is very rare in Japan, and Rozin, Poritsky, and Sotsky (1971) claimed striking success in teaching reading-disabled American children to read English represented by Chinese characters.

It should also be noted that both Chinese and Japanese are usually written in vertical columns and read from top to bottom. Left–right directional scanning is therefore not important. Besides this, there is no confusion created either in *Kanji* or in *Kana* by reversing a symbol, since no two symbols are left–right mirror images of one another. There can therefore be no mirror-image confusion in *reading* the symbols. Makita (1968) states that children frequently reverse a symbol in *writing,* but the error is regarded as relatively unimportant and is usually transient. These considerations suggest that Chinese and Japanese scripts would create much less difficulty than Western scripts for the dyseidetic as well as for the dysphonetic reader.

This advantage of Chinese and Japanese scripts is not achieved without cost. The disadvantage of these scripts compared with Western scripts is that they require a great many more symbols, since the number of morphemes and syllables greatly exceeds the number of phonemes. Hence, there are considerable pressures in both China and Japan for reform of the scripts, to reduce the number of symbols. However, the difficulties with ideographic or syllabic scripts are not so much human as technological. People actually have relatively little difficulty memorizing large amounts of information (e.g., words, places, faces), but it is comparatively difficult to construct mechanical or electronic devices for representing, storing, or transmitting the enormous variety of Chinese logographs. From the point of view of the potential dyslexic, it is perhaps unfortunate that scripts should evolve to conform to technological rather than to human needs.

To summarize this section, I have suggested that many people classified as dyslexic, especially those in the dysphonetic or auditory-linguistic category, might be better classified as dysphasic. The deficiency might be fundamentally at the level of precise sequential processing and reflect a deficiency in the left-hemispheric specialization for language, at least as reflected in visual hemifield differences in the identification of words.

Toward a Unified Characterization

The evidence reviewed so far is at least consistent with the view that many dyslexics have failed to establish a skill normally associated with left-cerebral specialization. Some may fail to establish clear cerebral dominance in the control or programming of the directional eye movements required for reading, or there may be an interhemispheric conflict in control of hand and eyes. In some cases, the deficit may be a more general one of sequencing, in which case the victim may reveal deficits in the processing of oral as well as of written language. Although somewhat variable, the evidence suggests on balance that the deficit is more often one of general sequencing than one of left–right confusions. That is, the common thread that seems to underlie a good deal of the evidence is that there is a deficit in some aspect of the praxic skills that normally characterize left-hemispheric specialization.

It is sometimes suggested that dyslexia is due to an inappropriate "right-hemispheric" processing strategy. For instance, Witelson (1977a) found that disabled readers did not show the usual left-handed advantage, implying right-hemispheric specialization, in the recognition of nonsense shapes presented to each hand. She proposed quaintly that dyslexics have "two right hemispheres and none left [p. 309]." Others have made similar proposals (e.g., Kershner, 1977; T. Marcel, Katz, & Smith, 1974; Olson, 1973). For instance, Gordon (1980) argued that dyslexics are "locked into" a right-hemispheric processing mode. He administered a battery of tests involving right-hemispheric skills, such as mental rotation, form completion, and block design, as well as left-hemispheric skills, such as perception of sequences, word production, and digit span. He then devised a Cognitive Laterality Quotient, in which standardized scores on the left-hemispheric tests were subtracted from those on the right-hemispheric tests. This quotient was normalized so that the average score for normal readers was zero. He then found that the average quotient for dyslexics (and their nondyslexic relatives) was nearly two standard deviations above zero, implying a strong bias in favor of right-hemispheric abilities.

The idea that dyslexics may be locked into a right-hemispheric mode of processing is very largely consistent with the theme already developed in this chapter. Notice that Witelson (1977a) did not claim a right-hemispheric *advantage;* rather, she suggested that dyslexics function as though possessing *two* right hemispheres. Again, Gordon's (1980) inference that dyslexics process information in right-hemispheric fashion is based not on tests of actual cerebral lateralization, but on tests thought to reflect the differential specializations of the hemispheres in normal subjects. In Chapter 3, it was suggested that right-hemispheric specialization is achieved by default, as a secondary consequence of left-hemispheric specialization. It might therefore be argued that the "right-hemispheric" cognitive style often detected in dyslexic subjects is due fundamentally to a lack of *left*-hemispheric specialization.

This cognitive style identified by Gordon need not result in reading disability. Gordon found that 90% of first-degree relatives of dyslexic children also showed this right-hemispheric profile of cognitive skills, even though most of them claimed never to have had any reading difficulties themselves. This again illustrates the probabilistic nature of reading disability.

Inheritance of Developmental Dyslexia

There is a good deal of evidence that developmental dyslexia tends to run in families, along with a tendency toward sinistrality or ambilaterality. We have just seen that, in the study by Gordon (1980), the so-called right-hemispheric cognitive style applied, not only to the dyslexic children, but to their nondyslexic relatives as well. Although Gordon did not observe an unusually high incidence of left-handedness among these children or their relatives, Denckla (1979) claimed that the majority of her dyslexic patients with crossed hand–eye dominance had at least one first-degree relative who was left-handed. Zangwill (1960) studied 20 disabled readers, and although he could find little evidence of familial disability, 10 of his cases came from families with an unusually high frequency of sinistrality, and one was also a stutterer. Orton (1930) charted the pedigrees of five dyslexic children, and among three generations of relatives, 19 out of 45 were described as left-handed or ambidextrous—very close to the proportion one would expect if these families belonged to Annett's RS− genotype.

The studies just described emphasize the high incidence of anomalies of lateralization among the families of dyslexics. Other studies emphasize the high incidence of dyslexia itself. For instance, Zangwill (1978a) recorded the family pedigrees of two dyslexic patients, one left-handed and the other predominantly but not exclusively right-handed; both families were remarkable for the high proportion of individuals with reading or spelling difficulties, and also included many who were left-handed or ambidextrous. In another study of 20 dyslexic children, Masland (1976) claimed that 45% of their first-degree relatives were also dyslexic. Naidoo (1972) studied 98 dyslexic boys and, in a cluster analysis of symptoms, identified two subgroups with familial reading and spelling difficulties associated with left-handedness. Hepworth (1971) estimated that in almost 40% of referrals two or more siblings were receiving help for reading problems at the same time.

Perhaps the most extensive and systematic investigation of familial dyslexia is that reported by Omenn and Weber (1978). These authors studied 21 families having multiple members with specific dyslexia. Following Boder (1971), they classified the dyslexic members as dysphonetic, dyseidetic, mixed, or in some cases "uncharacterized." The data are summarized in Figure 8.3. They are remarkable, not only for the high incidence of dyslexia in the families of dyslexics, but also for the fact that the *type* of dyslexia seems to run in families. Omenn and Weber note that their results "are consistent with transmission of autosomal dominant alleles strongly predisposing to dyslexia subtypes [p. 339]." They also observe, however, that their selection criteria would have biased the sample toward a high incidence of familial dyslexia.

Studies of twins suggest that the mechanism of inheritance is indeed genetic. Hallgren (1950) studied six pairs of twins, three dizygotic and three monozygotic. Of the dizygotic pairs, one was concordant and two discordant for dyslexia, whereas in all three monozygotic pairs, both twins were dyslexic. In a larger scale study of twins, Bakwin (1973) reported concordance for dyslexia in 84% of monozygotic twins but in only 29% of dizygotic twins.

But the most explicit claim for a genetic basis for dyslexia has come from S. D. Smith, Pennington, Kimberling, and Lubs (1981). They analyzed genetic linkage in leukocyte cultures derived from peripheral blood taken from a family of 12 kindreds, of whom 8 were dyslexic, covering three generations. Their analysis, they claim, "provides good evidence for an autosomal dominant locus on chromosome 15 responsible for one type of familial dyslexia [p. 3]." Smith *et al.* do not provide evidence on handedness or cerebral lateralization in this family, but in a larger sample of 49 dyslexics, 8 were non-right-handed compared with only 2 out of 30 nondyslexic relatives (S. D. Smith, personal communication, 24 June 1981).

These data conform reasonably well to the proposition that individuals inheriting the lack of consistent lateralization (Annett's RS— genotype) are more prone to developmental dyslexia than are the majority who inherit the usual disposition to asymmetry (RS+ genotype). In at least some cases, dyslexia is clearly a familial condition, and there is evidence that the mechanism of inheritance is very likely genetic. Moreover, some studies show it to be associated with familial sinistrality or other anomalies of lateralization. Yet there are some loose ends, and this simple account in terms of Annett's genetic model may be merely a first approximation. In some studies, for instance, there appears to be a high incidence of anomalous lateralization but little evidence of dyslexia in the families of dyslexic patients, whereas in other studies, the converse pattern holds. For instance, of the 21 present-generation dyslexic children in the study by Omenn and Weber (1978), only 2 were described as left-handed and 1 as ambidextrous. H. W. Gordon (1980) also reported that there was a low incidence of left-handedness in his study of the families of dyslexics, despite

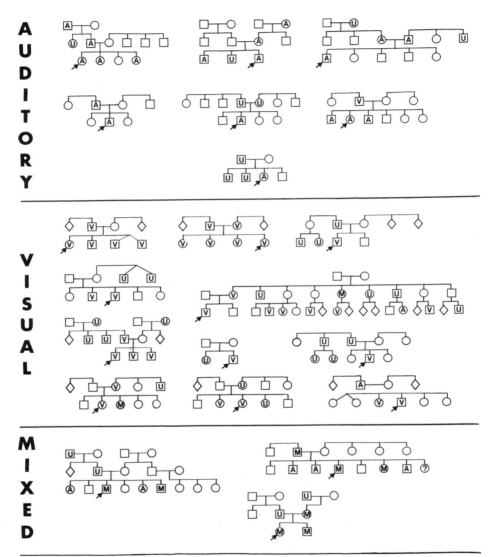

FIGURE 8.3. Pedigrees of 21 families, indicating incidence of auditory (A), visual (V), mixed (M), and unclassified (U) dyslexia. Arrows indicate the proband (child under study). The families are grouped according to whether the predominant pattern is visual, auditory, or mixed. [Adapted from Omenn & Weber, 1978.]

the high proportion of individuals displaying the "right-hemispheric" cognitive profile.

It is therefore possible that the inheritance of dyslexia, and perhaps of various anomalies of lateralization, is more specific than is implied by Annett's model. That is, the genetic locus responsible for one form of dyslexia might be different from that responsible for another. Alternatively, the gene locus inferred by Annett might indeed be the common element, and specificity of the phenotype within families might depend on nongenetic factors. It is perhaps worth noting that S. D. Smith *et al.* (1981), in an analysis of cognitive skills in the families of dyslexics, were unable to classify the dyslexic subjects according to Boder's scheme, and in this respect, their analysis fails to confirm Omenn and Weber's.

Both groups of investigators nevertheless suggest that dyslexia is inherited through the mechanism of an autosomal *dominant* allele, whereas Annett's model implies inheritance through a *recessive* allele. The data on inheritance of dyslexia are not definitive on this point, however, and the high incidence of familial dyslexia in these studies is undoubtedly due in part to bias in the selection of participants. Even so, this discrepancy in postulated mode of inheritance may well turn out to be critical.

Sex Differences in Reading Disability

One puzzling aspect of reading disability is that boys who suffer from it outnumber girls by perhaps as much as four to one (e.g., Critchley, 1975; Orton, 1925). This certainly poses difficulties for any simple theory based on Annett's model. Annett (1979) herself argued that the right shift is expressed more strongly in women than in men, implying that RS+ men are not so well lateralized on the whole as are RS+ women. Even if true, however, this would scarcely explain the extent of the difference between the sexes in the incidence of dyslexia. In any event, as we saw in the previous chapter, there is a good deal of evidence that women on the whole show the *lesser* degree of cerebral lateralization, for both verbal and nonverbal functions (McGlone, 1980), and on these grounds we might actually expect the higher incidence of reading difficulties to be among women.

Although reading difficulties are more common among boys than among girls, true dyslexia may not be. In the study by Omenn and Weber (1978), for instance, there was only a slightly higher incidence of dyslexia among the males than among the females, and the difference was not significant. Similarly, H. W. Gordon (1980) found no sex differences in his studies of dyslexia and cognitive style among the families of dyslexic children. In cases where reading difficulties are demonstrably familial, therefore, there is little evidence for a preponderance of males. This suggests that there may be factors other than the inherited disposition to dyslexia that contribute to the excess number of boys with reading problems. For instance, boys are notoriously more prone to hyperactivity than are girls (e.g., Cantwell, 1977), and it is likely that this contributes to difficulties in learning to read in ways unconnected with dyslexia itself. Moreover, boys are more likely than girls to suffer birth complications, such as anoxia, prematurity, miscarriages, and stillbirths (see Eme, 1979, for a review), which may also explain the slightly higher incidence of left-handedness among boys.

Naylor (1980) reviews evidence that reading-disabled children suffer attentional deficits, but this may well be due in part to the presence among reading-disabled samples of children who might better be classified as hyperactive rather than dyslexic. If the incidence of reading disability among boys is indeed inflated by extraneous factors of this sort, then the more accurate profile of the nature of developmental dyslexia might come, somewhat paradoxically, from the study of reading difficulties in girls rather than in boys. To my knowledge, however, such a strategy has not yet been explored.

Conclusions

This account has been by no means exhaustive. The literature on developmental dyslexia is at once vast and inconsistent, often to the point of contradiction, and it is not possible to capture all facets of it in a work of this kind. My concern has been to review only those studies that bear on the relation between developmental dyslexia and lateralization. Even within this limited domain, the evidence is often in conflict, perhaps partly because different investigators have used different criteria to define developmental dyslexia and partly because there are many different reasons why particular children have difficulty in reading. It is therefore possible to draw only broad general conclusions about the nature of developmental dyslexia.

At this broad level, it does seem reasonable to interpret developmental dyslexia in terms of a deficit in some aspect of the praxic skills that characterize left-hemispheric specialization. In some cases, the deficit may have to do with the control of eye movements in the directional scanning of script, leading to misperception of the sequences of letters or words. In other cases, the deficit may have more to do with a general difficulty in temporal sequencing, creating problems in the mapping of speech sounds onto written symbols. However, the evidence on these praxic disorders may be contaminated by the presence of some children, predominantly boys, who may have reading difficulties due to hyperactivity or to minimal brain pathology sustained at birth. True developmental dyslexia appears to be inherited genetically, and as a first approximation, it seems reasonable to conclude that those who possess Annett's RS−

genotype may be especially vulnerable. It remains possible, however, that the different categories of dyslexia are inherited in more specific fashion.

STUTTERING

Of all the disorders of language, stuttering is most obviously a deficit in sequential production. There is probably no satisfactory single definition of stuttering, however, since manifestations differ somewhat from individual to individual. In general, it may be described as an interference in the utterance of speech that may take the form of hesitations, spasms, or excessive repetition of individual sounds. Some authors regard symptoms of anxiety as part of the disorder; for instance, Despert (1943) describes it as "a neuromuscular dysfunction always associated with neurotic manifestations, and with anxiety always present [quoted in Morley, 1972, p. 429]." The critical question, however, is whether the anxiety is a result or a cause of the stuttering. Orton (1937) maintained that child stutterers who are investigated before secondary neurotic symptoms have developed do not display unusual psychological difficulties. Johnson (1961) could also find no research support for a psychoneurotic basis of stuttering, but at the same time, he rejected a constitutional basis, as we have seen; he described stuttering as "a type of learned behaviour pattern that is perpetuated and reinforced by the stutterer's anxiety or fear of its recurrence [quoted in Morley, 1972, p. 429]."

Stuttering and Cerebral Lateralization

The dominance theory of stuttering was not very precisely specified. Orton and Travis (1929) wrote of it as follows:

> Our anatomic hypothesis in explanation of stuttering is not so clear as that of strephosymbolia or disability in reading. . . . In general, however, it is that lack of establishment of clearcut or unilateral dominance might readily interfere with speech. The speech mechanism is an exceedingly complex integration of simpler reflex patterns, and this integration is probably not only cortical in origin but also entirely resident in the dominant hemisphere, under normal conditions. One of us [Travis, 1927] showed that striking dysintegration can be demonstrated in stuttering. This dysintegration appears as a lack of normal synchronism of various parts of the speech mechanism, as an antagonism between units of the breathing musculature, as tonic and clonic spasm of the muscles concerned, and as other such phenomena, and it seems conceivable that such dysintegration might result from confusion in dominant control [p. 62].

Thus, although Orton and Travis admitted that there was a vagueness to their theory, their final sentence suggests that the critical element may be a conflict, or "confusion," in cerebral control.

A common theme in explanations of stuttering is that it is related to the enforced use of the right hand in children who are naturally left-handed (e.g., Claiborne, 1917). Bryngelson and Rutherford (1937) claim that no fewer than 81% of 127 stutterers with a preference for the left hand had been taught to use the right hand. Orton and Travis (1929) measured muscle potentials in the forearms in response to simultaneous voluntary contractions of the hands and found that among normal right-handers the potential in the right arm usually preceded that in the left arm, whereas the reverse was true among ostensibly right-handed stutterers. Other authors have emphasized left-handedness per se, or mixed laterality, rather than any enforced switch in handedness. For instance, Burt (1950) reported the incidence of stuttering to be higher among left-handers (6.5%) than among right-handers (1.7%), and Morley (1972) measured handedness, footedness, and eyedness and observed higher incidences of uniform left-sidedness and of crossed laterality among stutterers than among a control group, although the differences were not great. The evidence relating stuttering to anomalies of handedness is extremely variable, however, and some studies have revealed no differences between stutterers and normals (Van Riper, 1971).

A study by Jones (1966) on the relation between cerebral dominance and stuttering offers rather direct support for the dominance theory. Jones described four patients referred for neurosurgical treatment of brain injury in the region of the presumed speech areas. All four had suffered from severe stuttering since childhood, but their neurological problems were of recent origin and unrelated to their stuttering. Three were left-handed, but all came from families with a high incidence of left-handedness. The cerebral hemisphere in which speech was represented was determined both pre- and postoperatively by means of the sodium amytal test (Wada & Rasmussen, 1960). Before the operation, this test revealed an unusual state of affairs: In each patient, speech was bilaterally controlled. Following surgery to the damaged hemisphere, each patient was able to speak without stuttering, and the postoperative test of speech representation now revealed unilateral control of speech by the unoperated hemisphere—the right hemisphere in three cases, and the left in the fourth.

There are also reported cases of stutterers regaining fluent speech following surgery to one or the other cerebral hemisphere for the relief of epilepsy (Guillaume, Mazars, & Mazars, 1957; Mazars, Hécaen, Tzavaras, & Merreune, 1970). In two cases, the patients, who were under local anaesthesia, began to speak fluently in the course of the surgery itself. One account reads as follows:

> During this operation, when we were starting the resection of the fusiform gyrus, we were astonished to hear the subject articulate with extraordinary ease and to express his surprise at no longer stuttering. Following this intervention, the patient was entirely

cured of his epileptic attacks and his stammer [Guillaume, *et al.*, 1957, p. 61; cited in translation by Van Riper, 1971, p. 352].

The neurological evidence on the association between stuttering and the bilateral representation of language is not quite so unequivocal as these studies might lead us to believe, however. G. Andrews, Quinn, and Sorby (1972) administered the sodium amytal test to three right-handed stutterers and found that all three had language representation restricted to the left cerebral hemisphere. These three patients showed no signs of cerebral pathology. In a fourth stutterer with evidence of unilateral cerebral insult, however, language was found to be represented bilaterally. In at least some cases, then, the bilateral representation of language in stutterers may be due to cerebral pathology rather than to any congenital lack of cerebral lateralization.

Studies based on more indirect measures of cerebral lateralization also provide some support for the dominance theory of stuttering, although again the findings are not uniformly positive. A number of investigators have reported a somewhat higher incidence of left-ear superiority in the perception of dichotically presented verbal stimuli among stutterers than among nonstutterers (Brady & Berson, 1975; Rosenfield & Goodglass, 1980; Sommers, Brady, & Moore, 1975; Tsunoda & Moriyama, 1972); others, however, have failed to observe this effect (Dorman & Porter, 1975; Herron, 1974; Pinsky & McAdam, 1980; Slorach & Noehr, 1973). Sussman and MacNeilage (1975a) also found no difference between stutterers and nonstutterers on a dichotic-listening test of perceptual asymmetry, but they did find a difference on a dichotic-tracking task thought to be sensitive to lateralization in vocal production. As a group, the stutterers showed no overall asymmetry, whereas normal controls showed evidence of a left-hemispheric advantage. This suggests that it is the lack of lateralization with respect to *production* that is most critical in the etiology of stuttering, as indeed one might expect on a prior grounds.

In a study of visual laterality, Moore (1976) reported that stutterers were more accurate in identifying words flashed tachistoscopically to the left than to the right of fixation, whereas the reverse was true among nonstutterers. Zimmerman and Knott (1974) measured slow potential shifts over the speech-motor areas on both sides of the brain and found larger changes during the moments preceding speech over the left side in 80% of nonstutterers but in only 20% of stutterers (but see Pinsky & McAdam, 1980, for negative results and a critique). Moore and Lang (1977) measured the blocking of alpha waves while subjects read out loud, and found that blocking was more pronounced over the right hemisphere in stutterers but over the left hemisphere in nonstutterers. Shenker (1979) averaged electroencephalographic responses over the left and right hemispheres and recorded greater amplitudes from the left than from the right hemisphere at speech onset and during speech among normal speakers, but among stutterers there was no consistent difference between hemispheres. Finally, F. Wood, Stump, McKeehan, Sheldon, and Proctor (1980) studied regional cerebral blood flow in two stutterers. While the patients were stuttering, activity in Broca's area was greater in the right than in the left hemispheres, whereas activity in Wernicke's area was greater in the left than in the right hemisphere. When the patients were under the influence of haloperidol, which controlled their stuttering, the greater activity in Broca's area shifted to the left hemisphere. These data suggest a conflict in cerebral control of speech between Broca's areas on the left and right.

Taken as a whole, then, the evidence does suggest that a significant proportion of stutterers do display evidence of reduced or anomalous lateralization, especially with respect to vocal production. Some of the studies cited here seem to suggest a reversal of the usual asymmetry rather than a lack of asymmetry among stutterers, although other studies do imply lack of asymmetry. There remains some doubt, therefore, as to precisely how stuttering might be related to anomalous lateralization—whether it is due to motor conflict between hemispheres, or to conflict between motor and perceptual asymmetries, or to inadequate motor control by the right cerebral hemisphere.

In a review of evidence, Rosenfield (1980) has also drawn attention to the high incidence of "altered cerebral laterality" among stutterers. He argues against the idea that stuttering is due to interhemispheric conflict in the control of speech:

> I do not believe that people stutter because language in one hemisphere "fights" language in the other, resulting in dysfluent speech. . . . there is no reason to suspect that bihemispheric language representation should make one stutter any more than it should make one more verbal or even mute. There is no reason to assume that "too much" language in the brain results in dysfluency any more than it will make one talk fast. Again, there are several individuals who do have language in both hemispheres but who do not stutter [p. 180].

Rosenfield argues that stuttering occurs because of a failure to overcome certain reflexes of the larynx that are incompatible with the actions required in speech. As evidence for this, he notes that stuttering is eliminated or reduced if the stutterer sings, or speaks with an accent, or speaks while inhaling instead of exhaling. All of these activities alter the pattern of laryngeal reflexes. Rosenfield suggests that those who are genetically predisposed toward abnormalities in cerebral dominance might have special difficulty in overcoming these reflexes. Yet this theory seems susceptible to the very criticisms that Rosenfield leveled against the conflict theory: It does not explain why those with bilateral representation of language, or with other anomalies of lateralization, should fail to overcome conflicting reflexes or why only some such individuals are affected.

What is clear from Rosenfield's account, however, is that speaking does require precise and intricate programming of the phonatory musculature in relation to reflexive adjustments of the larynx. It is this precise temporal sequencing that seems most fundamentally to characterize left-hemispheric specialization (see Chapter 3). Perhaps it is simply a question of having the neural mechanisms involved in this sequencing confined within a limited neural region, so that imprecision is not introduced by the integration of activity over a wide cortical area. Hence, programming is more precise if confined within a hemisphere than if spread between hemispheres. This argument is still essentially probabilistic, however. That is, the conditions for precise sequential control are more likely to be met if the brain develops functionally under the control of a consistent lateralizing influence than if allocation of functions to one or the other hemisphere is random. The lack of a consistent lateralizing influence need not result in failure of sequential programming, however; it all depends again on the "asymmetry lottery."

This is not a theory of stuttering, since it does not specify at all how the programming of speech works or how it may be disrupted. As Rosenfield remarks, "it is presumptuous for anyone to offer a truth-finding mechanism describing the etiology of stuttering [p. 180]." The point is simply that failure of cerebral lateralization may result in stuttering for the very reason that cerebral lateralization evolved in the first place, to ensure precise programming of sequential acts.

Inheritance of Stuttering

It is commonly asserted that Lewis Carroll was born left-handed and that his stuttering was brought about by an enforced switch in handedness (e.g., De Keyser, 1973), although M. Gardner (1965) has pointed out that there is little direct evidence for this. Stuttering, however, does appear to have been a familial condition in the Dodgson family, and according to one biographer, 8 of the 11 Dodgson children were afflicted by it (J. P. Wood, 1966).

Van Riper (1971) summarizes a great many studies indicating that stutterers are more likely than nonstutterers to have close relatives who stutter. In terms of scale, perhaps the most impressive survey is that of Bryant (1917), who reported that 50% of 20,000 stutterers had stuttering relatives. In other studies, the percentages ranged from 24% (Abe, 1934) to 80% (Trommer, 1929). Most of the earlier studies did not report figures for control groups of nonstutterers. Wepman (1939), however, found that 71% of 127 stutterers reported other cases of stuttering in their immediate families compared with only 13% of controls, and comparable data are reported by Bryngelson (1935) and Pierce and Lipcon (1959).

There is therefore overwhelming evidence that stuttering is at least as often as not a familial condition, which is consistent with the view that it is genetically inherited. It does not of course prove this, and it is perhaps worth noting a curious observation by Dalton and Hardcastle (1977): These authors sent questionnaires to 186 adult stutterers, 74 of whom reported that other members of their families also stuttered. Only two of these gave heredity as the cause of their stuttering!

There is evidence that concordance for stuttering is much higher in monozygotic twins than in dizygotic twins, further suggesting a genetic basis. According to Nelson, Hunter, and Walter (1945), when stuttering occurs in one monozygotic twin it also occurs in the other twin 9 times out of 10, but when it occurs in one dizygotic twin, it occurs in the other only once out of 15 times. Luchsinger (1944) makes a similar claim. There is also evidence, however, that the incidence of stuttering is considerably higher among twins than among the singly born. Estimates of the proportion of twins who stutter range from 1.9% (Graf, 1955), which is about twice the proportion in the general population, to as high as 20% (Nelson et al., 1945).

Stuttering is about three times as prevalent among men as among women (Van Riper, 1971). Contrary to what was the case with developmental dyslexia, however, this imbalance seems to apply to cases of stuttering that are clearly familial. Thus, G. Andrews and Harris (1964) reported that 19.1% of the fathers of stutterers also stuttered, compared with only 5.8% of mothers; again, 20% of brothers also stuttered, compared with only 8.4% of sisters. Orton (1930) also documents the families of four stutterers; of the total of 12 stutterers, 8 were male.

Conclusions

Again, the evidence reviewed here is broadly consistent with Annett's theory. Stuttering seems clearly to be a praxic disorder, and it often appears to be associated with a lack of the usual left-cerebral dominance in the control of speech. It is also clearly an inherited condition, at least in a sizable proportion of cases. One might therefore reasonably conclude that people belonging to Annett's RS− genotype might be more prone to stuttering than those who are genotypically RS+.

Again, however, it should be emphasized that Annett's model provides a framework rather than a theory. In particular, it provides no explanation for the striking preponderance of male stutterers over female ones. Hence, although the RS− genotype might provide a constant predisposing factor, there must be some other influence that causes boys to be affected more often than girls. Van Riper (1971) argues that this must have to do with a less stable neuromuscular control system for speech in boys than in girls during the early years of life. He concludes, charmingly, as follows: ''Even as the male has a constitutional predisposition to have a phallus, it is perhaps possible that he also has a minor one to have an unstable system for coordinating sequential speech in his early years [p. 48].''

DEVELOPMENTAL DYSPHASIA

Systematic research on developmental dysphasia is of fairly recent origin, and there appears to have been little direct attempt to relate it to cerebral lateralization. It is a somewhat more general category than either developmental dyslexia or stuttering; indeed, stuttering is sometimes included as a particular manifestation of it (e.g., Rapin & Wilson, 1978), and I have already suggested that those described as dyslexic in some studies may have been better described as more generally dysphasic. Nevertheless, developmental dysphasia is worthy of at least brief consideration, if only because it again seems most aptly described as a defect of sequencing, suggesting a failure to develop normal left-hemispheric specialization.

Lowe and Campbell (1965) showed that dysphasic children did not differ from normal children in their ability to perceive rapid pairs of sounds as two sounds rather than one, but were significantly worse than normals in their ability to determine which of two rapidly presented tones occurred first. The problem was thus not so much one of temporal acuity as one of temporal ordering, or sequencing. There is also evidence that dysphasic children are deficient in the processing of visual (Poppen, Stark, Eisenson, Forrest, & Wertheim, 1969) and tactile (Kracke, 1975) sequences, suggesting that the impairment is a general one of serial ordering, transcending particular sensory modalities.

This point is disputed by Tallal and Piercy (1973), who found that dysphasic children were not impaired in judging the serial order of pairs of visual stimuli. They argue that the deficit is primarily an auditory one, although Tallal, Stark, and Curtiss (1976) have shown a close relation among dysphasics between deficits of auditory perception and deficits in the production of elementary speech sounds. Tallal and Piercy (1978) go so far as to suggest that the auditory deficit might be a necessary and sufficient cause of developmental dysphasia. They note, for instance, that dysphasic children seem well able to learn a form of communication that bypasses the auditory modality, suggesting that the deficit is not primarily linguistic. But this point is disputed in turn by Cromer (1978), who argues for a more linguistic approach and suggests that the deficit is primarily one of hierarchical structuring.

Overriding these disputes is the question of whether developmental dysphasia can even be considered a unitary disorder or whether, as Rapin and Wilson (1978) maintain, it can take different forms that differ in etiology.

Some of the disputes may therefore be resolved in terms of a more fine-grained classification. But notwithstanding these issues, it seems generally true that dysphasic children are impaired on exactly the sorts of tasks that characterize the specialized capacities of the left cerebral hemisphere, be they linguistic or sequential. The evidence is of course indirect, since there appears to have been little attempt to directly assess cerebral lateralization in dysphasics, although Zangwill (1978b) notes that incomplete cerebral lateralization may well be the critical factor.

CONCLUSIONS

Although the evidence relating developmental disorders of language to anomalies of lateralization has not always been consistent, and has in some cases been criticized on methodological grounds, it has remained extraordinarily persistent. For instance, in a recent report mentioned briefly in the previous chapter, Geschwind and Behan (1982) claim that the incidence of learning disabilities (rather imprecisely defined as dyslexia and stuttering) was over 10 times more frequent among the strongly left-handed than among the strongly right-handed, and 3 times more frequent among the relatives of the left-handers. This study further highlights the heritability of developmental dyslexia and stuttering documented earlier. It therefore seems plausible to conclude that these disorders reflect the inherited lack of consistent lateralization, as postulated by Annett (1972, 1978). Presence of RS− genotype is scarcely prescriptive, however. Some RS− individuals display no disorders of language at all, and the patterns of disorders that do occur show considerable variability. This variability is also characteristic of left-handers themselves, as we have already seen. The common element, however, appears to be a deficit of sequencing, whether manifest in the control of lateral saccadic eye movements or of vocal speech. The erratic, regressive eye movements of the dyslexic may be regarded, in a sense, as a kind of visual stutter.

These conclusions are not very different from those reached by S. T. Orton over half a century ago. Despite the skepticism and even hostility with which Orton's theories have been treated over the years, many of his basic observations have been corroborated. In particular Annett's theory of lateralization, developed quite independently of considerations about disorders of language, seems to provide some theoretical justifications for Orton's views. It is only at the general level, however, that Orton's theorizing is upheld. There can no longer be any justification for taking his neurological theory of dyslexia seriously, since it does not make sense; moreover, Orton almost certainly overemphasized the role of left–right confusions in dyslexia, perhaps failing to observe that even normal readers make left–right confusions, especially when first learning to read. Problems of sequencing probably outweigh spatial problems, but they are more directly linked to deficiencies in left-hemispheric specialization. To my knowledge, there is little evidence that left–right confusions are related to the degree of cerebral lateralization.

It should also be clear from the evidence reviewed in this chapter that appealing to the inherited lack of consistent lateralization is neither diagnostic nor prescriptive. Many individuals in Annett's RS− category—perhaps the majority, in fact—suffer no obvious disorders of language. Moreover, lack of lateralization per se does not specify the nature of the disorder. Other factors, such as the sex of the subject or a familial history of some particular disorder, must also be taken into account. Indeed, in terms of Annett's model, the apparent specificity of language disorders within families is something of a puzzle. It is possible that the model itself is too simple and that different aspects of lateralization are under the control of different genetic loci, each perhaps operating in the manner proposed by Annett.

One theme that emerges from the evidence reviewed in this chapter is that there is indeed a class of developmental disorders of language and speech that are congenital rather than due to emotional maladjustment or to faulty teaching methods. Naidoo (1981) notes for instance that the incidence of reading disability has remained apparently constant despite marked changes in the techniques used to teach children to read:

> It is remarkable that whatever method is in use, most children learn to read, to spell and to write without undue difficulty. Yet teaching methods are often blamed for the poor progress of some children. Whole-word and "Look-and-Say" methods are condemned by the adherents of phonic methods, and phonics are regarded as stumbling blocks by those concerned primarily with reading for meaning. It is interesting to note that two large surveys in geographically different parts of the country [England] and separated by more than 30 years should find such similar percentages (approximately 4%) of children with severe retardation (Rutter, Tizard, & Whitmore, 1970; Schonell, 1942). Dyslexic children, whose reading and spelling problems are not the direct result of low intelligence, emotional disturbance, sensory deficiency or environmental disadvantage, have been and continue to be identified irrespective of which teaching method is in vogue [p. 263].

Similarly, the incidence of stuttering appears to have remained roughly constant despite different theories about it and despite changes in remedial techniques. Bloodstein (1975) summarizes the results of surveys ranging in time from 1893 to 1975 and concludes that the incidence has remained roughly constant over that interval. He also notes that the incidence appears to be slightly but consistently higher in Europe, where it is about 1% or more, than in America, where it tends to be slightly under 1%.

The idea that these disorders are congenital has often been resisted, perhaps because it provides a convenient excuse not to attempt remediation. If a child is diagnosed as congenitally dyslexic, for instance, there may seem an implicit suggestion that nothing can be done about it. On the other hand, it seems preferable to accept a congenital basis for a disorder than to lay the blame falsely on parents or teachers, or to seek some defect of motivation or character in the child. In any event, as Naidoo (1981) points out, to assert that dyslexia is a congenital problem does not mean that teaching methods are unimportant:

> The opposite is true especially for those to whom reading is a problem. But to blame a method of teaching or even a lack of method for the difficulties of dyslexic children is to overlook and misunderstand the nature of the problem [p. 264].

The reader interested in remedial techniques for dyslexic children is referred to Naidoo's article for a succinct, sensible discussion. She reviews the various methods that have been proposed, going back to those advocated by Orton (1937) and his colleagues, and notes that there are more similarities than differences among these methods. For instance, all tend to emphasize a phonic approach and to avoid the "whole-word" methods, and all pay attention to the details of the reading process. Normal readers can usually discover the rules for phoneme-to-grapheme correspondence for themselves, whatever the teaching method, but with the dyslexic child, nothing can be taken for granted. Given that reading is very largely automatic for the normal reader, it is difficult to appreciate precisely what the basic processes involved are and what it is that the dyslexic cannot do. In trying to help the dyslexic, therefore, it seems necessary to dissect the reading process in as minute a fashion as possible and to provide tuition in even the most elementary components.

The great variety of techniques for helping stutterers overcome their problem has been reviewed by Van Riper (1971). Although there is no miracle cure among them, many forms of treatment offer some relief, even if it is often only transitory. In some cases, the treatment is not so much a cure as a method of coping or of circumventing the problem.

A final point to stress is that, although developmental disorders of speech and language may be regarded as congenital and may be inherited genetically, they are not pathological in the sense that they imply disease or brain injury. The stutterer or the dyslexic may be deviant, but they are typically not intellectually or physically inferior to others. As I noted at the beginning of the chapter, our culture has been greatly enriched by such stutterers as Lewis Carroll and W. Somerset Maugham and by such dyslexics as Hans Christian Andersen and Auguste Rodin (or the actress Susan Hampshire). Such examples should help victims of these disorders understand their capricious nature and have confidence in their other abilities.

This has not been a tidy chapter, and I can only plead that the evidence itself is untidy. There has been much battering at the gate, but no breakthrough. Yet despite the inconsistencies in the evidence and the sense of un-resolved issues, there seems also a thread of continuity. In fact, our conception of disorders of speech and language has not altered greatly since the 1920s and 1930s, when Orton's theories held sway. Evidence relating these disorders to anomalies of cerebral lateralization has never been strong, but it has been extraordinarily persistent. Ideas about the cerebral representation of skills related to language will no doubt continue to provide a framework for research in this area.

9 Overview

For centuries, there has been dispute over whether human laterality, and in particular human handedness, is fundamentally biological or whether it is shaped by culture. At this particular point in history, it seems inescapable that the predominant pattern of right-handedness and left-hemispheric specialization for linguistic and praxic skills is essentially biological and programmed into the structure of the nervous system. This pattern appears to be universal among human beings of all cultures, in all parts of the globe, throughout recorded history, and possibly extending back in prehistory to our hominid ancestors of perhaps 2 or 3 million years ago. Precursors to human laterality can be detected in newborn infants, well before environmental or cultural influences could plausibly be thought to exert any systematic bias. In the normal course of events, and among the majority of people, environment or culture play only a minor role in modifying or reinforcing this biological disposition to lateralization.

Although this pattern of laterality is universally human, it is also uniquely human. The closest parallels come, not from other primates or even mammals, but from birds. Several species of parrot are predominantly left-footed, and several passerine birds show left-cerebral control of singing, but to my knowledge, there is no evidence for consistent footedness and cerebral lateralization in the same avian species. Although the *pattern* of laterality is unique to human beings, however, there is no reason to suppose that it depends on principles that differ from those underlying other asymmetries. The contingencies that led to the evolution of human cerebral lateralization may have been similar to those that led to the evolution of the lateralized control of bird song in passerine birds, for instance. A common ingredient in different manifestations of lateralization is that many of them have to do with manipulation or with the internal generation of sequentially organized actions. Skills with this property may be termed *praxic* skills.

I have argued that different manifestations of laterality in human beings are based on a single, biologically determined lateralizing influence. This influence determines the left-cerebral specialization for praxic skills, including language skills, so that right-hemispheric specializations are achieved by default. It need not follow, however, that there is a perfect correlation between handedness and cerebral lateralization, or between different aspects of cerebral lateralization, or between these asymmetries and other asymmetries, such as eye dominance, footedness, or preference for one or the other ear. One reason for this is simply that environmental influences may affect different manifestations of laterality differently. Presumably, the environment or culture in which people live is more likely to influence their cerebral lateralization. In other words, the phenotype need not reflect the unity of the genotype.

Following Annett, I have also argued that, in some minority of the human population, the lateralizing influence is absent, or is somehow denied expression, perhaps because of the presence of a recessive genetic allele. Among this minority, different manifestations of laterality are dictated independently and at random. The proportion of this so-called RS− minority would be higher among left-handers than among right-handers. This explains why different manifestations of laterality are more highly correlated among right-handers than among left-handers. The great majority of right-handers are right-footed, right-eyed, and right-eared, and have language and praxic skills represented predominantly in the left cerebral hemisphere, whereas left-handers show much more varied and unpredictable patterns of asymmetry. Another way to express this is to say that RS− individuals are less well buffered against environmental influences.

Laterality appears to embody those very talents that set us apart from other species—namely, our sophisticated abilities to communicate and to manipulate. It is of course tempting to stretch this theme further and to conclude that laterality provides the key to other uniquely human characteristics, such as consciousness or self-awareness. As I pointed out in Chapter 1, this conclusion goes beyond the evidence. If cerebral lateralization were a criterion for consciousness or self-awareness, we should have to grant these qualities to passerine birds and deny them to those left-handed humans who do not display the usual pattern or degree of cerebral asymmetry. In any event, Griffin (1976) has argued cogently for continuity of mental experience between human beings and other animals, so there must be serious question as to whether consciousness or even self-awareness are uniquely human qualities. Clearly, it will not do to appeal to cerebral asymmetry as evidence that they are, for this is merely a circular argument.

It seems likely then that laterality is a relatively surface manifestation of the evolution of language and other praxic skills. The most that might be attributed to the lack of consistent lateralization is an increased risk of certain specific disorders of language. Even this mild conclusion is somewhat in doubt, given the rather inconclusive nature of the evidence reviewed in Chapter 8. In any event, the very specificity of these disorders suggests that they have little to do with the deeper strata of language or cognition. Indeed, many stutterers and even dyslexics appear to possess superior literary, intellectual, or creative talents. Moreover, left-handers as a group appear to be no less intelligent, accomplished, or creative than are right-handers, even though they are not so clearly or consistently lateralized. These considerations make it very difficult to argue that cerebral lateralization was a necessary precursor to the evolution of language or higher cognitive functions.

I do not mean to imply that human laterality is unimportant. Laterality per se is not unique to human beings, but the particular pattern of right-handedness and left-cerebral specialization is distinctively human. It permeates our culture in manifold ways. As any left-hander will testify, such common objects as scissors, corkscrews, gearshifts, playing cards, saxophones, bowling balls, even books and magazines are constructed with an asymmetry designed for the convenience of right-handers. Our methods of writing are appropriate for right-handers, and left-handers are typically forced to improvise their own techniques for achieving legibility—some, like Leonardo da Vinci, evidently give up the struggle and write backward. It is customary, even obligatory, to carry out certain gestures, such as shaking hands, swearing on the Bible, or making the sign of the cross, with one's right hand even if one is left-handed.

Laterality even permeates the visual arts in subtle ways. Drawings and paintings change appearance, often quite dramatically, when left and right are reversed. Wolfflin (1941) argued that pictures are "read" from left to right, so that the diagonal that runs from bottom left to top right is seen as ascending and the other as descending. Arnheim (1974) notes that this and other asymmetries cannot be due to the actual eye movements made in scanning a picture, since viewers explore scenes in irregular fashion, without systematically directional movements. The left–right anisotropy may well be due in part to the experience of having learned to read from left to right; Van der Meer (1959) reports that it is more pronounced in university students than in those of limited education, but she also notes that it appears rather suddenly at age 15 years, which is curiously late if it depends on experience with reading and writing. It is also possible that the anisotropy reflects cerebral asymmetry. Gaffron (1950) notes that objects to the right in a picture tend to be more conspicuous than those to the left, and relates this to a left-cerebral dominance for vision. This is scarcely plausible, however, since the evidence suggests that the *right* hemisphere is typically the more specialized for perceptual processing (see Chapter 3).

In spite of the insidious and subtle ways in which laterality has infiltrated the human environment, I do not think that these environmental asymmetries have played a significant role in shaping human laterality. These asymmetries are the products of human laterality, not the cause. The natural world, as distinct from the artificial world created by human beings, does not exhibit consistent asymmetries, at least at the gross level at which it impinges upon our sense organs. For most of our evolutionary history, therefore, we have evolved as fundamentally symmetrical creatures, at least with respect to those structures involved with interactions with the natural environment. Handedness and cerebral asymmetry evolved in connection with internal programming demands rather than as adaptations to environmental asymmetries. Or so I have argued.

Laterality also raises important biological questions. It is by no means clear how left–right asymmetries are encoded biologically. The view I have taken in this book is that the principles governing different manifestations of asymmetry, from handedness to the asymmetries of the internal organs, are fundamentally the same. In this respect, human laterality is not unique. I have suggested, moreover, that there may be a common source of left–right information governing various manifestations of asymmetry and that this source is extrachromosomal. The genes may govern the expression of asymmetry, but they do not carry the directional information itself.

It is tempting to conclude that this source of asymmetry that enables differential specialization on the two sides of the body is related to the fundamental asymmetry of living molecules. Indeed, there seems no other possible source of left–right information. Thus, Wolpert (1978) writes:

> It is hard to see how [left–right asymmetry] could be specified at a cellular or tissue level other than by an underlying molecular or structural asymmetry that could bias the setting up of a gradient across the plane of bilateral symmetry. There are several macromolecules and organelles associated with cell structure and motility that have both a left–right asymmetry—and a polarity. Examples of these include the protein actin, microtubules that are built out of protein subunits, and cilia, which contain microtubules. It is attractive to think that the handedness of these structures underlies left–right asymmetry. The problem is to translate this structural asymmetry at the molecular or organelle level to the cellular and tissue level. My colleague, Dr. J. Lewis, has suggested that under certain conditions, the unwinding of a helix could exert an asymmetric force that might provide a directed bias to a structure like the heart or gut, which develops asymmetrically. Another possibility, suggested by Dr L. Honig, is that the molecular asymmetry could cause asymmetric transport [p. 325].

If laterality does indeed relate to molecular asymmetry, can we relate molecular asymmetry in turn to some yet more basic asymmetry? In 1957, Madam Chien-

Shiung Wu carried out a famous experiment demonstrating a fundamental asymmetry in the emission of electrons from the nucleus of cobalt-60, a highly radioactive isotope of cobalt. This confirmed an earlier suggestion by two other physicists of Chinese extraction, T. D. Lee and G. N. Yang, that the so-called weak interactions between subatomic particles do not obey the Law of Conservation of Parity. Up until that time, it had generally been thought that the laws of nature were essentially indifferent to left and right, and would remain the same if reflected in a mirror. Madam Wu's experiment demonstrated that this was not the case, at least with respect to weak interactions. (For a popular account, the reader is referred to Gardner, 1967.)

More recently, it has been demonstrated that fundamental asymmetries also exist at the level of electromagnetic interactions (e.g., Henley, 1969), and in the words of Ulbricht (1975, p. 313), this means that the nonconservation of parity has penetrated "into the heart of chemistry." It thus becomes reasonable to suppose that molecular asymmetries in biological tissue might well have come about because of a more fundamental asymmetry in the elementary forces of nature. Now, any asymmetrical influences at the molecular level are tiny compared with those at the level of weak interactions and are, for most practical purposes, negligible. However, such effects may not be negligible over the extremely long periods presumed to be involved in the evolution of life. Letokhov (1975) has calculated a minuscule difference in energy levels between molecular enantiomers (i.e., molecules that are mirror images of one another) and writes:

> The difference is quite negligible and cannot show itself in chemical reactions of any achievable duration. The chain of biochemical reactions of self-reproducing organisms the duration of which can reach 10^8–10^9 years is an exception to this rule. During such a long period of time even a relative difference in reaction rates of the order of 10^{-16} is quite sufficient for full selection of either of two stereoisomeric forms of all the amino acids that occur in animate nature [p. 275].

In short, there may be a common thread linking human laterality, other morphological asymmetries in plants and animals, the molecular asymmetries in living tissue, and the nonconservation of parity in the fundamental laws of physics.

For the most part, research on human laterality has focused on the human aspect, emphasizing discontinuity and human uniqueness. Attempts have been made to find all-embracing conceptions of laterality in terms of the dimensions of human consciousness or modes of thought. One might term this a *horizontal* strategy for elucidating the nature of laterality. Implicit in the strategy is the belief that there is some unitary dimension, or polarity, that characterizes human laterality, if only we could articulate it. I do not believe, however, that this approach is likely to yield further dividends.

The alternative strategy is *vertical,* emphasizing continuity with other species and other disciplines. This strategy has developed only recently, and in my view, it offers the greater prospects for advancing our understanding of laterality, if only because it has been relatively ignored. The study of laterality is too complex to be left to psychologists; it is truly interdisciplinary, involving psychology, neurology, physiology, biology, anthropology, and even biochemistry and nuclear physics, if the speculations outlined here have any validity. I am aware of my own inadequacy in covering all these aspects of this very far-reaching problem, but I hope to have at least steered it toward some new goals.

References

Aaron, P. G., Baxter, C. F., & Lucenti, J. Developmental dyslexia and acquired alexia: Two sides of the same coin? *Brain & Language*, 1980, *11*, 1–11.

Abe, N. Statistical observation of stutterers at the time of their draft in the army. *Naval Surgeon Magazine* (Japan), 1934, *23*, 232–234.

Achim, A., & Corballis, M. C. Mirror-image equivalence and the anterior commissure. *Neuropsychologia*, 1977, *15*, 475–478.

Akelaitis, A. J. Studies on the corpus callosum. II: The higher visual functions in each homonymous field following complete section of the corpus callosum. *Archives of Neurology & Psychiatry*, 1941, *45*, 788–796.

Akelaitis, A. J. The study of gnosis, praxis and language following section of the corpus callosum and anterior commissure. *Journal of Neurosurgery*, 1944, *1*, 95–102.

Alajouanine, J. Aphasia and artistic realization. *Brain*, 1948, *71*, 229–241.

Albert, M. C. A simple test of visual neglect. *Neurology*, 1973, *23*, 658–664.

Albert, M. L., & Obler, L. *The bilingual brain*. New York: Academic Press, 1978.

Anderson, A. L. The effect of laterality localization of focal brain lesions on the Wechsler-Bellevue subtests. *Journal of Clinical Psychology*, 1951, *7*, 149–153.

Anderson, J. R. Arguments concerning representations for mental imagery. *Psychological Review*, 1978, *85*, 249–277.

Andrews, G., & Harris, M. *The syndrome of stuttering*. London: Heinemann, 1964.

Andrews, G., Quinn, P. T., & Sorby, W. A. Stuttering: An investigation into cerebral dominance for speech. *Journal of Neurology, Neurosurgery, & Psychiatry*, 1972, *35*, 414–418.

Andrews, R. J. Aspects of language lateralization correlated with familial handedness. *Neurospsychologia*, 1977, *15*, 769–778.

Andrews, R. J., Mench, J., & Rainey, C. Right–left asymmetry of response to visual stimuli in the domestic chick. In D. J. Ingle, R. J. W. Mansfield, & M. A. Goodale (Eds.), *Advances in the analysis of visual behavior.* Cambridge, Mass.: MIT Press, 1980.

Annett, M. A model of the inheritance of handedness and cerebral dominance. *Nature,* 1964, *204,* 59–60.

Annett, M. The binomial distribution of right, mixed, and left handedness. *Quarterly Journal of Experimental Psychology,* 1967, *19,* 327–333.

Annett, M. The growth of manual preference and speed. *British Journal of Psychology,* 1970, *61,* 545–558.

Annett, M. The distribution of manual asymmetry. *British Journal of Psychology,* 1972, *63,* 343–358.

Annett, M. Handedness in families. *Annals of Human Genetics,* 1973, *37,* 93–105.

Annett, M. Handedness in the children of two left-handed parents. *British Journal of Psychology,* 1974, *65,* 129–131.

Annett, M. Hand preference and the laterality of cerebral speech. *Cortex,* 1975, *11,* 305–328.

Annett, M. A coordination of hand preference and skill replicated. *British Journal of Psychology,* 1976, *67,* 587–592.

Annett, M. *A single gene explanation of right and left handedness and brainedness.* Coventry, England: Lanchester Polytechnic, 1978.

Annett, M. Family handedness in three generations predicted by the right shift theory. *Annals of Human Genetics (London),* 1979, *42,* 479–491.

Annett, M. The genetics of handedness. *Trends in Neurosciences,* 1981, *3,* 256–258.

Annett, M., & Turner, A. Laterality and the growth of intellectual abilities. *British Journal of Educational Psychology,* 1974, *44,* 37–46.

Arnheim, R. *Art and visual perception* (The New Version). Berkeley, Ca.: Univ. of California Press, 1974.

The Art of Putting the Brain to Work. *Los Angeles Times,* November 6, 1977, Pt. 4, p. 20.

Atkinson, J., & Egeth, H. Right hemisphere superiority in visual orientation matching. *Canadian Journal of Psychology,* 1973, *27,* 152–158.

Bachofen, J. J. [*Myth, religion, and mother right*] (R. Manheim, Trans.). London: Routledge & Kegan Paul, 1967. (*Das Mutterecht* was originally published in Stuttgart in 1861.)

Badal, J. Contribution a l'étude des cécités psychiques: Alexie, agraphie, hémianopsie inférieure, trouble du sens de l'espace. *Archives d'Opthalmologie,* 1888, *8,* 97–117.

Baddeley, A. D., Ellis, N. C., Miles, T. R., & Lewis, V. J. Developmental and acquired dyslexia: A comparison. *Cognition,* 1982, *11,* 185–199.

Bakan, P. Birth order and handedness. *Nature,* 1971, *229,* 195.

Bakan, P. Left handedness and alcoholism. *Perceptual & Motor Skills,* 1973, *36,* 514.

Bakan, P. Left handedness and birth order revisited. *Neuropsychologia,* 1977, *15,* 837–839.

Bakan, P. Why left-handedness? *Behavioral & Brain Sciences,* 1978, *2,* 279–280.

Bakan, P., Dibb, G., & Reed, P. Handedness and birth stress. *Neuropsychologia,* 1973, *11,* 363–366.

Bakker, D. J. *Temporal order in disturbed reading.* Rotterdam: Rotterdam Univ. Press, 1972.

Bakker, D. J. Hemispheric specialization and stages in the learning-to-read process. *Bulletin of the Orton Society,* 1973, *23,* 15–27.

Bakker, D. J., Smink, T., & Reitsma, P. Ear dominance and reading ability. *Cortex,* 1973, *9,* 301–312.

Bakwin, H. Reading disability in twins. *Developmental Medicine & Child Neurology,* 1973, *15,* 184–187.

Baldwin, J. M. Origin of right or left handedness. *Science,* 1890, *16,* 247–248.

Baldwin, J. M. *Mental development in the child and the race* (3rd ed.). New York: Macmillan, 1906.

Bannatyne, A. *Language, reading and learning disabilities.* Springfield, Ill.: Thomas, 1971.

Barnsley, R. H., & Rabinovitch, M. S. Handedness: Proficiency versus stated preference. *Perceptual & Motor Skills*, 1970, *30*, 343–362.

Barsley, M. *Left-handed man in a right-handed world*. London: Pitman, 1970.

Barsley, M. *Left-handed people*. North Hollywood: Wilshire, 1976.

Basser, L. S. Hemiplegia of early onset and the faculty of speech with special reference to the effects of hemispherectomy. *Brain*, 1962, *85*, 427–460.

Bateson, G. *Mind and nature: A necessary unity*. Glasgow: Fontanta/Collins, 1980.

Battersby, W. S., Bender, M. B., Pollack, M., & Kahn, R. L. Unilateral "spatial agnosia" ("inattention") in patients with cerebral lesions. *Brain*, 1956, *88*, 675–686.

Bell, D. Speech functions of the thalamus inferred from the effects of thalamotomy. *Brain*, 1968, *91*, 619–638.

Belmont, L., & Birch, H. G. Lateral dominance, lateral awareness, and reading disability. *Child Development*, 1965, *36*, 57–71.

Benson, D. F., Sheramata, W. A., Bouchard, R., Segarra, J., Price, D., & Geschwind, N. Conduction aphasia. *Archives of Neurology*, 1973, *28*, 339–346.

Benton, A. L. Constructional apraxia and the minor hemisphere. *Confinia Neurologica*, 1967, *29*, 1–16.

Benton, A. L. Differential behavioral effects in frontal lobe disease. *Neuropsychologia*, 1968, *6*, 53–60.

Benton, A. L. Visuoconstructive disability in patients with cerebral disease: Its relationship to side of lesion and aphasic disorder. *Documenta Opthalmologica*, 1973, *34*, 67–76.

Benton, A. L. Developmental dyslexia: Neurological aspects. In W. J. Friedlander (Ed.), *Advances in neurology* (Vol. 7). New York: Raven, 1975.

Benton, A. L. Some conclusions about dyslexia. In A. L. Benton & D. Pearl (Eds.), *Dyslexia*. New York: Oxford Univ. Press, 1978.

Benton, A. L. Visuoperceptive, visuospatial, and visuoconstructive disorders. In K. M. Heilman & E. Valenstein (Eds.), *Clinical neuropsychology*. Oxford: Oxford Univ. Press, 1979.

Benton, A. L. The neuropsychology of facial recognition. *American Psychologist*, 1980, *35*, 176–180.

Benton, A. L., Hannay, H. J. & Varney, N. R. Visual perception of line direction in patients with unilateral brain disease. *Neurology*, 1975, *25*, 907–910.

Benton, A. L., & Kemble, J. D. Right–left orientation and reading disability. *Psychiatria et Neurologia* (Basel), 1960, *139*, 49–60.

Bever, T. G., & Chiarello, R. J. Cerebral dominance in musicians and non-musicians. *Science*, 1974, *185*, 537–539.

Bhalla, V., & Kaul, S. S. Occipital hair whorl as a racial criterion. *American Journal of Physical Anthropology*, 1968, *29*, 99–104.

Bingley, T. Mental symptoms in temporal lobe epilepsy and temporal lobe glioma. *Acta Psychologica Neurologica Scandinavia*, 1958, *33*, Suppl. 120.

Bisiach, E., Capitani, E., Luzzatti, C., & Perani, D. Brain and conscious representation of reality. *Neuropsychologia*, 1981, *19*, 543–552.

Bisiach, E., & Luzzatti, C. Unilateral neglect of representational space. *Cortex* 1978, *14*, 129–133.

Bisiach, E., Luzzatti, C., & Perani, D. Unilateral neglect, representational schema, and consciousness. *Brain*, 1979. *102*, 609–618.

Blau, A. *The master hand*. Research Monograph No. 5. New York: American Orthopsychiatric Association, 1946.

Bloodstein, O. *A handbook on stuttering* (Rev. Ed.). Chicago: National Easter Seal Society for Crippled Children and Adults, 1975.

Blumstein, S., & Cooper, W. E. Hemisphere processing of intonation contours. *Cortex*, 1974, *10*, 146–158.

Blumstein, S. Goodglass, H., & Tartter, V. The reliability of ear advantage in dichotic listening. *Brain & Language*, 1975, *2*, 226–236.

Bodamer, J. Die Prosop-Agnosie (die Agnosie des Physiognomieerkennens). *Archiv für Psychiatrie and Nervenkrankheit*, 1941, *179*, 6–53.

Boder, E. Developmental dyslexia: Prevailing diagnostic concepts and a new diagnostic approach. In H. Myklebust (Ed.), *Progress in learning disabilities*. New York: Grune & Stratton, 1971.

Boder, E. Developmental dyslexia: A diagnostic approach based on three atypical reading–spelling patterns. *Developmental Medicine & Child Neurology*, 1973, *15*, 663–687.

Bogen, J. E. The other side of the brain I: Dysgraphia and dyscopia following cerebral commissurotomy. *Bulletin of the Los Angeles Neurological Society*, 1969, *34*, 73–105. (a)

Bogen, J. E. The other side of the brain II: An appositional mind. *Bulletin of the Los Angeles Neurological Society*, 1969, *34*, 135–162. (b)

Bogen, J. E., & Bogen, G. M. The other side of the brain III: The corpus callosum and creativity. *Bulletin of the Los Angeles Neurological Society*, 1969, *34*, 191–220.

Bogen, J. E., & Vogel, P. J. Treatment of generalized seizures by cerebral commissurotomy. *Surgical Forum*, 1963, *14*, 431.

Boklage, C. E. The sinistral blastocyst: An embryological perspective on the development of brain-function asymmetries. In J. Herron (Ed.), *Neuropsychology of left-handedness*. New York: Academic Press, 1980.

Borod, J. C., & Caron, H. S. Facedness and emotion related to lateral dominance, sex and expression type. *Neuropsychologia*, 1980, *18*, 237–242.

Borowy, T., & Goebel, R. Cerebral lateralization of speech: The effects of age, sex, race, and socioeconomic class. *Neuropsychologia*, 1976, *14*, 363–370.

Bosshardt, H. G., & Hörmann, H. Temporal precision of coding as a basic factor of laterality effects in the octention of verbal auditory stimuli. *Acta Psychologica*, 1975, *39*, 1–12.

Bouma, H., & Legein, C. P. Foveal and parafoveal recognition of letters and words by dyslexics and average readers. *Neurophsychologia*, 1977, *15*, 69–80.

Bowers, D., & Heilman, K. M. Pseudoneglect: Effects of hemispace on a tactile line bisection task. *Neuropsychologia*, 1980, *18*, 491–498.

Boyd, W. *Emile for today: The Emile of Jean Jacques Rousseau*. London: Heinemann, 1956.

Brackenridge, C. J. Secular variation in handedness over ninety years. *Neuropsychologia*, 1981, *19*, 459–462.

Bradshaw, J. L. Right hemisphere language: Familial and non-familial sinistrals, cognitive deficits and writing hand position in sinistrals, and concrete–abstract imageable–non-imageable dimensions in word recognition. A review of related issues. *Brain & Language*, 1980, *10*, 172–188.

Bradshaw, J. L., & Nettleton, N. C. The nature of hemisphere specialization in man. *Behavioral & Brain Sciences*, 1981, *4*, 51–63.

Bradshaw, J. L., Nettleton, N. C., & Taylor, M. J. Right hemisphere language and cognitive deficit in sinistrals? *Neuropsychologia*, 1981, *19*, 113–132.

Brady, J. P., & Berson, J. Stuttering, dichotic listening, and cerebral dominance. *Archives of General Psychiatry*, 1975, *32*, 1449–1452.

Brain, R. Speech and handedness. *Lancet*, 1945, *249*, 837–841.

Braun, A. W., & Myers, R. E. Central nervous system findings in the newborn monkey following severe *in utero* partial asphyxia. *Neurology*, 1975, *25*, 327–338.

Broca, P. Remarques sur le siège de la faculté du langage articulé, suivies d'une observation d'aphémie (perte de la parole). *Bulletins de la Société Anatomique*, 1861, *6*, 330–357.

Broca, P. Sur le siège de la faculté du langage articulé. *Bulletins de la Société d'Anthropologie de Paris*, 1865, *6*, 377–393.

Browne, T. *Pseudodoxia epidemica, or Enquiries into very many received tenets, and commonly presumed truths.* London, printed by T. H. for Edward Dod, 1646.

Bruens, J. H., Gastaut, H., & Giove, G. Electroencephalographic study of the signs of chronic vascular insufficiency of the sylvin region in aged people. *EEG and Clinical Neurophysiology,* 1960, *12,* 283–295.

Bruner, J. S. *Processes of cognitive growth: Infancy* (vol. 3). Heinz Werner Memorial Lecture Series. Worcester, Mass.: Clark Univ. Press, 1968.

Brust, J. C. M. Music and language: Musical alexia and agraphia. *Brain,* 1980, *103,* 367–392.

Bryant, F. A. Influence of heredity in stuttering. *Journal of Heredity,* 1917, *8,* 46–47.

Bryden, M. P. Tachistoscopic recognition, handedness, cerebral dominance. *Neuropsychologia,* 1965, *3,* 1–8.

Bryden, M. P. Laterality effects in dichotic listening. Relations with handedness and reading ability in children. *Neuropsychologia,* 1970, *8,* 443–450.

Bryden, M. P. Speech lateralization in families: A preliminary study using dichotic listening. *Brain & Language,* 1975, *2,* 201–211.

Bryden, M. P. Response bias and hemispheric differences in dot localization. *Perception & Psychophysics,* 1976, *19,* 23–28.

Bryden, M. P. Measuring handedness with questionnaires. *Neuropsychologia,* 1977, *15,* 617–624.

Bryden, M. P. Sex differences in brain organization: Different brains or different strategies? *Behavioral & Brain Sciences,* 1980, *3,* 230–231.

Bryden, M. P., & Allard, F. Visual hemifield differences depend on typeface. *Brain & Language,* 1976, *3,* 191–200.

Bryden, M. P., & Allard, F. Dichotic listening and the development of linguistic processes. In M. Kinsbourne (Ed.), *Asymmetrical function of the brain.* Cambridge: Cambridge Univ. Press, 1978.

Bryden, M. P., & Sprott, D. A. Statistical determination of degree of laterality. *Neuropsychologia,* 1981, *19,* 571–581.

Bryngelson, B. Sidedness as an etiological factor in stuttering. *Journal of Genetic Psychology,* 1935, *47,* 204–217.

Bryngelson, E., & Rutherford, B. A comparative study of laterality of stutterers and nonstutterers. *Journal of Speech Disorders,* 1937, *2,* 15–16.

Buchanan, A. Mechanical theory of the predominance of the right hand over the left; or, more generally, of the limbs of the right side over the left side of the body. *Proceedings of the Philosophical Society of Glasgow,* 1862, *5,* 142–167.

Buckingham, H. W. Jr., & Kertesz, A. A linguistic analysis of fluent aphasia. *Brain & Language,* 1974, *1,* 29–42.

Bureš, J., Burešová, O. & Křivánek, J. An asymmetric view of brain laterality. *Behavioral & Brain Sciences,* 1981, *4,* 22–23.

Burnett, S. A., Lane, D. M., & Dratt, L. M. Spatial ability and handedness. *Intelligence,* 1982, *6,* 57–68.

Burt, C. *The backward child.* New York: Appleton, 1937.

Burt, C. *The backward child* (3rd ed.). London: Univ. of London Press, 1950.

Cain, P., & Wada, J. A. An anatomical asymmetry in the baboon brain. *Brain, Behavior, & Evolution,* 1979, *16,* 222–226.

Cameron, R., Currier, R., & Haeper, A. Aphasia and literacy. *British Journal of Disorders of Communication,* 1971, *6,* 161–163.

Campbell, R. Asymmetries in interpreting and expressing a posed facial expression. *Cortex,* 1978, *14,* 327–342.

Cantwell, D. Hyperkinetic syndrome. In M. Rutter & L. Hersov (Eds.), *Child psychiatry.* Oxford: Blackwell, 1977.

Caplan, D. On the cerebral localization of linguistic issues surrounding deficit analysis and functional localization. *Brain & Language,* 1981, *14,* 120–137.

Caplan, P. J., & Kinsbourne, M. Baby drops the rattle: Asymmetry of duration of grasp by infants. *Child Development,* 1976, *47,* 532–534.

Carey, S., & Diamond, R. From piecemeal to configurational representation of faces. *Science,* 1977, *195,* 312–314.

Carmon, A., & Bechtold, H. P. Dominance of the right cerebral hemisphere for stereopsis. *Neuropsychologia,* 1969, *7,* 29–39.

Carmon, A., & Nachshon, I. Ear asymmetry in perception of emotional non-verbal stimuli. *Acta Psychologica,* 1973, *37,* 351–357.

Carter, R. L., Hohenegger, M., & Satz, P. Handedness and aphasia: An inferential method for determining the mode of cerebral speech specialization. *Neuropsychologia,* 1980, *18,* 569–574.

Carter-Saltzman, L. Mirror twinning: reflection of a genetically mediated embryological event? *Behavior Genetics,* 1979, *9,* 442–443.

Carter-Saltzman, L. Biological and sociocultural effects on handedness: Comparison between biological and adoptive families. *Science,* 1980, *209,* 1263–1265.

Chamberlain, H. D. The inheritance of left handedness. *Journal of Heredity,* 1928, *19,* 557–559.

Chan, K. S. F., Hsu, F. K., Chan, S. T., & Chan, Y. B. Scrotal asymmetry and handedness. *Journal of Anatomy,* 1960, *94,* 543–548.

Chaney, R. B., & Webster, J. C. Information in certain multidimensional sounds. *Journal of the Acoustical Society of America,* 1966, *40,* 449–455.

Chase, R. A. In discussion following B. Milner: Brain mechanisms suggested by studies of temporal lobes. In C. H. Millikan & F. L. Darley (Eds.), *Brain mechanisms underlying speech and language.* New York: Grune & Stratton, 1967.

Chaurasia, B. D., & Goswami, H. K. Functional asymmetry in the face. *Acta Anatomica,* 1975, *91,* 154–160.

Chesher, E. Some observations concerning the relation of handedness to the language mechanism. *Bulletin of the Neurological Institute of New York,* 1936, *4,* 556–562.

Chi, J. E., Dooling, E. C., & Gilles, F. H. Left-right asymmetries of the temporal speech areas of the human fetus. *Archives of Neurology,* 1977, *34,* 346–348.

Chiarello, C. A house divided? Cognitive functioning with callosal agenesis. *Brain & Language,* 1980, *11,* 128–158.

Chomsky, N. *Syntactic structures.* The Hague: Mouton, 1957.

Chomsky, N. Review of *Verbal Behavior* by B. F. Skinner. *Language,* 1959, *35,* 26–58.

Chomsky, N. *Aspects of a theory of grammar.* Cambridge, Mass.: MIT Press, 1965.

Christensen, I. P., & Gregory, A. H. Further study of an auditory illusion. *Nature,* 1977, *268,* 630.

Claiborne, J. H. Stuttering relieved by reversal of manual dexterity. *New York Medical Journal,* 1917, *105,* 577–581; 619–621.

Clark, M. M. *Left-handedness.* London: Univ. of London Press, 1957.

Clark, W. E. Le Gros. Description of cerebral hemispheres of the brain of the gorilla. *Journal of Anatomy,* 1927, *61,* 467–475.

Cohen, A. Hand preference and developmental status of infants. *Journal of Genetic Psychology,* 1966, *108,* 337–345.

Cole, J. Paw preference in cats related to hand preference in animals and man. *Journal of Comparative and Physiological Psychology,* 1955, *48,* 137–140.

Cole, J. Laterality in the use of the hand, foot, and eye in monkeys. *Journal of Comparative & Physiological Psychology,* 1957, *50,* 296–299.

Coleman, R. L., & Deutsch, C. P. Lateral dominance and right–left discrimination: A comparison of normal and retarded readers. *Perceptual & Motor Skills*, 1964, *19*, 43–50.

Collins, R. L. On the inheritance of handedness: II. Selection for sinistrality in mice. *Journal of Heredity*, 1969, *60*, 117–119.

Collins, R. L. The sound of one paw clapping: An inquiry into the origins of left handedness. In G. Lindzey, D. D. Thiessen (Eds.), *Contributions to behavior-genetic analysis—the mouse as a prototype*. New York: Meredith Corporation, 1970.

Collins, R. L. When left-handed mice live in right-handed worlds. *Science*, 1975, *187*, 181–184.

Collins, R. L. Origins of the sense of asymmetry: Mendelian and non-Mendelian models of inheritance. *Annals of the New York Academy of Sciences*, 1977, *299*, 283–305.

Collins, R. L. In the beginning was the asymmetry, even when it was null: A propositional framework for a general theory of the inheritance of asymmetry. *Behavioral & Brain Sciences*, 1978, *2*, 290–291.

Coltheart, M. Deep dyslexia: A right-hemisphere hypothesis. In M. Coltheart, K. E. Patterson, & J. C. Marshall (Eds.), *Deep dyslexia*. London: Routledge & Kegan Paul, 1980.

Coltheart, M., Patterson, K. E., & Marshall, J. C. (Eds.), *Deep dyslexia*. London: Routledge & Kegan Paul, 1980.

Comte, A. J. Recherches anatomies-physiologiques, relative à la prédominance du bras droite sur le bras gauche. Paris, chez l'auteur, 1828. (No. 7 in a volume of pamphlets with binder's title: *Mémoires. Physiologie. Système Nerveux*. ''Mémoire lue à l'Academie des Sciences le 25 février 1828.'')

Conrad, K. Uber aphasiche Sprachtsorungen bei Hiruverlezten Linkshanderm. *Nervenarzt*, 1949, *20*, 148–154.

Cooper, W. E. The analytic/holistic distinction applied to the speech of patients with hemispheric brain damage. *Behavioral & Brain Sciences*, 1981, *4*, 68–69.

Corballis, M. C. The left–right problem in psychology. *Canadian Psychologist*, 1974, *15*, 16–33.

Corballis, M. C. Is left-handedness genetically determined? In J. Herron (Ed.), *Neuropsychology of left-handedness*. New York: Academic Press, 1980. (a)

Corballis, M. C. Laterality and myth. *American Psychologist*, 1980, *35*, 284–295. (b)

Corballis, M. C., Anuza, T., & Blake, L. Tachistoscopic perception under head tilt. *Perception & Psychophysics*, 1978, *24*, 274–284.

Corballis, M. C., & Beale, I. L. Bilateral symmetry and behavior. *Psychological Review*, 1970, *77*, 451–464.

Corballis, M. C., & Beale, I. L. *The psychology of left and right*. Hillsdale, N. J.: Erlbaum, 1976.

Corballis, M. C., & Morgan, M. J. On the biological basis of human laterality: I. Evidence for a maturational left–right gradient. *The Behavioral & Brain Sciences*, 1978, *1*, 261–269.

Coren, S., & Porac, C. Fifty centuries of right-handedness: The historical record. *Science*, 1977, *198*, 631–632.

Coren, S., Porac, C., & Duncan, P. Lateral preference behaviors in preschcool children and young adults. *Child Development*, 1981, *52*, 443–450.

Corkin, S. Serial-order deficits in inferior readers. *Neuropsychologia*, 1974, *12*, 347–354.

Coryell, J., & Michel, G. F. How supine postural preferences of infants can contribute towards the development of handedness. *Infant Behavior & Development*, 1978, *1*, 245–257.

Craig, J. D. Asymmetries in processing auditory nonverbal information. *Psychological Bulletin*, 1979, *86*, 1339–1349.

Crichton-Browne, J. On the weight of the brain and its component parts in the insane. *Brain*, 1880, *2*, 42–67.

Critchley, M. *The parietal lobes*. London: Arnold, 1953.

Critchley, M. Parietal syndromes in ambidextrous and left-handed subjects. *Zentralblatt für Neurochirurgie*, 1954, *14*, 4–16.

Critchley, M. *Developmental dyslexia.* London: Heinemann, 1964.

Critchley, M. Aphasiology nomenclature and definitions. *Cortex,* 1967, *3,* 3–25.

Critchley, M. *The dyslexic child.* London: Heinemann, 1970.

Critchley, M. Developmental dyslexia: Its history, nature, and prospects. In D. D. Duane & M. B. Rawson (Eds.), *Reading, perception and language.* Baltimore, Md.: York Press, 1975.

Cromer, R. F. The basis of childhood dysphasia: A linguistic approach. In M. A. Wyke (Ed.), *Developmental dysphasia.* London: Academic Press, 1978.

Crovitz, H. F., & Zener, K. A group-test for assessing hand and eye dominance. *American Journal of Psychology,* 1962, *75,* 271–276.

Cunningham, D. J. *Contribution to the surface anatomy of the cerebral hemispheres, with a chapter upon cranio-cerebral topography by Victor Horsley.* Dublin: Royal Irish Academy, 1892.

Cunningham, D. J. Right-handedness and left-brainedness. The Huxley lecture for 1902. *Journal of the Royal Anthropological Institute of Great Britain and Ireland,* 1902, *32,* 273–296.

Curry, F. K. W. A comparison of left-handed and right-handed subjects on verbal and nonverbal listening tasks. *Cortex,* 1967, *3,* 343–352.

Curry, F. K. W., & Rutherford, D. R. Recognition and recall of dichotically presented verbal stimuli by right- and left-handed persons. *Neuropsychologia,* 1967, *5,* 119–126.

Dahlberg, G. Genotypic asymmetries. *Proceedings of the Royal Society of Edinburgh,* 1943, *63,* 20–31.

Dalton, P., & Hardcastle, W. J. *Disorders of fluency and their effects on communication.* London: Arnold, 1977.

Damasio, A. R., Castro-Caldas, A., Grosso, J., & Ferro, J. Brain specialization for language does not depend on literacy. *Archives of Neurology,* 1976, *33,* 300–301.

Damasio, A. R., Damasio, H., & Chui, H. C. Neglect following damage to frontal lobe or basal ganglia. *Neuropsychologia,* 1980, *18,* 123–132.

Danforth, C. H. Resemblance and difference in twins. *Journal of Heredity,* 1919, *10,* 399–409.

Darley, F. L., Brown, J. R., & Swenson, W. M. Language changes after neurosurgery for parkinsonism. *Brain & Language,* 1975, *2,* 65–69.

Dart, R. A. The predatory implemental technique of *Australopithecus. American Journal of Physical Anthropology,* 1949, *7,* 1–38.

Dart, R. A. (with D. Craig) *Adventures with the missing link.* London: H. Hamilton, 1959.

Darwin, C. A biographical sketch of an infant. *Mind,* 1877, *2,* 285–294.

Davidoff, J. B. Hemispheric differences in the perception of lightness. *Neuropsychologia,* 1975, *13,* 121–124.

Davidoff, J. B. Hemispheric sensitivity differences in the perception of colour. *Quarterly Journal of Experimental Psychology,* 1976, *28,* 387–394.

Davis, A. E., & Wada, J. A. Hemispheric asymmetries in human infants: Spectral analysis of flash and click evoked potentials. *Brain & Language,* 1977, *4,* 23–31.

Davis, L., Foldi, N. S., Gardner, H., & Zurif, E. B. Repetition in the transcortical aphasias. *Brain & Language,* 1978, *6,* 226–238.

Davis, T. A. Reversible and irreversible lateralities in some animals. *Behavioral & Brain Sciences,* 1978, *2,* 291–293.

Dax, M. Lesions de la moitié gauche de l'encéphale coïncident avec l'oubli des signes de la pensée. *Gazette Hebdomadaire de Médecine et de Chirurgie* (Paris), 1865, *2,* 259–260.

Day, J. Right-hemisphere language processing in normal right-handers. *Journal of Experimental Psychology: Human Perception & Performance,* 1977, *3,* 518–528.

Dearborn, W. F. Structural factors which condition special disability in reading. *Proceedings of the 57th Annual Session of the American Association for Mental Deficiency,* 1933, *38,* 266–283.

De Bono, E. *The use of lateral thinking*. London: Cape, 1967.

De Bono, E. *Lateral thinking: A textbook of creativity*. London: Ward Lock Educational, 1970.

De Bono, E. *Teaching thinking*. London: Temple Smith, 1976.

Dejerine, J. Sur un cas de cecité verbale avec agraphie suivi d'autopsie. *Mémoires de la Société de Biologie*, 1891, *3*, 197–201.

Dejerine, J. Contribution a l'étude anatomo-pathologique et clinique des différents variétés de cécité verbale. *Mémoires de la Société de Biologie*, 1892, *4*, 61–90.

De Keyser, J. The stuttering of Lewis Carroll. In Y. Lebrun & R. Hoops (Eds.), *Neurolinguistic approaches to stuttering*. The Hague: Mouton, 1973.

de Mortillet, G. *Le préhistorique antiquité de l'homme*. Paris: Reinwald, 1882.

de Mortillet, G. Formations des variétés, albinisme et gauchissement. *Bulletin de la Société d'Anthropologie de Paris*, Séance de 3 Juillet, 1890.

Denckla, M. B. Childhood learning disabilities. In K. M. Heilman & E. Valenstein (Eds.), *Clinical neuropsychology*. New York: Oxford Univ. Press, 1979.

Denckla, M. B., Rudel, R. G., & Broman, M. Tests that discriminate between dyslexic and other learning-disabled boys. *Brain & Language*, 1981, *13*, 118–129.

Denenberg, V. H. Hemispheric laterality in animals and the effects of early experience. *Behavioral & Brain Sciences*, 1981, *4*, 1–21.

Dennis, M., & Kohn, B. Comprehension of syntax in infantile hemiplegics after cerebral hemidecortication: Left hemisphere superiority. *Brain & Language*, 1975, *2*, 472–482.

Dennis, M., & Whitaker, H. A. Language acquisition following hemidecortication: Linguistic superiority of the left over the right hemisphere. *Brain & Language*, 1976, *3*, 404–433.

Dennis, M., & Whitaker, H. A. Hemispheric equipotentiality and language acquisiton. In S. J. Segalowitz & F. Gruber (Eds.), *Language development and neurological theory*. New York: Academic Press, 1977.

Dennis, W. Early graphic evidence of dextrality in man. *Perceptual & Motor Skills*, 1958, *8*, 147–149.

De Renzi, E. Hemispheric asymmetry as evidenced by spatial disorders. In M. Kinsbourne (Ed.), *Asymmetrical function of the human brain*. New York: Academic Press, 1978.

De Renzi, E., & Faglioni, P. The relationship between visuo-spatial impairment and constructional apraxia. *Cortex*, 1967, *3*, 327–342.

DeSante, D. F. *An analysis of the fall occurrences and nocturnal orientations of vagrant wood warblers (Parulidae) in California*. Unpublished doctoral dissertation, Stanford University, 1973.

Descartes, R. *Oeuvres de Descartes: VIII. Principia philosophiae*. Paris: Leopold Cerf, 1905. (Originally published, 1644).

Despert, J. L. Stuttering in children. *Nervous Child*, 1943, *2*, 79–207.

Deutsch, D. An auditory illusion. *Nature*, 1974, *251*, 307–309.

Deutsch, D. Pitch memory: An advantage for the left-handed. *Science*, 1978, *199*, 559–560.

Deutsch, D. The octave illusion and the what–where connection. In R. S. Nickerson (Ed.), *Attention and performance VIII*. Hillsdale, N.J.: Erlbaum, 1980.

Dewson, J. H. III. Some behavioral effects of removal of superior temporal cortex in the monkey. In D. Chivers & J. Herbert (Eds.), *Recent advances in primatology*. New York: Academic Press, 1978.

Dimond, S., & Beaumont, G. Hemispheric function and paired associate learning. *British Journal of Psychology*, 1974, *65*, 275–278.

Dimond, S., & Farrington, L. Emotional response to films shown to the right and left hemispheres of the brain as measured by heartrate. *Acta Psychologica*, 1977, *41*, 255–260.

Diver, C. D., & Andersson-Kottö, I. Sinistrality in *Limnaea peragra* (Mollusca, Pulmonata): The problem of mixed broods. *Journal of Genetics*, 1938, *35*, 447–525.

Dobzhansky, T. *Genetics of the evolutionary process*. New York: Columbia Univ. Press, 1970.

Dorman, M. F., & Porter, R. J. Hemispheric lateralization for speech perception in stutterers. *Cortex*, 1975, *11*, 181–185.

Doyle, J. C. Ornstein, R., & Galin, D. Lateral specialization of cognitive mode: II. EEG frequency analysis. *Psychophysiology*, 1973, *11*, 567–578.

Dunlop, D. B., Dunlop, P., & Fenelon, B. Visual laterality analysis in children with reading disability: The results of new techniques of examination. *Cortex*, 1973, *9*, 227–236.

Dunlop, P. An interdisciplinary approach to dyslexia—the orthoptic approach. *Australian Orthoptic Journal*, 1972, *12*, 16–20.

Dunn, T. D. Double hemiplegia with double hemianopsia and loss of geographic centre. *Transactions of the College of Physicians of Philadelphia*, 1895, *17*, 45–46.

Durnford, M., & Kimura, D. Right hemisphere specialization for depth perception reflected in visual field differences. *Nature*, 1971, *231*, 394–395.

Eames, T. H. The anatomical basis of lateral dominance anomalies. *American Journal of Orthopsychiatry*, 1934, *4*, 524–528.

Eccles, J. C. *The brain and the unity of conscious experience.* Cambridge: Cambridge Univ. Press, 1965.

Eccles, J. C. Mental dualism and commissurotomy. *Behavioral & Brain Sciences*, 1981, *4*, 105.

Efron, R. The effect of handedness on the perception of simultaneity and temporal order. *Brain*, 1963, *86*, 261–284. (a)

Efron, R. The effect of stimulus intensity on the perception of simultaneity in right- and left-handed subjects. *Brain*, 1963, *86*, 285–294. (b)

Efron, R. Temporal perception, aphasia, and déjà vu. *Brain*, 1963, *86*, 403–424. (c)

Efron, R., & Yund, E. W. Ear dominance and intensity independence in the perception of dichotic chords. *Journal of the Acoustical Society of America*, 1976, *59*, 889–898.

Eling, P., Marshall, J. C., & van Galen, G. The development of language lateralization as measured by dichotic listening. *Neuropsychologia*, 1981, *19*, 767–773.

Eme, R. F. Sex differences in childhood psychopathology: A review. *Psychological Bulletin*, 1979, *86*, 574–595.

Entus, A. K. Hemispheric asymmetry in processing of dichotically presented speech and nonspeech by infants. In S. J. Segalowitz & G. Gruber (Eds.), *Language development and neurological theory.* New York: Academic Press, 1977.

Erman, A. [*Life in ancient Egypt*] (H. M. Tirard, Trans.). London: Macmillan, 1894.

Farrell, W. S. Coding left and right. *Journal of Experimental Psychology: Human Perception & Performance*, 1979, *5*, 42–51.

Finch, G. Chimpanzee's handedness. *Science*, 1941, *94*, 117–118.

Fincher, J. *Sinister people: The looking-glass world of the left-hander.* New York: Putnam, 1977.

Fischer, F. W., Liberman, I. Y., & Shankweiler, D. Reading reversals and developmental dyslexia: A further study. *Cortex*, 1978, *14*, 496–510.

Fliess, W. *Der Ablauf des Lebens.* Vienna: Deuticke, 1923.

Freud, S. *Zur Auffasung der Aphasien. Eine Kritische Studie.* Leipzig: Deuticke, 1891.

Freud, S. *Leonardo da Vinci: A psychological study of an infantile reminiscence.* London: Routledge, 1948.

Freud, S. *The origins of psychoanalysis. Letters to Wilhelm Fliess, drafts and notes: 1887–1902.* London: Imago Publishing, 1954.

Friedlander, W. J. Some aspects of eyedness. *Cortex*, 1971, *7*, 357–371.

Friedman, H., & Davis, M. Left handedness in parrots. *Auk*, 1938, *55*, 478–480.

Friedman, J. H., Golomb, J., & Mora, M. N. The hair whorl sign for handedness. *Diseases of the Nervous System*, 1952, *13*, 208–216.

Fritsch, V. *Left and right in science and life.* London: Barrie & Rockliff, 1968.

Froehlich, J. The quantitative genetics of fingerprints. In E. Giles & J. S. Friedlaender (Eds.), *The measures of man*. Cambridge, Mass.: Peabody Museum Press, 1976.

Fromkin, V. A., Krashen, S., Curtiss, S., Rigler, D., & Rigler, M. The development of language in Genie: A case of language acquisition beyond the "critical period." *Brain & Language*, 1974, *1*, 81–107.

Frost, F. T. Tool behavior and the origins of laterality. *Journal of Human Evolution*, 1980, *9*, 447–459.

Froude, J. A. *Thomas Carlyle in London, 1834–1881*. London: Longmans, Green 1884.

Fry, D. B. Right ear advantage for speech presented monaurally. *Language & Speech*, 1974, *17*, 142–151.

Gaffron, M. Right and left in pictures. *Art Quarterly*, 1950, *13*, 312–313.

Gainotti, G. Emotional behavior and the hemispheric side of the lesion. *Cortex*, 1972, *8*, 41–54.

Gainotti, G., Caltagirone, C., & Miceli, G. Semantic disorders of auditory language comprehension in right brain-damaged patients. *Journal of Psycholinguistic Research*, 1979, *8*, 13–20.

Gainotti, G., Caltagirone, C., Miceli, G., & Masullo, C. Selective semantic-lexical impairment of language comprehension in right brain-damaged patients. *Brain & Language*, 1981, *13*, 201–211.

Galaburda, A. M., LeMay, M., Kemper, T. L., & Geschwind, N. Right–left asymmetries in the brain. *Science*, 1978, *199*, 852–856.

Gardiner, M. F., & Walter, D. O. Evidence of hemispheric specialization from infant EEG. In S. Harnad, R. Doty, L. Goldstein, J. Jaynes, & G. Krauthamer (Eds.), *Lateralization in the nervous system*. New York: Academic Press, 1977.

Gardner, B. T., & Gardner, R. A. Two-way communication with an infant chimpanzee. In A. Schrier & F. Stollnitz (Eds.), *Behavior of nonhuman primates* (Vol. 4). New York: Academic Press, 1971.

Gardner, H. What we know (and don't know) about the two halves of the brain. *Harvard Magazine*, 1978, *78*, 24–27.

Gardner, J., Lewkowicz, E., & Turkewitz, G. Development of postural asymmetry in premature infants. *Developmental Psychology*, 1977, *10*, 471–480.

Gardner, M. *The annotated Alice*. Harmondsworth, England: Penguin Books, 1965.

Gardner, M. *The ambidextrous universe*. London: Allen Lane, The Penguin Press, 1967,

Gardner, R. A., & Gardner, B. T. Teaching sign language to a chimpanzee. *Science*, 1969, *165*, 664–672.

Garrett, S. V. Putting our whole brain to use: A fresh look at the creative process. *Journal of Creative Behavior*, 1976, *10*, 239–249.

Gates, A., & Bradshaw, J. L. The role of the cerebral hemispheres in music. *Brain & Language*, 1977, *4*, 403–431.

Gates, A. I., & Bond, G. L. Reading readiness: A study of factors determining success and failure in beginning reading. *Teacher's College Record*, 1936, *37*, 679–685.

Gazzaniga, M. S. Effects of commissurotomy on a preoperatively learned visual discrimination. *Experimental Neurology*, 1963, *8*, 14–19.

Gazzaniga, M. S. *The bisected brain*. New York: Appleton, 1970.

Gazzaniga, M. S., Bogen, J. E., & Sperry, R. W. Some functional effects of sectioning the cerebral commissures in man. *Proceedings of the National Academy of Sciences*, 1962, *48*, 1765–1769.

Gazzaniga, M. S., Bogen, J. E., & Sperry, R. W. Dyspraxia following division of the cerebral hemispheres. *Archives of Neurology*, 1967, *16*, 606–612.

Gazzaniga, M. S., & Sperry, R. W. Language after section of the cerebral commissures. *Brain*, 1967, *90*, 131–148.

Gazzaniga, M. S., Volpe, B. T., Smylie, C. S., Wilson, D. H ., & LeDoux, J. E. Plasticity in speech organization following commissurotomy. *Brain*, 1979, *102*, 808–815.

Geffen, G. The development of hemispheric specialization for speech perception. *Cortex*, 1976, *12*, 337–346.

Geffen, G. The development of the right ear advantage in dichotic listening with focused attention. *Cortex*, 1978, *14*, 169–177.

Geffen, G., Bradshaw, J. L., & Wallace, G. Interhemispheric effects on reaction times to verbal and nonverbal stimuli. *Journal of Experimental Psychology*, 1971, *87*, 415–422.

Geffen, G., & Sexton, M. A. The development of auditory strategies of attention. *Developmental Psychology*, 1978, *14*, 11–17.

Geffen, G., & Traub, E. Preferred hand and familial sinistrality in dichotic monitoring. *Neuropsychologia*, 1979, *17*, 527–532.

Geffen, G., Traub, E., & Stierman, I. Language laterality assessed by unilateral ECT and dichotic monitoring. *Journal of Neurology, Neurosurgery, & Psychiatry*, 1978, *41*, 354–360.

Geffen, G., & Wale, J. Development of selective listening and hemispheric asymmetry. *Developmental Psychology*, 1979, *15*, 138–146.

Geffner, D. S., & Hochberg, I. Ear laterality performance of children from low and middle socioeconomic levels on a verbal dichotic listening task. *Cortex*, 1971, *7*, 193–203.

Geschwind, N. Problems in the anatomical understanding of the aphasias. In A. L. Benton (Ed.), *Contributions to clinical neuropsychology*. Chicago: Aldine, 1969.

Geschwind, N. The apraxias: Neural mechanisms of disorders of learned movement. *American Scientist*, 1975, *63*, 188–195.

Geschwind, N. Specializations of the human brain. *Scientific American*, 1979, *241*(3), 108–119.

Geschwind, N. The perverseness of the right hemisphere. *Behavioral & Brain Sciences*, 1981, *4*, 106–107.

Geschwind, N. & Behan, P. Left-handedness: Association with immune disease, migraine, and developmental learning disorder. *Proceedings of the National Academy of Sciences*, 1982, *79*, 5097–5100.

Geschwind, N., & Levitsky, W. Human brain: Left–right asymmetries in temporal speech region. *Science*, 1968, *161*, 186–187.

Gesell, A., & Ames, L. B. The development of handedness. *Journal of Genetic Psychology*, 1947, *70*, 155–175.

Gilbert, C. Nonverbal perceptual abilities in relation to left-handedness and cerebral lateralization. *Neuropsychologia*, 1977, *15*, 779–791.

Ginsberg, G. P., & Hartwick, A. Directional confusion as a sign of dyslexia. *Perceptual & Motor Skills*, 1971, *32*, 535–543.

Glanville, B. B., Best, C. T., & Levenson, R. A cardiac measure of cerebral asymmetries in infant auditory perception. *Developmental Psychology*, 1977, *13*, 54–59.

Gloning, I., & Quatember, R. Statistical evidence of neuropsychological syndrome in left-handed and ambidextrous patients. *Cortex*, 1966, *2*, 484–488.

Godfrey, J. J. Perceptual difficulty and the right ear advantage for vowels. *Brain & Language*, 1974, *1*, 323–336.

Goldstein, K. *Language and language disturbances*. New York: Grune & Stratton, 1948.

Goldstein, L. Is cerebral laterality a myth? *Research Communications in Psychology, Psychiatry & Behavior*, 1980, *5*, 291–299.

Goodglass, H., & Kaplan, E. Disturbance of gesture and pantomime in aphasia. *Brain*, 1963, *86*, 703–720.

Goodglass, H., & Quadfasel, F. A. Language laterality in left handed aphasics. *Brain*, 1954, *77*, 521–548.

Gordon, D. P. The influence of sex and handedness on the development of lateralization of function. Unpublished manuscript, 1980.

Gordon, H. W. Hemispheric asymmetries in the perception of musical chords. *Cortex*, 1970, *6*, 387–398.

Gordon, H. W. Verbal and nonverbal cerebral processing in man for audition. Unpublished doctoral dissertation, California Institute of Technology, 1973. (Cited in Nebes, 1978.)

Gordon, H. W. Hemispheric asymmetry for dichotically presented chords in musicians and nonmusicians, males and females. *Acta Psychologica*, 1978, *42*, 383–395. (a)

Gordon, H. W. Left hemisphere dominance for rhythmic elements in dichotically-presented melodies. *Cortex*, 1978, *14*, 58–70. (b)

Gordon, H. W. Cognitive asymmetry in dyslexic families. *Neuropsychologia*, 1980, *18*, 645–656.

Gordon, M. C. Reception and retention factors in tone duration discriminations by brain-damaged and control patients. *Cortex*, 1967, *3*, 233–249.

Gott, P. S. Language after dominant hemispherectomy. *Journal of Neurology, Neurosurgery, & Psychiatry*, 1973, *36*, 1082–1088.

Gott, P. S., & Saul, R. E. Agenesis of the corpus callosum: Limits of functional compensation. *Neurology*, 1978, *28*, 1272–1279.

Graf, O. I. Incidence of stuttering among twins. In W. Johnson & R. Lentenneger (Eds.), *Stuttering in children and adults*. Minneapolis: Univ. of Minnesota Press, 1955.

Granet, M. La droite et la gauche en Chine. In M. Granet (Ed.), *Études sociologiques sur la Chine*. Paris: Presses Universitaires de France, 1953.

Griffin, D. R. *The question of animal awareness*. New York: Rockefeller Univ. Press, 1976.

Groden, S. Q. *The symposuim of Plato*. Amherst: Univ. of Massachusetts Press, 1970.

Guillaume, J., Mazars, G. Mazars, Y. Intermédiaire épileptique dans certains types de bégaiement. *Revue Neurologiques*, 1957, *96*, 59–61.

Haggard, M. P., & Parkinson, A. M. Stimulus task factors as determinants of ear advantages. *Quarterly Journal of Experimental Psychology*, 1971, *23*, 168–177.

Hall, G. S. Notes on the study of infants. *Pedagogical Seminary*, 1891, *1*, 128–138.

Hallgren, B. Specific dyslexia (congenital word blindness). *Acta Psychiatrica et Neurologica, Supplementum 65*. Copenhagen, 1950.

Hamilton, C. R. Investigations of perceptual and mnemonic lateralization in monkeys. In S. Harnad, R. W. Doty, L. Goldstein, J. Jaynes, & G. Krauthamer (Eds.), *Lateralization in the nervous system*. New York: Academic Press, 1977.

Hamilton, C. R., & Lund, J. S. Visual discrimination of movement: Midbrain or forebrain? *Science*, 1970, *170*, 1428–1430.

Hamilton, C. R., Tieman, S. B., & Farrell, W. S. Cerebral dominance in monkeys. *Neuropsychologia*, 1974, *12*, 193–197.

Hannay, H. J., Varney, N. R., & Benton, A. L. Visual localization in patients with unilateral brain disease. *Journal of Neurology, Neurosurgery, & Psychiatry*, 1976, *39*, 307–313.

Hardyck, C., & Petrinovich, L. F. Left-handedness. *Psychological Bulletin*, 1977, *84*, 385–404.

Hardyck, C., Petrinovich, L., & Goldman, R. Left handedness and cognitive deficit. *Cortex*, 1976, *12*, 266–278.

Harris, A. J. *How to increase reading ability* (3rd ed.). New York: Longmans, Green, 1956.

Harris, C. W. (Ed.). *Problems in measuring change*. Madison: Univ. of Wisconsin Press, 1963.

Harris, L. J. Left-handedness: early theories, facts, and fancies. In J. Herron (Ed.), *Neuropsychology of left-handedness*. New York: Academic Press, 1980. (a)

Harris, L. J. The human infant as focus in theories of handedness: Some lessons from the past. Paper read at NATO Advanced Study Institute on Neuropsychology and Cognition, Augusta, Georgia, September 1980. (b)

Harris, L. J. Which hand is the "eye" of the blind?—A new look at an old question. In J. Herron (Ed.), *Neuropsychology of left handedness*. New York: Academic Press, 1980. (c)

Haslam, R. H. A., Dalby, J. T., Johns, R. D., & Rademaker, A. W. Cerebral asymmetry in developmental dyslexia. *Archives of Neurology*, 1981, *38*, 679–682.

Hatta, T. Recognition of Japanese *kanji* in the left and right visual field. *Neuropsychologia*, 1977, *15*, 685–688.

Hawn, P., & Harris, L. J. Hand asymmetries in grasp duration and reaching in two- and five-month-old human infants. Paper presented at Annual Meeting of the International Neuropsychology Society, New York, February 3, 1979.

Hay, D. A., & Howie, P. M. Handedness and differences in birthweight of twins. *Perceptual & Motor Skills*, 1980, *51*, 666.

Haydon, S. P., & Spellacy, F. J. Monaural reaction time asymmetries for speech and non-speech sounds. *Cortex*, 1973, *9*, 288–294.

Head, H. *Aphasia and kindred disorders of speech* (2 vols.). London: Cambridge Univ. Press, 1926.

Hécaen, H. Acquired aphasia in children and the ontogenesis of hemispheric functional specialization. *Brain & Language*, 1976, *3*, 114–134.

Hécaen, H., & Ajuriaguerra, J. de. *Left handedness*. New York: Grune & Stratton, 1964.

Hécaen, H., & Angelergues, R. *La cécité psychique*. Paris: Masson, 1963.

Hécaen, H., De Agostini, M., & Monzon-Montes, A. Cerebral organization in left handers. *Brain & Language*, 1981, *12*, 261–284.

Hécaen, H., & Sauguet, J. Cerebral dominance in left-handed subjects. *Cortex*, 1971, *7*, 19–48.

Heilman, K. M. Apraxia. In K. M. Heilman & E. Valenstein (Eds.), *Clinical neuropsychology*. Oxford: Oxford Univ. Press, 1979. (a)

Heilman, K. M. Neglect and related disorders. In K. M. Heilman & E. Valenstein (Eds.), *Clinical neuropsychology*. Oxford; Oxford Univ. Press, 1979. (b)

Heilman, K. M., Scholes, P., & Watson, R. Auditory affective agnosia. *Journal of Neurology, Neurosurgery, & Psychiatry*, 1975, *38*, 69–72.

Heilman, K. M., Watson, R. T., Valenstein, E., & Bowers, D. Neglect in man: Hemispheric asymmetries and hemispatial neglect. *Behavioral & Brain Sciences*, 1980, *3*, 505–506.

Hellige, J. B. Visual laterality patterns for pure- versus mixed-list presentations. *Journal of Experimental Psychology: Human Perception & Performance*, 1978, *4*, 121–131.

Henley, E. M. Parity and time-reversal invariance in nuclear physics. *Annual Review of Nuclear Science*, 1969, *19*, 367–427.

Hepworth, T. S. *Dyslexia: The problem of reading retardation*. London: Angus & Robertson, 1971.

Herron, J. EEG alpha asymmetry and dichotic listening in stutterers. Paper presented at Fourteenth Annual Meeting of the Society for Psychophysiological Research, Salt Lake City, Utah, 1974.

Herron, J., Galin, D., Johnstone, J., & Ornstein, R. Cerebral specialization, writing posture, and motor control of writing in left-handers. *Science*, 1979, *205*, 1285–1289.

Hertz, R. La prééminence de la main droite: Étude sur la polarité religieuse. *Revue Philosophique*, 1909, *68*, 553–580. (Translated in Hertz, 1960.)

Hertz, R. [*Death and the right hand.*] (R. & C. Needham, Trans.). Aberdeen: Cohen & West, 1960.

Hewes, G. W. Lateral dominance, culture, and writing systems. *Human Biology*, 1949, *21*, 233–245.

Hewes, G. W. Primate communication and the gestural origin of language. *Current Anthropology*, 1973, *14*, 5–24.

Hicks, R. E., Evans, E. A., & Pellegrini, R. J. Correlation between handedness and birth order. *Perceptual & Motor Skills*, 1978, *46*, 53–54.

Hicks, R. E., & Kinsbourne, M. Human handedness: A partial cross-fostering study. *Science*, 1976, *192*, 908–910.

Hier, D. B., LeMay, M., Rosenberger, P. B., & Perlo, V. P. Developmental dyslexia: Evidence for a subgroup with a reversal of cerebral asymmetry. *Archives of Neurology*, 1978, *35*, 90–92.

Hines, D., & Satz, P. Cross-modal asymmetries in perception related to asymmetry in cerebral function. *Neuropsychologia*, 1974, *12*, 239–247.

Holt, S. B. *Genetics of dermal ridges.* Springfield, Ill.: Thomas, 1968.

Howard, K. J., Rogers, L. J., & Boura, A. L. A. Functional lateralization of the chicken forebrain revealed by the use of intracranial glutamate. *Brain Research*, 1980, *188*, 369–382.

Hubbard, J. I. Handedness is not a function of birth order. *Nature*, 1971, *232*, 276–277.

Hudson, P. T. W. The genetics of handedness—a reply to Levy and Nagylaki. *Neuropsychologia*, 1975, *13*, 331–339.

Hummel, K. P., & Chapman, D. B. Visceral asymmetry and associate anomalies in the mouse. *Journal of Heredity*, 1959, *50*, 9–13.

Humphrey, M. E. Consistency of hand usage: A preliminary enquiry. *British Journal of Educational Psychology*, 1951, *21*, 214–225.

Humphrey, M. E., & Zangwill, O. L. Cessation of dreaming after brain injury. *Journal of Neurology, Neurosurgery, & Psychiatry*, 1951, *14*, 322–325.

Humphrey, M. E., & Zangwill, O. L. Dysphasia in left-handed patients with unilateral brain lesions. *Journal of Neurology, Neurosurgery, & Psychiatry*, 1952, *15*, 184–193.

Hung, D. L., & Tzeng, O. J. L. Orthographic variations and visual information processing. *Psychological Bulletin*, 1981, *90*, 377–414.

Hyvarinen, J., & Poranen, A. Function of the parietal associative area 7 as revealed by cellular discharges in alert monkeys. *Brain*, 1974, *97*, 673–692.

Ibbotson, N. R., & Morton, J. Rhythm and dominance. *Cognition*, 1981, *9*, 125–138.

Irwin, R. J., & Newland, J. K. Children's knowledge of left and right. *Journal of Child Psychology & Psychiatry*, 1977, *18*, 271–277.

Jackson, J. *Ambidexterity or two-handedness and two-brainedness.* London: Kegan Paul, Trench, Trubner, 1905.

Jackson, J. A survey of psychological, social, and environmental differences between advanced and retarded readers. *Journal of Genetic Psychology*, 1944, *65*, 113–131.

Jackson, J. H. Clinical remarks on cases of defects of expression (by words, writing, signs, etc.) in diseases of the nervous system. *Lancet*, 1864, *2*, 604.

Jackson, J. H. Defect of intellectual expression (aphasia) with left hemiplagia. *Lancet*, 1868, *1*, 457.

Jackson, J. H. Case of large tumour without optic neuritis and with left hemiplegia and imperception. *Royal London Opthalmic Hospital Report*, 1876, *8*, 434. (Reprinted in Taylor, 1932.)

Jahoda, G. On the nature of difficulties in spatial perceptual tasks: Ethnic and sex differences. *British Journal of Psychology*, 1979, *70*, 351–363.

Janet, P. *The major symptoms of hysteria.* New York: MacMillan, 1907.

Jantz, R. L., Fohl, F. H., & Zahler, J. W. Finger ridge-counts and handedness. *Human Biology*, 1979, *51*, 91–99.

Jaynes, J. *The origin of consciousness in the breakdown of the bicameral mind.* Boston: Houghton, 1976.

Johnson, W. (Ed.). *Stuttering in children and adults.* Minneapolis: Univ. of Minnesota Press, 1955.

Johnson, W. Measurements of oral reading and speaking rate and disfluency of adult male and female stutterers and nonstutterers. *Journal of Speech and Hearing Disorders, Monograph Supplement 7*, 1961, 1–20.

Jones, R. K. Observations on stammering after localized cerebral injury, *Journal of Neurology, Neurosurgery, & Psychiatry*, 1966, *29*, 192–195.

Jorm, A. F. The cognitive and neurological bases of developmental dyslexia: A theoretical framework and a review. *Cognition*, 1979, *7*, 19–33.

Kail, R., Pellegrino, J., & Carter, P. Developmental changes in mental rotation. *Journal of Experimental Child Psychology*, 1980, *29*, 102–116.

Kallman, H. J., & Corballis, M. C. Ear asymmetry in reaction time to musical sounds. *Perception & Psychophysics*, 1975, *17*, 368–370.

Keeley, L. H. The functions of paleolithic flint tools. *Scientific American*, 1977, *237* (November), 108–127.

Kelly, R. R., & Tomlinson-Keasey, C. The effect of auditory input on cerebral laterality. *Brain & Language*, 1981, *13*, 67–77.

Kelso, J. A. S., & Tuller, B. Toward a theory of apractic syndromes. *Brain & Language*, 1981, *12*, 224–245.

Kennedy, F. Stock-brainedness,the causative factor in the so-called "crossed aphasics." *American Journal of Medical Science*, 1916, *152*, 849–859.

Kershner, J. R. Lateralization in normal six-year-olds as related to later reading disability. *Developmental Psychobiology*, 1977, *11*, 303–319.

Kertesz, A., & Geschwind, N. Patterns of pyramedal decussation and their relationship to handedness. *Archives of Neurology*, 1971, *24*, 326–332.

Kertesz, A., & McCabe, P. Recovery patterns and prognosis in aphasia. *Brain*, 1977, *100*, 1–18.

Kim, Y., Royer, F., Bonstelle, C., & Boller, F. Temporal sequencing of verbal and nonverbal materials: The effect of laterality of lesion. *Cortex*, 1980, *16*, 135–143.

Kimura, D. Some effects of temporal-lobe damage on auditory perception. *Canadian Journal of Psychology*, 1961, *15*, 156–165. (a)

Kimura, D. Cerebral dominance and the perception of verbal stimuli. *Canadian Journal of Psychology*, 1961, *15*, 166–171. (b)

Kimura, D. Speech lateralization in young children as determined by an auditory test. *Journal of Comparative & Physiological Psychology*, 1963, *56*, 899–902.

Kimura, D. Left–right differences in the perception of melodies. *Quarterly Journal of Experimental Psychology*, 1964, *16*, 355–358.

Kimura, D. Dual functional asymmetry of the brain in visual perception. *Neuropsychologia*, 1966, *4*, 275–285.

Kimura, D. Functional asymmetry of the brain in dichotic listening. *Cortex*, 1967, *3*, 163–178.

Kimura, D. Manual activity during speaking. I. Right-handers. *Neuropsychologia*, 1973, *11*, 45–50. (a)

Kimura, D. Manual activity during speaking. II. Left-handers. *Neuropsychologia*, 1973, *11*, 51–55. (b)

Kimura, D. Neuromotor mechanisms in the evolution of human communication. In H. D. Steklis & M. J. Raleigh (Eds.), *Neurobiology of social communication in primates*. New York: Academic Press, 1979.

Kimura, D. Sex differences in intrahemispheric organization of speech. *Behavioral & Brain Sciences*, 1980, *3*, 240–241.

Kimura, D. Neural mechanisms of manual signing. *Sign Language Studies*, 1981, *33*, 291–312.

Kimura, D., & Archibald, Y. Motor functions of the left hemisphere. *Brain*, 1974, *97*, 337–350.

Kimura, D., & Folb, S. Neural processing of backwards-speech sounds. *Science*, 1968, *161*, 395–396.

King, F. L., & Kimura, D. Left-ear superiority in dichotic perception of vocal nonverbal sounds. *Canadian Journal of Psychology*, 1972, *26*, 111–116.

Kinsbourne, M. The mechanism of hemispheric control of the lateral gradient of attention, In P. M. A. Rabbitt & S. Dornic (Eds.), *Attention and performance V*. New York: Academic Press, 1975.

Kinsbourne, M. If sex differences in brain lateralization exist, they have yet to be discovered. *Behavioral & Brain Sciences*, 1980, *3*, 241–242.

Kinsbourne, M., & Hiscock, M. Does cerebral dominance develop? In S. J. Segalowitz & F. Gruber (Eds.), *Language development and neurological theory*. New York: Academic Press, 1977.

Klein, B. von E. Inferring functional localization from neurological evidence. In E. Walker (Ed.), *Explorations in the biology of language*. Montgomery, Vt.: Bradford Books, 1978.

Kleist, K. Kriegverletzungen des Gehirns in ihrer Bedeutng für die Hirnlodalisation and Hirn- pathologie. In O. von Schjerning (Ed.), *Handbuch der Arztlichen Erfahrung in Weltkriege, 1914/1918, Vol. 4*. Liepzig: Barth, 1923.

Kopell, H. P. Letter in *Scientific American*, 1971, *224* (June), 9.

Kohn, B., & Dennis, M. Patterns of hemispheric specialization after hemidecortication for infantile hemiplegia. In M. Kinsbourne & W. L. Smith (Eds.), *Hemispheric disconnection and cerebral function*. Springfield, Ill.: Charles C Thomas, 1974.

Kosslyn, S. M., & Pomerantz, J. R. Imagery, propositions, and the form of internal representa- tions. *Cognitive Psychology*, 1977, *9*, 52–76.

Kracke, I. Perception of rhythmic sequences by receptive aphasic and deaf children. *British Journal of Disturbed Communication*, 1975, *10*, 43–51.

Krashen, S. D. Language and the left hemisphere. *UCLA Working Papers in Phonetics*, 1972, *24*, 1–72.

Ladavas, E., Umilta, C., & Ricci-Bitti, P. E. Evidence for sex differences in right-hemisphere dom- inance for emotions. *Neuropsychologia*, 1980, *18*, 361–366.

Laitinen, L. V., & Vilkki, J. Observations on physiological and psychological functions of the ventral oral nucleus of the human thalamus. *Acta Neurologica Scandinavia*, 1977, *55*, 198– 212.

Lancaster, J. B. On the evolution of tool-using behavior. In C. L. Brace & J. Metress (Eds.), *Man in evolutionary perspective*. New York: Wiley, 1973.

Lassonde, M. C., Lortie, J., Ptito, M., & Geoffroy, G. Hemispheric asymmetry in callosal agenesis as revealed by dichotic listening performance. *Neuropsychologia*, 1981, *19*, 455–458.

Lauterbach, C. E. Studies of twin resemblance. *Genetics*, 1925, *10*, 535–568.

Lauterbach, C. E., & Knight, J. B. Variations in the whorl of the head hair. *Journal of Heredity*, 1927, *18*, 107–115.

Layton, W. M. Random determination of a developmental process: Reversal of normal visceral asymmetry in the mouse. *Journal of Heredity*, 1976, *67*, 336–338.

Leakey, M. D. *Olduvai Gorge* (Vol. 3). Cambridge: Cambridge, Univ. Press, 1971.

Leakey, R. E., & Lewin, R. *Origins*. New York: Dutton, 1977.

LeDoux, J. E., Wilson, D. H., & Gazzaniga, M. S. Manipulo-spatial aspects of cerebral laterali- zation: Clues to the origin of lateralization. *Neuropsychologia*, 1977, *15*, 743–750.

Leehey, S. C. Development of right-hemisphere specialization in children. Paper presented at Eastern Psychological Association, New York, April 1976.

Lehman, R. A. W. The handedness of rhesus monkeys. *Neuropsychologia*, 1978, *16*, 33–42.

Leiber, L., & Axelrod, S. Not all sinistrality is pathological. *Cortex*, 1981, *17*, 259–272.

LeMay, M. Morphological cerebral asymmetries of modern man, fossil man, and nonhuman pri- mate. *Annals of the New York Academy of Sciences*, 1976, *280*, 349–366.

LeMay, M. Asymmetries of the skull and handedness: Phrenology revisited. *Journal of Neurological Sciences*, 1977, *32*, 243–253.

LeMay, M. Prominence of the right side of the brain. *Behavioral & Brain Sciences*, 1980, *3*, 304.

LeMay, M., & Culebras, A. Human brain—morphological differences in the hemispheres de- monstrable by carotid arteriography. *New England Journal of Medicine*, 1972, *287*, 168–170.

Lemon, R. E. Nervous control of the syrinx in white-throated sparrows (*Zonotrichia albicollis*). *Journal of Zoology (London)*, 1973, *71*, 131–140.

Lenneberg, E. H. *Biological foundations of language.* New York: Wiley, 1967.

Leong, C. K. Lateralization in severely disabled readers in relation to functional cerebral development and synthesis of information. In R. M. Knights & D. J. Bakker (Eds.), *The neuropsychology of learning disorders: Theoretical approaches.* Baltimore, Md.: Univ. Park Press, 1976.

Lepori, N. G. Sur la genèse des structures asymétriques chez l'embryon des oiseaux. *Monitore Zoologico Italiano,* 1969, *3,* 33–53.

Lepori, N. G. Asymmetric blastomere movement during gastrulation. *Behavioral & Brain Sciences,* 1978, *2,* 304–305.

Lesèvre, N. L'organization du regard chez les enfants d'age scolaire lecteurs normaux et dyslexiques (étude électrooculographique). *Revue de Neuropsychiatrie Infantile,* 1968, *16,* 323–349.

Lesser, R. Verbal comprehension in aphasia: An English version of three Italian tests. *Cortex,* 1974, *10,* 247–263.

Letokhov, V. S. On difference of energy levels of left and right molecules due to weak interactions. *Physics Letters,* 1975, *53A,* 275–276.

Levy, J. Possible basis for the evolution of lateral specialization in the human brain. *Nature,* 1969, *224,* 614–615.

Levy, J. Information processing and higher psychological functions in the disconnected hemispheres of human commissurotomy patients. Unpublished doctoral dissertation, California Institute of Technology, 1970. (Cited in Nebes, 1978.)

Levy, J. Psychobiological implications of bilateral asymmetry. In S. Dimond & J. G. Beaumont (Eds.), *Hemispheric function in the human brain.* London: Paul Elek, 1974.

Levy, J. A review of evidence for a genetic component in the determination of handedness. *Behavior Genetics,* 1976, *6,* 429–453.

Levy, J. The origins of lateral asymmetry. In S. Harnad, R. W. Doty, L. Goldstein, J. Jaynes, & G. Krauthamer (Eds.), *Lateralization in the nervous system.* New York: Academic Press, 1977.

Levy, J., & Levy, J. M. Human lateralization from head to foot: Sex-related factors. *Science,* 1978, *200,* 1291–1292.

Levy, J., & Nagylaki, T. A model for the genetics of handedness. *Genetics,* 1972, *72,* 117–128.

Levy, J., & Reid, M. Variations in writing posture and cerebral organization. *Science,* 1976, *194,* 337–339.

Levy, J., & Reid, M. Variations in cerebral organization as a function of handedness, hand posture in writing, and sex. *Journal of Experimental Psychology: General,* 1978, *107,* 119–144.

Ley, R. G., & Bryden, M. P. Hemispheric differences in processing emotions and faces. *Brain & Language,* 1979, *7,* 127–138.

Liberman, A. M., Cooper, F. S., Shankweiler, D. P., & Studdert-Kennedy, M. Perception of the speech code. *Psychological Review,* 1967, *74,* 431–461.

Liberman, I. Y., Shankweiler, D., Orlando, C., Harris, K. S., & Berti, F. B. Letter confusions and reversals of sequence in the beginning reader: Implications for Orton's theory of developmental dyslexia. *Cortex,* 1971, *7,* 127–142.

Lieberman, P. *On the origins of language.* New York: MacMillan, 1975.

Liederman, J., & Kinsbourne, M. Rightward motor bias in newborns depends upon parental right-handedness. *Neuropsychologia,* 1980, *18,* 579–584. (a)

Liederman, J., & Kinsbourne, M. The mechanism of neonatal rightward turning bias: A sensory or motor asymmetry? *Infant Behavior & Development,* 1980, *3,* 223–238. (b)

Liepmann, H. *Drei Aufsätze aus dem Apraxiegebiet.* Berlin: Karger, 1908.

Liepmann, H., & Maas, O. Fall von linksseitiger Agraphie und Apraxie bei rechtsseitiger Lähmung. *Zeitschrift für Psychologie und Neurologie,* 1907, *10,* 214–227.

Lissauer, H. Ein fall von Seelenblindhert nebst einem Beitrage zur Theorie derselben. *Archiv für Psychiatrie und Nervenkrankheiten,* 1890, *21,* 222–270.

Lloyd, G. Right and left in Greek philosophy. *Journal of Hellenic Studies*, 1962, *82*, 56–66.

Loesch, D. Genetics of dermatoglyphic patterns on palms. *Annals of Human Genetics*, 1971, *34*, 277–290.

Loesch, D. Genetical studies of sole and palmar dermatoglyphics. *Annals of Human Genetics*, 1974, *37*, 405–420.

Longden, K., Ellis, C., & Iversen, D. S. Hemispheric differences in the perception of curvature. *Neuropsychologia*, 1976, *14*, 195–202.

Lowe, A. D., & Campbell, R. A. Temporal discrimination in aphasoid and normal children. *Journal of Speech and Hearing Research*, 1965, *8*, 313–314.

Luchsinger, R. Biological studies on monozygotic twins relative to size and form of the larynx. *Archiv Julius Klaus-Stiftung für Vererbungsforschung*, 1944, *19*, 3–4. (Cited with title translated into English in Van Riper, 1971.)

Luria, A. R. *Traumatic aphasia: Its syndromes, psychopathology, and treatment.* Moscow: Academy of Medical Sciences, 1947.

Luria, A. R., Tsvetkova, L. S., & Futer, D. S. Aphasia in a composer. *Journal of Neurological Science*, 1965, *2*, 288–292.

Lynch, J. C. The functional organization of posterior parietal association cortex. *Behavioral & Brain Sciences*, 1980, *3*, 485–499.

Mach, E. *The analysis of sensations.* Chicago, Ill.: Open Court Publishing House, 1897.

Makita, K. The rarity of reading disability in Japanese children. *American Journal of Orthopsychiatry*, 1968, *38*, 599–614.

Marcel, A. J., & Rajan, P. Lateral specialization for recognition of words and faces in good and poor readers. *Neuropsychologia*, 1975, *13*, 489–498.

Marcel, T., Katz, L., & Smith, M. Laterality and reading proficiency. *Neuropsychologia*, 1974, *12*, 131–139.

Marie, P. Existe-t-il dans le cerveau humain des centres innés ou préformés de langage? *La Presse Médicale*, 1922, *17*, 117–181.

Marks, C. E. *Commissurotomy, consciousness, and unity of mind.* Montgomery, Vt.: Bradford Books, 1980.

Marzi, C. A., & Berlucchi, G. Right visual field superiority for accuracy of recognition of famous faces in normals. *Neuropsychologia*, 1977, *15*, 751–756.

Mascie-Taylor, C. G. N., MacLarnon, A. M., Lanigan, P. M., & McManus, I. C. Foot-length asymmetry, sex, and handedness. *Science*, 1981, *212*, 1416–1417.

Masland, R. Paper read at the proceedings of the Orton Society. Reported in *APA Monitor*, December 1976, p. 10.

Massis, H. Defence of the West, II. (F. S. Flint, Trans.). *The Criterion*, 1926, *4*, 476–493.

Mateer, C. Asymmetric effects of thalamic stimulation on rate of speech. *Neuropsychologia*, 1978, *16*, 497–499.

Mazars, G., Hécaen, H., Tzavaras, A., & Merreune, L. Contribution à la chirurgie de certains bégaiements et la compréhension de leur physiopathologie. *Revue Neurologique*, 1970, *122*, 213–220.

McFarland, K., & Anderson, J. Factor stability of the Edinburgh Handedness Inventory as a function of test–retest performance, age, and sex. *British Journal of Psychology*, 1980, *71*, 135–142.

McFie, J. The effects of hemispherectomy on intellectual functioning in cases of infantile hemiplegia. *Journal of Neurology, Neurosurgery, & Psychiatry*, 1961, *24*, 240–249.

McGlone, J. Sex differences in the cerebral organization of verbal functions in patients with unilateral brain lesions. *Brain*, 1977, *100*, 775–793.

McGlone, J. Sex differences in functional brain asymmetry. *Cortex*, 1978, *14*, 122–128.

McGlone, J. Sex differences in human brain asymmetry: A critical survey. *Behavioral & Brain Sciences,* 1980, *3,* 215–263.

McKeever, W. F. Evidence against the hypothesis of right hemisphere language dominance in the native American Navajo. *Neuropsychologia,* 1981, *19,* 595–598. (a)

McKeever, W. F. On laterality research and dichotomania. *Behavioral & Brain Sciences,* 1981, *4,* 73–74. (b)

McKeever, W. R., & Dixon, M. S. Right-hemisphere superiority for discriminating memorized from nonmemorized faces: Affective imagery, sex, and perceived emotionality effects. *Brain & Language,* 1981, *12,* 246–260.

McKeever, W. F., & Huling, M. D. Lateral dominance in tachistoscopic word recognitions of children at two levels of ability. *Quarterly Journal of Experimental Psychology,* 1970, *22,* 600–604.

McKeever, W. F., & Huling, M. D. Lateral dominance in tachistoscopic word recognition performance obtained with simultaneous visual input. *Neuropsychologia,* 1971, *9,* 15–20.

McKeever, W. F., & Van Deventer, A. D. Dyslexic adolescents: Evidence of impaired visual and auditory language processing associated with normal lateralization and visual responsivity. *Cortex,* 1975, *11,* 361–378.

McKeever, W. F., & Van Deventer, A. D. Visual and auditory language processing asymmetries: Influence of handedness, familial sinistrality, and sex. *Cortex,* 1977, *13,* 225–241.

McManus, I. C. Handedness in twins: A critical review. *Neuropsychologia,* 1980, *18,* 347–355.

McRae, D. L., Branch, C. L., & Milner, B. The occipital horns and cerebral dominance. *Neurology,* 1968, *18,* 95–98.

Melekian, B. Lateralization in the human newborn at birth: Asymmetry of the stepping reflex. *Neuropsychologia,* 1981, *19,* 707–711.

Meyer, M. Left-handedness and right-handedness in infancy. *Psychological Bulletin,* 1913, *10,* 52–53.

Michel, G. F. Right-handedness: A consequence of infant supine head-orientation preference? *Science,* 1981, *212,* 685–687.

Michel, G. F., & Goodwin, R. Intrauterine birth position predicts newborn supine head position preferences. *Infant Behavior & Development,* 1979, *2,* 29–38.

Milisen, R., & Van Riper, C. Differential transfer of training in a rotary activity. *Journal of Experimental Psychology,* 1939, *24,* 640–646.

Milner, B. Laterality effects in audition. In V. B. Mountcastle (Ed.), *Interhemispheric relations and cerebral dominance.* Baltimore: Johns Hopkins Press, 1962.

Milner, B. Visually-guided maze learning in man: Effects of bilateral hippocampal, bilateral frontal, and unilateral cerebral lesions. *Neuropsychologia,* 1965, *3,* 317–338.

Milner, B. Visual recognition and recalll after right temporal lobe excision in man. *Neuropsychologia,* 1968, *6,* 191–209.

Milner, B. Interhemispheric differences in the localization of psychological processes in man. *British Medical Bulletin,* 1971, *27,* 272–277.

Milner, B. Psychological aspects of focal epilepsy and its neurosurgical management. In D. P. Purpura, J. K. Penry, & R. D. Walters (Eds.), *Advances in neurology* (Vol. 8). New York: Raven, 1975.

Milner, B. Clues to the cerebral organization of memory, In P. A. Buser & A. Rougeul-Buser (Eds.), *Cerebral correlates of conscious experience.* (INSERM Symposium No. 6). Amsterdam: Elsevier/North Holland, 1978.

Milner, B., Taylor, L., & Sperry, R. W. Lateralized suppression of dichotically presented digits after commissural section in man. *Science,* 1968, *161,* 184–186.

Mittwoch, U. To be born right is to be born male. *New Scientist,* 1977, *73,* 74–76.

Mittwoch, U. Changes in the direction of the lateral growth gradient in human development—left to right and right to left. *Behavioral & Brain Sciences,* 1980, *3,* 306–307.

Mohr, J. P. Broca's area and Broca's aphasia. In H.Whitaker & H. A. Whitaker (Eds.), *Studies in neurolinguistics* (Vol. 1). New York: Academic Press, 1976.

Molfese, D. L. Electrophysiological correlates of categorical speech perception in adults. *Brain & Language,* 1978, *5,* 25–35.

Molfese, D. L., Freeman, R. B. Jr., & Palermo, D. S. The ontogeny of brain lateralization for speech and nonspeech sounds. *Brain & Language,* 1975, *2,* 356–368.

Molfese, D. L., & Hess, T. Hemispheric specialization for VOT perception in the preschool child. *Journal of Experimental Child Psychology,* 1978, *26,* 71–84.

Molfese, D. L., & Molfese, V. J. Hemisphere and stimulus differences as reflected in the cortical responses of newborn infants to speech stimuli. *Developmental Psychology,* 1979, *15,* 505–511. (a)

Molfese, D. L., & Molfese, V. J. VOT distinctions in infants: Learned or innate? In H. Whitaker (Ed.), *Studies in neurolinguistics* (Vol. 6). New York: Academic Press, 1979. (b)

Monod, J. On symmetry and function in biological systems. In A. Engstrom & B. Strandberg (Eds.), *Symmetry and function of biological systems at the macromolecular level.* New York: Wiley, 1969.

Mononen, L. J., & Seitz, M. R. An AER analysis of contralateral advantage in the transmission of auditory information. *Neuropsychologia,* 1977, *15,* 165–174.

Monroe, M. Methods for diagnosis and treatment of cases of reading disability. *Genetic Psychology Monographs* 1928, *4,* (4,5).

Monroe, M. *Children who cannot read.* Chicago: Univ. of Chicago Press, 1932.

Moore, W. H. Bilateral tachistoscopic word perception of stutterers and normal subjects. *Brain & Language,* 1976, *3,* 434–443.

Moore, W. H., & Lang, M. K. Alpha asymmetry over the right and left hemispheres of stutterers and control subjects preceding massed oral readings: A preliminary investigation. *Perceptual & Motor Skills,* 1977, *44,* 223–230.

Morais, J., & Bertelson, P. Spatial position versus ear of entry as determinant of the auditory laterality effect: A stereophonic test. *Journal of Experimental Psychology: Human Perception & Performance,* 1975, *1,* 253–262.

Morais, J., & Darwin, C. J. Ear differences for same–different reaction times to monaurally presented speech. *Brain & Language,* 1974, *1,* 383–390.

Morgan, L. Y., Juberg, R. C., & Faust, C. C. Digital dermatoglyphics correlated with laterality. Paper presented at the Harold Cummins Memorial Symposium, Gulf Shores, Alabama, March 1977.

Morgan, M. J. Embryology and inheritance of asymmetry. In S. Harnad, R. W. Doty, L. Goldstein, J. Jaynes, & G. Krauthamer (Eds.), *Lateralization in the nervous system.* New York: Academic Press, 1977.

Morgan, M. J. Genetic models of asymmetry should by asymmetrical. *Behavioral & Brain Sciences,* 1978, *1,* 325–331.

Morgan, M. J. Influences of sex on variation in human brain asymmetry. *Behavioral & Brain Sciences,* 1980, *3,* 244–245.

Morgan, M. J. Hemispheric specializations and spatiotemporal interactions. *Behavioral & Brain Sciences,* 1981, *4,* 74–75.

Morgan, M. J., & Corballis, M. C. On the biological basis of human laterality: II. The mechanisms of inheritance. *Behavioral & Brain Sciences,* 1978, *1,* 270–277.

Morgan, W. P. A case of congenital word-blindness. *British Medical Journal,* 1896, *2,* 1378.

Morley, M. E. *The development and disorders of speech in childhood.* London: Churchill Livingstone, 1972.

Morrow, L., Vrtunski, P. B., Kim, Y., & Boller, F. Arousal responses to emotional stimuli and laterality of lesion. *Neuropsychologia*, 1981, *19*, 65–71.

Morse, P. A. The infancy of infant speech perception: The first decade of research. *Brain, Behavior, & Evolution*, 1979, *16*, 351–373.

Moscovitch, M. Language and the cerebral hemispheres: Reaction time studies and their implications for models of cerebral dominance. In P. Pliner, L. Krames, & T. Alloway (Eds.), *Communication and affect: Language and thought*. New York: Academic Press, 1973.

Moscovitch, M. On the representation of language in the right hemisphere of right-handed people. *Brain & Language*, 1976, *3*, 47–71.

Moscovitch, M. The development of lateralization of language functions and its relation to cognitive and linguistic development: A review and some theoretical speculations. In S. J. Segalowitz & F. Gruber (Eds.), *Language development and neurological theory*. New York: Academic Press, 1977.

Moss, F. A. *Applications of psychology*. Boston: Houghton, 1929.

Mountcastle, V. B., Lynch, J. C., Georgopoulos, A., Sakata, H., & Acuna, C. Posterior parietal association areas of the monkey: Command functions for operations in extrapersonal space. *Journal of Neurophysiology*, 1975, *38*, 871.

Munk, H. Ueber die Functionen der Grosshirnrinde. *Gesammelte Mittheilungen aus den Jahren, 1877–80*. Berlin: Huschwald, 1881.

Nagylaki, T., & Levy, J. "The sound of one paw clapping" isn't sound. *Behavior Genetics*, 1973, *3*, 279–292.

Naidoo, S. *Specific dyslexia*. London: Pitman, 1972.

Naidoo, S. Teaching methods and their rationale. In G. Th. Pavlidis & T. R. Miles (Eds.), *Dyslexia research and its applications to eduction*. New York: Wiley, 1981.

Naylor, H. Reading disability and lateral asymmetry: An information-processing analysis. *Psychological Bulletin*, 1980, *87*, 531–545.

Naylor, H., Lambert, N. M., Sassone, D. M., & Hardyck, C. Lateral asymmetry in perceptual judgments of reading disabled, hyperactive, and control children. *International Journal of Neuroscience*, 1980, *10*, 135–143.

Nebes, R. D. Direct examination of cognitive function in the right and left hemispheres. In M. Kinsbourne (Ed.), *Asymmetrical function of the brain*. London: Cambridge Univ. Press, 1978.

Nebes, R. D., & Sperry, R. W. Hemispheric deconnection syndrome with cerebral birth injury in the dominant arm area. *Neuropsychologia*, 1971, *9*, 247–259.

Needham, E. C., & Black, J. W. The relative ability of aphasic persons to judge the duration and intensity of pure tones. *Journal of Speech & Hearing Research*, 1970, *13*, 725–730.

Needham, R. Right and left in Nyoro Symbolic classification. *Africa*, 1967, *37*, 425–451.

Needham, R. *Right and left: Essays on dual symbolic classification*. Chicago: Univ. of Chicago Press, 1973.

Nelson, S. E., Hunter, H. & Walter, M. Stuttering in twin types. *Journal of Speech Disorders*, 1945, *10*, 335–343.

Neville, A. C. *Animal asymmetry*. London: Arnold, 1976.

Newcombe, F., & Ratcliff, G. Handedness, speech lateralization, and ability. *Neuropsychologia*, 1973, *11*, 399–407.

Newman, H. H. *Physiology of twinning*. Chicago: Chicago Press, 1923.

Newman, H. H. Dermatoglyphics and the problem of handedness. *American Journal of Anatomy*. 1934, *55*, 277–322.

Newman, H. H. *Multiple human births*. New York: Doubleday, Doran, 1940.

Nottebohm, F. Ontogeny of bird song. *Science*, 1970, *167*, 950–956.

Nottebohm, F. Neural lateralization of vocal control in a passerine bird, I. Song. *Journal of Experimental Zoology*, 1971, *177*, 229–262.

Nottebohm, F. Neural lateralization of vocal control in a passerine bird, II. Subsongs, calls, and a theory of vocal learning. *Journal of Experimental Zoology,* 1972, *179,* 25–50.

Nottebohm, F. Asymmetries in neural control of vocalization in the canary. In S. Harnad, R. W., Doty, L. Goldstein, J. Jaynes, & G. Krauthamer (Eds.), *Lateralization in the nervous system.* New York: Academic Press, 1977.

Nottebohm, F. A continuum of sexes bedevils the search for sexual differences? *Behavioral & Brain Sciences,* 1980, *3,* 245–246.

Nottebohm, F., & Nottebohm, M. E. Left hypoglossal dominance in the control of canary and white-crowned sparrow song. *Journal of Comparative Physiology,* 1976, *108,* 171–192.

Obrzut, J. E. Dichotic listening and bisensory memory skills in qualitatively diverse dyslexic readers. *Journal of Learning Disabilities,* 1979, *12,* 304–314.

Ojemann, G. A., & Whitaker, H. A. Language localization and variability. *Brain & Language,* 1978, *6,* 239–260.

Ojemann, G. A., & Ward, A. A. Speech representation in ventrolateral thalamus. *Brain,* 1971, *94,* 669–680.

Oldfield, R. C. The assessment and analysis of handedness: The Edinburgh Inventory. *Neuropsychologia,* 1971, *9,* 97–114.

Olson, M. E. Laterality in tachistoscopic word recognition in normal and delayed readers in elementary schools. *Neuropsychologia,* 1973, *11,* 343–350.

Omenn, G. S., & Weber, B. A. Dyslexia: Search for phenotypic and genetic heterogeneity. *American Journal of Medical Genetics,* 1978, *1,* 333–342.

Oppenheimer, J. M. Asymmetry revisited. *American Zoologist,* 1974, *14,* 867–879.

Orbach, J. Retinal locus as a factor in the recognition of visually perceived words. *American Journal of Psychology,* 1953, *65,* 555–562.

Ornstein, R. E. *The psychology of consciousness.* San Francisco: Freeman, 1972.

Orton, S. T. ''Word-blindess'' in school children. *Archives of Neurology & Psychiatry,* 1925, *14,* 581–615.

Orton, S. T. A physiological theory of reading disability and stuttering in children. *New England Journal of Medicine,* 1928, *199,* 1046–1052.

Orton, S. T. Familial occurrence of disorders in acquisition of language. *Eugenics,* 1930, *3,* 140–147.

Orton, S. T. Special disability in reading. *Bulletin of the Neurological Institute of New York,* 1931, *1,* 159–192.

Orton, S. T. *Reading, writing, and speech problems in children.* New York: Norton, 1937.

Orton, S. T., & Travis, L. E. Studies in stuttering. IV. Studies of action currents in stutterers. *Archives of Neurology & Psychiatry,* 1929, *21,* 61–68.

Overstreet, R. An investigation of prenatal position and handedness. *Psychological Bulletin,* 1938, *35,* 520–521.

Paivio, A. Images, propositions, and knowledge. In J. M. Nicholas (Ed.), *Images, perception, and knowledge.* (The Western Ontario Series in the Philosophy of Science). Dordrecht, The Netherlands: Reidel, 1976.

Patterson, F. Conversations with a gorilla. *National Geographic,* 1978, *154,* 438–466.

Patterson, K., & Bradshaw, J. L. Differential hemispheric mediation of nonverbal stimuli. *Journal of Experimental Psychology: Human Perception & Performance,* 1975, *1,* 246–252.

Patterson, K. E. Neuropsychological approaches to the study of reading. *British Journal of Psychology,* 1981, *72,* 151–174.

Patterson, K. E., & Marcel, A. J. Aphasia, dyslexia, and the phonological coding of written words. *Quarterly Journal of Experimental Psychology,* 1977, *29,* 307–318.

Pavlidis, G. Th. Do eye movements hold the key to dyslexia? *Neuropsychologia,* 1981, *19,* 57–64.

Penfield, W., & Jasper, H. H. *Epilepsy and the functional anatomy of the human brain.* Boston: Little, Brown, 1954.

Penfield, W., & Roberts, L. *Speech and brain mechanisms.* Princeton: Princeton Univ. Press, 1959.

Peters, M. Why the preferred hand taps more quickly than the non-preferred hand: Three experiments on handedness. *Canadian Journal of Psychology,* 1980, *34,* 62–71.

Peters, M., & Durding, B. M. Handedness measured by finger tapping: A continuous variable. *Canadian Journal of Psychology.* 1978, *32,* 257–261.

Peters, M., & Durding, B. M. Footedness of left- and right-handers. *American Journal of Psychology,* 1979, *92,* 133–142.

Peters, M., & Petrie, B. F. Functional asymmetries of the stepping reflex of human neonates. *Canadian Journal of Psychology,* 1979, *33,* 198–200.

Peters, M., Petrie, B., & Oddie, D. Foot-length asymmetry, sex, and handedness. *Science,* 1981, *212,* 1417–1418.

Peterson, G. M. Mechanisms of handedness in the rat. *Comparative Psychology Monographs,* 1934, *9*(46).

Peterson, J. M., & Lansky, L. M. Left-handedness among architects: Some facts and speculation. *Perceptual & Motor Skills,* 1974, *38,* 547–550.

Peterson, M.R., Beecher, M. D., Zoloth, S. R., Moody, D. B., & Stebbins, W. C. Neural lateralization of species-specific vocalizations by Japanese macaques (*Macaca fuscata*). *Science,* 1978, *202,* 324–327.

Petrie, B. F., & Peters, M. Handedness: Left/right differences in intensity of grasp response and duration of rattle holding in infants. *Infant Behavior & Development,* 1980, *3,* 215–221.

Phippard, D. Hemifield differences in visual perception in deaf and hearing subjects. *Neuropsychologia,* 1977, *15,* 555–562.

Pierce, C. M., & Lipcon, H. H. Stuttering: Clinical and electroencephalographic findings. *Military Medicine,* 1959, *12,* 511–519.

Pinsky, S. D., & McAdam, D. W. Electroencephalographic and dichotic indices of cerebral laterality in stutterers. *Brain & Language,* 1980, *11,* 374–397.

Pirozzolo, F. J. *The neuropsychology of developmental reading disorders.* New York: Praeger, 1979.

Poizner, H., Battison, R., & Lane, H. Cerebral asymmetry for American Sign Language: The effects of moving stimuli. *Brain & Language,* 1979, *7,* 351–362.

Policansky, D. Flatfishes and the inheritance of asymmetries. *Behavioral & Brain Sciences,* 1982, *5,* 264–267.

Poppen, R., Stark, J., Eisenson, J., Forrest, T., & Wertheim, G. Visual sequencing performance of aphasic children. *Journal of Speech & Hearing Research,* 1969, *12,* 288–300.

Popper, K., & Eccles, J. C. *The self and its brain.* Berlin: Springer, 1977.

Pratt, R. T. C., & Warrington, E. K. The assessment of cerebral dominance with unilateral E.C.T. *British Journal of Psychiatry,* 1972, *121,* 327–328.

Premack, D. A functional analysis of language. *Journal of the Experimental Analysis of Behavior,* 1970, *14,* 107–125.

Puccetti, R. The alleged manipulospatiality explanation of right hemisphere visuospatial superiority. *Behavioral & Brain Sciences,* 1981, *4,* 75–76.

Pylyshyn, Z. W. What the mind's eye tells the mind's brain: A critique of mental imagery. *Psychological Bulletin,* 1973, *80,* 1–24.

Pylyshyn, Z. W. Imagery and artifical intelligence. In W. Savage (Ed.), *Perception and cognition: Issues in the foundation of psychology. (The Minnesota studies in the philosophy of science,* Vol. 9). Minneapolis: The Univserity Press, 1978.

Ramaley, F. Inheritance of left handedness. *American Naturalist,* 1913, *47,* 730–738.

Ramsay, D. S. Manual preference for tapping in infants. *Developmental Psychology*, 1979, *15*, 437–442.

Ramsay, D. S. Beginnings of bimanual handedness and speech in infants. *Infant Behavior & Development*, 1980, *3*, 67–77. (a)

Ramsay, D. S. Emergence of unimanual handedness and repetitive babbling in infants. Paper presented at the International Conference on Infant Studies, New Haven, Connecticut, April 1980. (b)

Ramsay, D. S. Onset of unimanual handedness in infants. *Infant Behavior & Development*, 1980, *3*, 377–385. (c)

Ramsay, D. S., Campos, J. J., & Fenson, L. Onset of bimanual handedness in infants. *Infant Behavior & Development*, 1979, *2*, 69–76.

Rapin, I., & Wilson, B. C. Children with developmental language disability: Neurological aspects and assessment. In M. Wyke (Ed.), *Developmental dysphasia*. New York: Academic Press, 1978.

Ratcliff, G. Spatial thought, mental rotation, and the right cerebral hemisphere. *Neuropsychologia*, 1979, *17*, 49–54.

Reade, C. "The coming man." Letter to the Editor, *Harper's Weekly*, March 2, 1878, pp. 174–175.

Reuter-Lorenz, P., & Davidson, R. J. Differential contributions of the two cerebral hemispheres to the perception of happy and sad faces. *Neuropsyhologia*, 1981, *19*, 609–613.

Reynolds, M. McQ., & Jeeves, M. A. A developmental study of hemispheric specialization for recognition of faces in normal subjects. *Cortex*, 1978, *14*, 511–520.

Richardson, J. T. E. How to measure laterality. *Neuropsychologia*, 1976, *14*, 135–136.

Riese, W. The early history of aphasia. *Bulletin of the History of Medicine*, 1947, *21*, 322–334.

Rife, D. C. Genetic studies of monozygotic twins. I, II, III. *Journal of Heredity*, 1933, *24*, 339–345, 407–414, 443–446.

Rife, D. C. Handedness with special reference to twins. *Genetics*, 1940, *25*, 178–186.

Rife, D. C. Genetic interrelations between dermatoglyphics and functional handedness. *Genetics*, 1943, *28*, 41–48.

Rife, D. C. Application of gene frequency analysis to the interpretation of data from twins. *Human Biology*, 1950, *22*, 136–145.

Rife, D. C. Handprints and handedness. *American Journal of Human Genetics*, 1955, *7*, 170–179.

Rigal, R. A. Determination of handedness using hand-efficiency tests. *Perception & Motor Skills*, 1974, *39*, 253–254. (a)

Rigal, R. A. Hand efficiency and right–left discrimination. *Perceptual & Motor Skills*, 1974, *38*, 219–224. (b)

Rigby, P. Dual symbolic classification among the Gogo of Central Tanzania. *Africa*, 1966, *36*, 1–16.

Roberts, W. W. The interpretation of some disorders of speech. *Journal of Mental Science*, 1949, *95*, 567–588.

Robinson, D. L., Goldberg, M. E., & Stanton, G. B. Parietal association cortex in the primate: Sensory mechanisms and behavioral modulations. *Journal of Neurophysiology*, 1978, *41*, 910–932.

Robinson, D. N. What sort of persons are hemispheres? Another look at split-brain man. *British Journal for the Philosophy of Science*, 1976, *27*, 73–78.

Robinson, G. M., & Solomon, D. J. Rhythm is processed by the speech hemisphere. *Journal of Experimental Psychology*, 1974, *102*, 508–511.

Rock, I. *Orientation and form*. New York: Academic Press, 1973.

Rogers, L., TenHouten, W., Kaplan, C., & Gardiner, M. Hemispheric specialization and language: An EEG study of Hopi children. Unpublished manuscript, 1976. (Cited in Scott *et al.*, 1979.)

Rogers, L. J. Lateralization in the avian brain. *Bird Behaviour*, 1980, *2*, 1–12.

Rogers, L. J. Environmental influences on brain lateralization. *Behavioral & Brain Sciences*, 1981, *4*, 35–36.

Rogers, L. J., & Anson, J. M. Lateralization of function in the chicken forebrain. *Pharmacology, Biochemistry, & Behavior*, 1979, *10*, 679–686.

Rosenberger, P. B., & Hier, D. B. Cerebral asymmetry and verbal intellectual deficits. *Annals of Neurology*, 1981, *38*, 300–304.

Rosenfield, D. B. Cerebral dominance and stuttering. *Journal of Fluency Disorders*, 1980, *5*, 171–185.

Rosenfield, D. B., & Goodglass, H. Dichotic testing of cerebral dominance in stutterers. *Brain & Language*, 1980, *11*, 170–180.

Rossi, G. F., & Rosadini, G. Experimental analysis of cerebral dominance in man. In C. H. Millikan & F. L. Darley (Eds.), *Brain mechanisms underlying speech and language*. New York: Grune & Stratton, 1967.

Rozin, P., Poritsky, S., & Sotsky, R. American children with reading problems can easily learn to read English represented by Chinese characters. *Science*, 1971, *171*, 1264–1267.

Rubens, A. B. Transcortical motor aphasia. In H. Whitaker & H. A. Whitaker (Eds.), *Studies in neurolinguistics* (Vol. 1). New York: Academic Press, 1976.

Rubens, A. B. Agnosia. In K. M. Heilman & E. Valenstein (Eds.), *Clinical neuropsychology*. Oxford: Oxford Univ. Press, 1979.

Russell, B. *A history of Western philosophy*. London: Allen & Unwin, 1946.

Russo, M., & Vignolo, L. A. Visual figure–ground discrimination in patients with unilateral cerebral disease. *Cortex*, 1967, *3*, 113–127.

Rutter, M., Tizard, J., & Whitmore, K. *Education, health and behaviour*. London: Longman, 1970.

Sackeim, H. A., & Gur, R. C. Lateral asymmetry in intensity of emotional expression. *Neuropsychologia*, 1978, *16*, 473–481.

Safer, M. A., & Leventhal, H. Ear differences in evaluating emotional tones of voice and verbal content. *Journal of Experimental Psychology: Human Perception & Performance*, 1977, *3*, 75–82.

Saffran, E. M., Bogyo, L. C., Schwartz, M. F., & Marin, O. S. M. Does deep dyslexia reflect right-hemisphere reading? In M. Coltheart, K. E. Patterson, & J. C. Marshall (Eds.), *Deep dyslexia*. London: Routledge & Kegan Paul, 1980.

Sagan, C. *The dragons of Eden*. New York: Random House, 1977.

St. James-Roberts, I. A reinterpretation of hemispherectomy data without functional plasticity of the brain. I. Intellectual function. *Brain & Language*, 1981, *13*, 31–53.

Sanders, B., Wilson, J. R., & Vandenberg, S.G. Handedness and spatial ability. *Cortex*, 1982, *18*, 79–90.

Sarasin, P. Über rechts- und links-Händigkeit in der Praehistorie und die rechts-Händigkeit in der historischen Zeit. *Naturforschende Gesellschaft in Basel, Verhandlungen*, 1918, *29*, 122–196.

Sasanuma, S. Itoh, M., Mori, K., & Kobayashi, Y. Tachistoscopic recognition of Kana and Kanji words. *Neuropsychologia*, 1977, *15*, 547–533.

Satz, P. Pathological left handedness: An explanatory model. *Cortex*, 1972, *8*, 121–135.

Satz, P. Cerebral dominance and reading disability: An old problem revisited. In R. M. Knights & D. J. Bakker (Eds.), *The neuropsychology of learning disorders*. Baltimore, Md.: Univ. Park Press, 1976.

Satz, P., Achenbach, K., Pattishall, E., & Fennel, E. Order of report, ear asymmetry and handedness in dichotic listening. *Cortex*, 1965, *1*, 377–396.

Satz, P., Fennel, E., & Jones, M. B. Comments on: A model of inheritance of handedness and cerebral dominance. *Neuropsychologia*, 1969, *7*, 101–103.

Satz, P., Rardin, D., & Ross, J. An evaluation of a theory of specific developmental dyslexia. *Child Development*, 1971, *42*, 2009–2021.

Schaller, G. B. *The mountain gorilla: Ecology and behavior.* Chicago: Univ. of Chicago Press, 1963.

Scheinfeld, A. *The new you and heredity.* London: Chatto & Windus, 1956.

Schlumberger, H. G., & Gotwals, J. E. *Ischiopagus tripus.* Report of two cases. *Archives of Pathology*, 1945, *39*, 142–147.

Scholes, R. J., & Fischler, I. Hemispheric function and linguistic skill in the deaf. *Brain & Language*, 1979, *7*, 336–350.

Schonell, F. J. The relation of reading disability to handedness and certain ocular factors: Part 1. *British Journal of Educational Psychology*, 1940, *10*, 227–237.

Schonell, F. J. The relation of reading disability to handedness and certain ocular factors: Part 2. *British Journal of Educational Psychology*, 1941, *11*, 20–27.

Schonell, F. J. *Backwardness in the basic subjects.* Edinburgh: Oliver & Boyd, 1942.

Schwartz, M. Left-handedness and high-risk pregnancy. *Neuropsychologia*, 1977, *15*, 341–344.

Scott, S., Hynd, G. W., Hunt, L., & Weed, W. Cerebral speech lateralization in the native American Navajo. *Neuropsychologia*, 1979, *17*, 80–92.

Scotti, G., & Spinnler, H. Colour imperception in unilateral hemisphere-damaged patients. *Journal of Neurology, Neurosurgery, & Psychiatry*, 1970, *33*, 22–28.

Searleman, A. A review of right hemisphere linguistic capabilities. *Psychological Bulletin*, 1977, *84*, 503–528.

Segalowitz, S. J., & Chapman, J. S. Cerebral asymmetry for speech in neonates: A behavioral measure. *Brain & Language*, 1980, *9*, 281–288.

Semenov, S. A. *Prehistoric technology.* London: Cory, McAdams, & MacKay, 1964.

Sergent, J., & Bindra, D. Differential hemispheric processing of faces: Methodological considerations and reinterpretation. *Psychological Bulletin*, 1981, *89*, 541–554.

Seth, G. Eye–hand co-ordination and 'handedness': a developmental study of visuo-motor behaviour in infancy. *British Journal of Educational Psychology*, 1973, *43*, 35–49.

Shankweiler, D., Liberman, I. Y., Mark, L. S., Fowler, C. A., & Fischer, F. W. The speech code and learning to read. *Journal of Experimental Psychology: Human Learning & Memory*, 1979, *5*, 531–545.

Shanon, B. Writing positions in Americans and Israelis. *Neuropsychologia*, 1978, *16*, 587–591.

Shenker, R. C. Motor potentials of stutterers and non-stutterers during speech (Doctoral dissertation, McGill University, 1979). *Dissertation Abstracts International*, 1979, *40*, 4624B.

Sidman, M., & Kirk, B. Letter reversals in naming, writing, and matching to sample. *Child Development*, 1974, *45*, 616–625.

Silverberg, R., Obler, L. K., & Gordon, H. W. Handedness in Israel. *Neuropsychologia*, 1979, *17*, 83–92.

Skinner, B. F. *Verbal behavior.* New York: Appleton, 1957.

Slorach, N., & Noehr, B. Dichotic listening in stuttering and dyslalic children. *Cortex*, 1973, *9*, 295–300.

Smith, A. Speech and other function after left (dominant) hemispherectomy. *Journal of Neurology, Neurosurgery, & Psychiatry*, 1966, *29*, 467–471.

Smith, L. C. A study of laterality characteristics of retarded readers and reading achievers. *Journal of Experimental Education*, 1950, *18*, 321–329.

Smith, S. D., Pennington, B. F., Kimberling, W. J., & Lubs, H. A. An investigation of familial dyslexia using both genetic and cognitive analysis. Paper presented to the Society for Research in Child Development, Boston, April 1981.

Sommers, R. K., Brady, W., & Moore, W. H., Jr. Dichotic ear preferences of stuttering children and adults. *Perceptual & Motor Skills*, 1975, *41*, 931–938.

Sparks, R., & Geschwind, N. Dichotic listening in man after section of neocortical commissures. *Cortex*, 1968, *4*, 3–16.

Sparrow, S. S., & Satz, P. Dyslexia, laterality, and neuropsychological development. In D. J. Bakker & P. Satz (Eds.), *Specific reading disability: Advances in theory and method*. Rotterdam: Univ. of Rotterdam Press, 1970.

Spemann, H., & Falkenberg, H. Über asymmetrische Entwicklung und Situs inversus bei Zwillingen und Doppelbildungen. *Wilhelm Roux Archiv für Entwicklungsmechanik*, 1919, *45*, 371–422.

Sperry, R. W., Zaidel, E., & Zaidel, D. Self recognition and social awareness in the deconnected minor hemisphere. *Neuropsychologia*, 1979, *17*, 153–166.

Spreen, O., Benton, A. L., & Fincham, R. Auditory agnosia without aphasia. *Archives of Neurology*, 1965, *13*, 84.

Springer, S. P. Ear asymmetry in a dichotic detection task. *Perception & Psychophysics*, 1971, *10*, 239–241.

Springer, S. P. Handedness and cerebral organization in twins—implications for the biological basis of human laterality. *Behavioral & Brain Sciences*, 1978, *2*, 316–317.

Springer, S. P. & Deutsch, G. *Left brain, right brain*. San Francisco: Freeman, 1981.

Springer, S. P., & Searleman, A. Left handedness in twins: Implications for the mechanisms underlying cerebral asymmetry of function. In J. Herron (Ed.), *Neuropsychology of left-handedness*. New York: Academic Press, 1980.

Steel, K. B., & Javert, C. T. Mechanism of labor for transverse positions of the vertex. *Surgical Gynecology & Obstetrics*, 1942, *75*, 477–480.

Stein, G. M., Gibbons, R. D., & Meldman, M. J. Lateral eye movement and handedness as measure of functional brain asymmetry in learning disability. *Cortex*, 1980, *16*, 223–230.

Stein, J., & Fowler, S. Visual dyslexia. *Trends in Neurosciences*, 1981, *4*, 77–80.

Strauss, E., & Moscovitch, M. Perception of facial expressions. *Brain & Language*, 1981, *13*, 308–322.

Strub, R. L., & Gardner, H. The repetition deficit in conduction aphasia. *Brain & Language*, 1974, *1*, 241–256.

Studdert-Kennedy, M. Dichotic studies II: Two questions. *Brain & Language*, 1975, *2*, 123–130.

Studdert-Kennedy, M. The beginnings of speech. In G. B. Barlow, K. Immelmann, M. Main, & L. Petrinovich (Eds.), *Behavioral development: An interdisciplinary approach*. New York: Cambridge Univ. Press, 1980.

Studdert-Kennedy, M. Cerebral hemispheres: Specialized for the analysis of what? *Behavioral & Brain Sciences*, 1981, *4*, 76–77.

Studdert-Kennedy, M., & Shankweiler, D. Hemispheric specialization for speech perception. *Journal of the Acoustical Society of America*, 1970, *48*, 579–594.

Sturtevant, A. H. Inheritance of direction of coiling in *Limnaea*. *Science*, 1923, *58*, 269.

Suberi, M., & McKeever, W. F. Differential right hemispheric memory storage of emotional and non-emotional faces. *Neuropsychologia*, 1977, *15*, 757–768.

Subirana, A. The prognosis in aphasia in relation to cerebral dominance and handedness. *Brain*, 1958, *81*, 415–425.

Sussman, H. M. The laterality effect in lingual-auditory tracking. *Journal of the Acoustical Society of America*, 1971, *49*, 1874–1880.

Sussman, H. M., & MacNeilage, P. F. Hemispheric specialization for speech production and perception in stutterers. *Neuropsychologia*, 1975, *13*, 19–26. (a)

Sussman, H. M., & MacNeilage, P. F. Studies of hemispheric specialization for speech production. *Brain & Language*, 1975, *2*, 131–151. (b)

Sussman, H. M., MacNeilage, P. F., & Lumbley, J. Pursuit auditory tracking of dichotically presented tonal amplitudes. *Journal of Speech & Hearing Research*, 1975, *18*, 74–81.

Tallal, P. Auditory temporal perception, phonics, and reading disabilities in children. *Brain & Language*, 1980, *9*, 182–198.

Tallal, P., & Piercy, M. Developmental aphasia: Impaired rate of non-verbal processing as a function of sensory modality. *Neuropsychologia*, 1973, *11*, 389–398.

Tallal, P., & Piercy, M. Developmental aphasia: Rate of auditory processing and selective impairment of consonant perception. *Neuropsychologia*, 1974, *12*, 83–93.

Tallal, P., & Piercy, M. Defects of auditory perception in children with developmental dysphasia. In M. Wyke (Ed.), *Developmental dysphasia*. New York: Academic Press, 1978.

Tallal, P., Stark, R. E., & Curtiss, B. Relation between speech perception and speech production in children with developmental dysphasia. *Brain & Language*, 1976, *3*, 305–317.

Taylor, D. C. Differential rates of cerebral maturation between sexes and between hemispheres. *Lancet*, 1969 (July 19), 140–142.

Taylor, J. (Ed.), *Selected writings of John Hughlings Jackson* (Vol. 2). London: Staples, 1958.

Teng, E. L., Lee, P.-H. Yang, K.-S., & Chang, P. C. Handedness in a Chinese population: Biological, social, and pathological factors. *Science*, 1976, *193*, 1148–1150.

Terrace, H. S., Petitto, L. A., Saunders, R. J., & Bever, T. G. Can an ape create a sentence? *Science*, 1979, *206*, 891–900

Terzian, H. Behavioral and EEG effects of intracarotid sodium amytal injection. *Acta Neurochirurgia* (Vienna), 1964, *12*, 230–239.

Teuber, H.-L., & Weinstein, S. Ability to discover hidden figures after cerebral lesions. *Archives of Neurology & Psychiatry*, 1956, *76*, 369–379.

Thompson, L. J. Language disabilities in men of eminence. *Journal of Learning Disabilities*, 1971, *4*, 39–50.

Thomson, M. E. A comparison of laterality effects in dyslexics and controls using verbal dichotic listening tasks. *Neuropsychologia*, 1976, *14*, 243–246.

Tomlinson-Keasey, C., Kelly, R. R., & Burton, J. K. Hemispheric changes in information processing during development. *Developmental Psychology*, 1978, *14*, 214–223.

Torgerson, J. Situs inversus, asymmetry, and twinning. *American Journal of Human Genetics*, 1950, *2*, 361–370.

Touwen, B. C. L., & Sporrel, T. Soft signs and minimal brain damage. *Developmental Medicine & Child Neurology*, 1979, *21*, 528–530.

Trankell, A. Aspects of genetics in psychology. *American Journal of Human Genetics*, 1955, *7*, 264–276.

Travis, L. E. Dysintegration of the breathing movements during stuttering. *Archives of Neurology & Psychiatry*, 1927, *18*, 673.

Travis, L. E. *Speech pathology*. New York: Appleton, 1931.

Treisman, A., & Geffen, G. Selective attention and cerebral dominance in perceiving and responding to speech messages. *Quarterly Journal of Experimental Psychology*, 1968, *20*, 139–150.

Trevarthen, C. B. Functional relations of disconnected hemispheres with the brain stem and with each other: Monkey and man. In M. Kinsbourne & W. L. Smith (Eds.), *Hemispheric disconnection and cerebral function*. Springfield, Ill.: Thomas, 1974.

Trevarthen, C. B. Manipulative strategies of baboons and origins of cerebral asymmetry. In M. Kinsbourne (Ed.), *Asymmetrical function of the brain*. London: Cambridge Univ. Press, 1978.

Trommer, E. *Das Stottern, die Sprachzwangneurose: II. Versammlung der Deutschen Gesellschaft für Sprach und Stimmheilkunde*. Liepzig: Kabitzsch, 1929.

Tsunoda, T., & Moriyama, H. Specific patterns of cerebral dominance for various sounds in adult stutterers. *Journal of Auditory Research,* 1972, *12,* 216–227.

Turkewitz, G. The development of lateral preferences in the human infant. In S. Harnad, R. W. Doty, L. Goldstein, J. Jaynes, & G. Krauthamer (Eds.), *Lateralization in the nervous system.* New York: Academic Press, 1977.

Turkewitz, G., Gordon, E. W., & Birch, H. G. Head-turning in the human neonate: Effect of prandial condition and lateral preference. *Journal of Comparative & Physiological Psychology,* 1965, *59,* 189–192.

Tzavaras, A., Hécaen, H., & Le Bras, H. Le problème de la spécificité du déficit de la reconnaissance du visage humain lors des lésions hémisphériques unilatérales. *Neuropsychologia,* 1970, *8,* 403–416.

Tzavaras, A., Kaprinis, G., & Gatzoyas, A. Literacy and hemispheric specialization for language: Digit dichotic listening in illiterates. *Neuropsychologia,* 1981, *19,* 565–570.

Ulbricht, T. L. V. The origin of optical asymmetry on earth. *Origins of Life,* 1975, *6,* 303–315.

Underwood, J. K., & Paulson, C. J. Aphasia and congenital deafness: A case study. *Brain & Language,* 1981, *12,* 285–291.

Van Allen, M. W., Benton, A. L., & Gordon, M. C. Temporal discrimination in brain-damaged patients. *Neuropsychologia,* 1966, *4,* 159–167.

Van der Meer, H. C. *Die Links-Rechts-Polarisation des phänomenalen Raumes: Eine Experiment.* Groningen: Wolters, 1959.

Van Dongen, H. R., & Loonen, M. C. B. Factors related to the prognosis of acquired aphasia in children, *Cortex,* 1977, *13,* 131–136.

Van Riper, C. *The nature of stuttering.* Englewood Cliffs: N. J.: Prentice-Hall, 1971.

Van Wagenen, W., & Herren, R. Surgical division of commissural pathways in the corpus callosum. *Archives of Neurology & Psychiatry,* 1940, *44,* 740–759.

Vargha-Khadem, F., & Corballis, M. C. Cerebral asymmetry in infants. *Brain & Language,* 1979, *8,* 1–9.

Varney, N. R., & Benton, A. L. Tactile perception of direction in relation to handedness and familial handedness. *Neuropsychologia,* 1975, *13,* 449–454.

Vermeij, G. J. Left asymmetry in the animal kingdom. *Behavioral & Brain Sciences,* 1978, *2,* 320–322.

Vernon, M. D. *Backwardness in reading* (2nd ed.). Cambridge: Cambridge Univ. Press, 1960.

Von Kraft, A. On the problem of the origin of asymmetric organs and human laterality. *Behavioral & Brain Sciences,* 1980, *3,* 478–479.

Von Monakow, C. *Die lokalisation im Grosshirurinde und der Abbau der Funktion durch Korticale Herde.* Wiesbaden: Bergmann, 1914.

von Woellwarth, C. Experimentelle Untersuchungen über dem Situs inversus der Eingeweide und der Habenula des Zwischenhirns bei Amphibien. *Wilhem Roux Archiv für Entwicklungsmechanik,* 1950, *144,* 178–256.

Waber, D. Sex differences in cognition: A function of maturation rate. *Science,* 1976, *192,* 572–574.

Waber D. Sex differences in mental abilities, hemisphere lateralization, and rate of physical growth at adolescence. *Developmental Psychology,* 1977, *13,* 29–38.

Wada, J. A., Clarke, R., & Hamm, A. Cerebral hemispheric asymmetry in humans. *Archives of Neurology,* 1975, *32,* 239–246.

Wada, J. A., & Rasmussen, T. Intracarotid injection of sodium amytal for the lateralization of cerebral speech dominance: Experimental and clinical observations. *Journal of Neurosurgery,* 1960, *17,* 266–282.

Wagner, M. T., & Hannon, R. Hemispheric asymmetries in faculty and student musicians and non-musicians during melody recognition tasks. *Brain & Language,* 1981, *13,* 379–388.

Walker, E. Current studies of animal communication as paradigms for the biology of language. In E. Walker (Ed.), *Explorations in the biology of language.* Montgomery, Vt.: Bradford Books, 1978.

Wall, W. D. Reading backwardness among men in the army. I. *British Journal of Educational Psychology,* 1945, *15,* 28–40.

Wall, W. D. Reading backwardness among men in the army. II. *British Journal of Educational Psychology,* 1946, *16,* 133–148.

Warren, J. M. Handedness and cerebral dominance in monkeys. In S. Harnad, R. W. Doty, L. Goldstein, J. Jaynes, & G. Krauthamer (Eds.), *Lateralization in the nervous system.* New York: Academic Press, 1977.

Warren, J. M. The left force: homology or analogy. *Behavioral & Brain Sciences,* 1978, *1,* 322.

Warrington, E. K., & James, M. An experimental investigation of facial recognition in patients with unilateral lesions. *Cortex,* 1967, *3,* 317–326.

Warrington, E. K., James, M., & Kinsbourne, M. Drawing disability in relation to laterality of cerebral lesion. *Brain,* 1966, *89,* 53–82.

Warrington, E. K., & Pratt, R. T. C. Language laterality in left handers assessed by unilateral E.C.T. *Neuropsychologia,* 1973, *11,* 423–428.

Watson, J. B. *Behaviorism.* New York: The People's Institute, 1924.

Weber, A. M., & Bradshaw, J. L. Levy and Reid's neurological model in relation to writing hand/posture: An evaluation. *Psychological Bulletin,* 1981, *90,* 74–88.

Weber, E. Das Schreiben als Ursache der einseitigen Lage des Sprachzentrums. *Zentralblatt für Physiologie,* 1904, *18,* 341–347.

Webster, W. G. Functional asymmetry between the cerebral hemispheres of the cat. *Neuropsychologia,* 1972, *10,* 75–87.

Webster, W. G. Territoriality and the evolution of brain symmetry. In S. J. Dimond, & D. A. Blizard (Eds.), *Evolution and lateralization of the brain.* New York: New York Academy of Sciences, 1977.

Webster, W. G. Morphological asymmetries of the cat brain. *Brain, Behavior & Evolution,* 1981, *18,* 72–79.

Webster, W. G., & Webster, I. H. Anatomical asymmetries of the cerebral hemispheres of the cat brain. *Physiology & Behavior,* 1975, *14,* 867–869.

Wechsler, A. The effect of organic brain disease on recall of emotionally charged versus neutral narrative tests. *Neurology,* 1973, *23,* 130–135.

Wehrmaker, A. Left-handedness: Etiological cues from *situs inversus. Behavioral & Brain Sciences,* 1978, *2,* 322–323.

Weisenberg, T. H., & McBride, K. E. *Aphasia: A clinical and psychological study.* New York: The Commonwealth Fund, 1935.

Weiss, M. S., & House, A. S. Perception of dichotically presented vowels. *Journal of the Acoustical Society of America,* 1973, *53,* 51–58.

Wepman, J. M. Familial incidence in stammering. *Journal of Speech Disorders,* 1939, *4,* 199–204.

Wernicke, C. Der aphasische symptomencomplex. *Eine psychologische studie auf anatomischer basis.* Breslau: Cohen & Weigert, 1874.

Weyl, H. *Symmetry.* Princeton, N. J.: Princeton Univ. Press, 1952.

Whitaker, H. A case of the isolation of the language function. In H. Whitaker & H. A. Whitaker (Eds.), *Studies in neurolinguistics, Vol. 1.* New York: Academic Press, 1976.

White, K., & Ashton, R. Handedness assessment inventory. *Neuropsychologia,* 1976, *14,* 261–264.

White, M. J. Laterality differences in perception: A review. *Psychological Bulletin,* 1969, *72,* 387–405.

White, M. J. Hemispheric asymmetries in tachistoscopic information-processing. *British Journal of Psychology,* 1972, *63,* 497–508.

Wieschhoff, H. A. Concepts of right and left in African cultures. *Journal of the American Oriental Society,* 1938, *58,* 202–217.

Wilbrand, H. *Die Seelenblindheit als Herderscheinung und ihre Beziehungen zur Homonymen Hemianopsie.* Wiesbaden: Bergmann, 1887.

Wilde, W. *Practical observations on aural surgery.* Philadelphia: Blanchard & Lea, 1853.

Wile, I.S. *Handedness: Right and left.* Boston: Lothrop, Lee, & Shepard, 1934.

Wilson, D. Righthandedness. *The Canadian Journal,* 1872, No. 75, 193–203.

Wilson, E. B. Notes on the reversal of asymmetry in the regeneration of chelae in Alpheus heterochelis. *Biological Bulletin* (of the Marine Biological Laboratory, Woods Hole, Mass.), 1903, *4,* 197–210.

Wilson, P. T., & Jones, H. E. Left-handedness in twins. *Genetics,* 1932, *17,* 560–571.

Witelson, S. F. Sex and the single hemisphere: Specialization of the right hemisphere for spatial processing. *Science,* 1976, *193,* 425–427.

Witelson, S. F. Developmental dyslexia: Two right hemispheres and none left. *Science,* 1977, *195,* 309–311. (a)

Witelson, S. F. Early hemispheric specialization and interhemispheric plasticity: An empirical and theoretical review. In S. J. Segalowitz & F. A. Gruber (Eds.), *Language development and neurological theory.* New York: Academic Press, 1977. (b)

Witelson, S. F., & Pallie, W. Left hemisphere specialization for language in the newborn: Neuroanatomical evidence of asymmetry. *Brain,* 1973, *96,* 641–646.

Witelson, S. F., & Rabinovitch, M. S. Hemispheric speech lateralization in children with auditory-linguistic deficits. *Cortex,* 1972, *8,* 412–426.

Wolfe, L. S. Differential factors in specific reading disability. *Journal of Genetic Psychology,* 1941, *58,* 45–70.

Wolff, P. H., Hurwitz, I., & Moss, H. Serial organization of motor skills in left- and right-handed adults. *Neuropsychologia,* 1977, *15,* 539–546.

Wolfflin, H. *Gedanken zur Kunstgeschichte, Gedrucktes und Ungedrucktes* (3rd Edition). Basel: Schwabe, 1941.

Wolpert, L. Positional information and the spatial pattern of cellular differentiation. *Journal of Theoretical Biology,* 1969, *25,* 1–47.

Wolpert, L. The problem of directed left–right asymmetry in development. *Behavioral & Brain Sciences,* 1978, *2,* 324–325.

Woo, T. L., & Pearson, K. Dextrality and sinistrality of hand and eye. *Biometrika,* 1927, *19,* 165–199.

Wood, F., Stump, D., McKeehan, A., Sheldon, S., & Proctor, J. Patterns of regional cerebral blood flow during attempted reading aloud by stutterers both on and off haloperidol medication: Evidence for inadequate left frontal activation during stuttering. *Brain & Language,* 1980, *9,* 141–144.

Wood, J. P. *The snark was a boojum: A life of Lewis Carroll.* New York: Pantheon Books, 1966.

Woolley, H. T. The development of right handedness in a normal infant. *Psychological Review,* 1910, *17,* 37–41.

Wunderlich, R. C., & Heerema, N. A. Hair crown patterns of human newborns. *Clinical Pediatrics,* 1975, *14,* 1045–1049.

Wyke, M. A. (Ed.). *Developmental dysphasia.* London: Academic Press, 1978.

Yakovlev, P. I. A proposed definition of the limbic system. In C. H. Hockman (Ed.), *Limbic system mechanisms and autonomic function.* Springfield, Ill.: Thomas, 1972.

Yakovlev, P. I., & Rakic, P. Patterns of decussation of bulbar pyramids and distribution of pyramidal tracts on two sides of the spinal cord. *Transactions of the American Neurological Association,* 1966, *91,* 366–367.

Yanowitz, J. S., Satz, P., & Heilman, K. M. Foot-length asymmetry, sex, and handedness. *Science,* 1981, *212,* 1418.

Yeni-Komshian, G. H., & Benson, D. A. Anatomical study of cerebral asymmetry in the temporal lobes of humans, chimpanzees,and rhesus monkeys. *Science,* 1976, *192,* 387–389.

Yeni-Komshian, G. H., Isenberg, D., & Goldberg, H. Cerebral dominance and reading disability: Left visual field deficit in poor readers. *Neuropsychologia,* 1975, *13,* 83–94.

Young, A. W., & Ellis, A. W. Asymmetry of cerebral hemispheric function in normal and poor readers. *Psychological Bulletin,* 1981, *89,* 183–190.

Young, G. Manual specialization in infancy: Implications for lateralization of brain function. In S. J. Segalowitz & F. A. Gruber (Eds.), *Language development and neurological theory.* New York: Academic Press, 1977.

Young, J. Z. Why do we have two brains? In V. B. Mountcastle (Ed.), *Interhemispheric relations and cerebral dominance.* Baltimore, Md.: Johns Hopkins Press, 1962.

Youngren, O. M., Peek, F. W., & Phillips, R. E. Repetitive vocalizations evoked by local electrical stimulation of avian brains. *Brain, Behavior, and Evolution,* 1974, *9,* 393–421.

Zaidel, E. Linguistic competence and related functions in the right cerebral hemisphere of man following commissurotomy and hemispherectomy. Unpublished doctoral dissertation, California Institute of Technology, 1973. (Cited in Nebes, 1978.)

Zaidel, E. A technique for presenting lateralized visual input with prolonged exposure. *Vision Research,* 1975, *15,* 283–289.

Zaidel, E. Auditory vocabulary of the right hemisphere following brain bisection or hemidecortication. *Cortex,* 1976, *12,* 191–211.

Zaidel, E. Lexical organization in the right hemisphere. In P. A. Buser & A. Rougeul-Buser (Eds.), *Cerebral correlates of conscious experience.* Amsterdam: Elsevier/ North Holland, 1978.

Zaidel, E. Reading by the disconnected right hemisphere: An aphasiology perspective. In Y. Zotterman (Ed.), *The Wenner-Gren symposium on dyslexia.* London: Plenum, 1981.

Zaidel, E., & Peters, A. M. Phonological encoding and ideographic reading by the disconnected right hemisphere: Two case studies. *Brain & Language,* 1981, *14,* 205–234.

Zangwill, O. L. Agraphia due to a left parietal glioma in left-handed man. *Brain,* 1954, *77,* 510–520.

Zangwill, O. L. *Cerebral dominance and its relation to psychological function.* Edinburgh: Oliver & Boyd, 1960.

Zangwill, O. L. Thought and the brain. *British Journal of Psychology,* 1976, *67,* 301–314.

Zangwill, O. L. Dyslexia and cerebral dominance: A reassessment. In L. Oettinger, Jr., and L. V. Majovski (Eds.), *The psychologist, the school, and the child with MBD/LD.* New York: Grune & Stratton, 1978. (a)

Zangwill, O. L. The concept of developmental dysphasia. In M. Wyke (Ed.), *Developmental dysphasia.* New York: Academic Press, 1978. (b)

Zangwill, O. L., & Blakemore, C. Dyslexia: Reversal of eye-movements during reading. *Neuropsychologia,* 1972, *10,* 371–373.

Zazzo, R. *Les jumeaux: Le couple et la personne.* Paris: Presses Universitaires de France, 1960.

Zimmerman, G. W., & Knott, J. R. Slow potentials of the brain related to speech processing in normal speakers and stutterers. *EEG & Clinical Neurophysiology,* 1974, *37,* 599–607.

Zurif, E. B. Auditory lateralization: Prosodic and syntactic factors. *Brain & Language,* 1974, *1,* 391–404.

Zurif, E. B., & Bryden, M. P. Familial handedness and left–right differences in auditory and visual perception. *Neuropsychologia,* 1969, *7,* 179–187.

Zurif, E. B., & Caramazza, A. Psycholinguistic structures in aphasia: Studies in syntax and semantics. In H. Whitaker & H. A. Whitaker (Eds.), *Studies in neurolinguistics* (Vol. 1). New York: Academic Press, 1976.

Zurif, E. B., & Carson, G. Dyslexia in relation to cerebral dominance and temporal analysis. *Neuropsychologia,* 1970, *8,* 351–361.

Author Index

Numbers in italics refer to pages on which the complete references are listed.

Subject Index

PERSPECTIVES IN
NEUROLINGUISTICS, NEUROPSYCHOLOGY, AND
PSYCHOLINGUISTICS: A Series of Monographs and Treatises

Harry A. Whitaker, Series Editor
DEPARTMENT OF HEARING AND SPEECH SCIENCES
UNIVERSITY OF MARYLAND
COLLEGE PARK, MARYLAND 20742

HAIGANOOSH WHITAKER and HARRY A. WHITAKER (Eds.).
Studies in Neurolinguistics, Volumes 1, 2, 3, and 4

NORMAN J. LASS (Ed.). Contemporary Issues in Experimental Phonetics

JASON W. BROWN. Mind, Brain, and Consciousness: The Neuropsychology of Cognition

SIDNEY J. SEGALOWITZ and FREDERIC A. GRUBER (Eds.). Language Development and Neurological Theory

SUSAN CURTISS. Genie: A Psycholinguistic Study of a Modern-Day "Wild Child"

JOHN MACNAMARA (Ed.). Language Learning and Thought

I. M. SCHLESINGER and LILA NAMIR (Eds.). Sign Language of the Deaf: Psychological, Linguistic, and Sociological Perspectives

WILLIAM C. RITCHIE (Ed.). Second Language Acquisition Research: Issues and Implications

PATRICIA SIPLE (Ed.). Understanding Language through Sign Language Research

MARTIN L. ALBERT and LORAINE K. OBLER. The Bilingual Brain: Neuropsychological and Neurolinguistic Aspects of Bilingualism

TALMY GIVÓN. On Understanding Grammar

CHARLES J. FILLMORE, DANIEL KEMPLER, and WILLIAM S-Y. WANG (Eds.). Individual Differences in Language Ability and Language Behavior

JEANNINE HERRON (Ed.). Neuropsychology of Left-Handedness

FRANÇOIS BOLLER and MAUREEN DENNIS (Eds.). Auditory Comprehension: Clinical and Experimental Studies with the Token Test

R. W. RIEBER (Ed.). Language Development and Aphasia in Children: New Essays and a Translation of "Kindersprache und Aphasie" by Emil Fröschels

GRACE H. YENI-KOMSHIAN, JAMES F. KAVANAGH, and CHARLES A. FERGUSON (Eds.). Child Phonology, Volume 1: Production and Volume 2: Perception